Strategies and Policies in Digital Convergence

Sangin Park
Seoul National University, Korea

IDEA GROUP REFERENCE
Hershey · London · Melbourne · Singapore

Acquisitions Editor:	Kristin Klinger
Development Editor:	Kristin Roth
Senior Managing Editor:	Jennifer Neidig
Managing Editor:	Sara Reed
Assistant Managing Editor:	Sharon Berger
Copy Editor:	Julie LeBlanc
Typesetter:	Sara Reed
Cover Design:	Lisa Tosheff
Printed at:	Yurchak Printing Inc.

Published in the United States of America by
Idea Group Reference (an imprint of Idea Group Inc.)
701 E. Chocolate Avenue, Suite 200
Hershey PA 17033
Tel: 717-533-8845
Fax: 717-533-8661
E-mail: cust@idea-group.com
Web site: http://www.idea-group-ref.com

and in the United Kingdom by
Idea Group Reference (an imprint of Idea Group Inc.)
3 Henrietta Street
Covent Garden
London WC2E 8LU
Tel: 44 20 7240 0856
Fax: 44 20 7379 0609
Web site: http://www.eurospanonline.com

Library of Congress Cataloging-in-Publication Data

Strategies and policies in digital convergence / Sangin Park, editor.

p. cm.

Summary: "This book addresses and positions the issues in business strategy and public policy rising from digital convergence, especially in the areas of mobile communications, broadband networks, and digital multimedia broadcast services. It presents new business opportunities generated by digital convergence, and raises governance issues in digital convergence"--Provided by publisher.

Includes bibliographical references and index.

ISBN 1-59904-156-1 (hbk.) -- ISBN 1-59904-157-X (softcover) -- ISBN 1-59904-158-8 (ebook)

1. Telecommunication--Technological innovations. 2. Digital communications--Economic aspects. I. Park, Sangin, 1965-

HE7631.S74 2007

384.3--dc22

2006033669

British Cataloguing in Publication Data
A Cataloguing in Publication record for this book is available from the British Library.

Table of Contents

Section I
Deployment of Broadband Technology

Section II
New Business Opportunities

Section III
Root and Content Governance

Detailed Table of Contents

Section I
Deployment of Broadband Technology

This chapter provides an overview of challenges and opportunities of broadband technology. The focus of the chapter is on the control of transmission capacity with the coalition in favor of an open network (network neutrality) and its impacts on the future of the global Internet as well as terrestrial networks, radio spectrum and satellite broadband.

This chapter pays attention specifically to the social and cultural impacts of VoIP, which is expected to alleviate economic or geographic restrictions, enabling individuals to communicate on a broader scale at a reasonable financial cost. This chapter discusses the core components of VoIP and how it facilitates communication, and examines whether we are entering a truly "global village" through greater use of VoIP technologies.

Digital convergence requires an efficient utilization of radio spectrum. As one possibility, this chapter proposes a modified lease auction (MLA) in which the government leases the spectrum competitively to business and public users. The chapter also discusses the process of transition from the current system to MLA as well as a provision of insurance as a way to protect incumbents from excessive risk of losing spectrum rights.

Chapter IV

The Mobile Virtual Network Operators (MVNOs) can be an alternative way to efficiently utilize the radio spectrum and to increase competition in the mobile communications industry. This chapter presents simulations of quantitative figures such as net present value, pay-back period, investment cost, revenues and running cost under different MVNO business cases in the 3G mobile communications market.

Section II
New Business Opportunities

Chapter V

This chapter examines Internet auctions and provides some intuitive persepctives on the evolution of e-commerce. The chapter finds the existence of the network effect between Web site usage and listings, which explains the dominance of eBay even with higher fees in the Internet auctions market. The first-mover's advantage of eBay established by network effects is suggestive of the possible evolution of e-commerce in which clicks generate some values.

Chapter VI

As digital convergence proceeds, m-commerce takes shape and mobile banking becomes a front runner of m-commerce. In the mobile payment system, mobile network operators are on the verge of turning into non-bank financial institutions, which raises a serious public policy issue in financial and banking sectors. This chapter analyzes mobile payment issues and policy implications in Korea.

Chapter VII

This chapter studies the innovation strategy of Nokia, a major telecom company, in the emerging digital home market. The chapter finds that on the one hand, Nokia follows a niche creation strategy, relying on its existing technological competencies in the areas of handset design and open device architecture, and on the other hand, Nokia builds new market competencies either developed in-house or through collaboration with its industry partners.

Chapter VIII

This chapter directs our attention to the importance of a variety of systems in digital convergence, and proceeds farther to put an emphasis on open systems which assure variety and interoperability. The chapter then explores the different meanings and criteria suggested by the term "open systems" and the many ways openness is viewed.

Section III
Root and Content Governance

Chapter IX

Internet governance refers to the complex interaction of root servers, software, and public and private entities through which content is made available over the World Wide Web. This chapter discusses the outcome of largely libertarian origins of Internet management and the future structure of Internet governance, which will have significant geo-political repercussions in the process of digital convergence.

Chapter X

This chapter takes on the major regulatory challenges for digital content services in digital convergence. The chapter details the regulatory approach of the European Union in the wider electronic (mainly Internet-based) communications areas, which aims to promote that different forms of contents should be legally available for use, treatment, storage and distribution in various technological platforms.

Chapter XI

This chapter reviews and compares the copyright history in the U.S. and China, and explores major rationales behind copyright policies of these two countries as well as main reasons that they were able to avert potential Intellectual Property trade wars in recent years. The chapter makes some specific suggestions on how to achieve a sound balance of Intellectual Property protection and social development in the digital age.

Chapter XII

This chapter explains the public policy constraints on the deployment of most technology in digital convergence. Specifically, privacy and security are a balance between individual interests in secrecy/solitude and society's interests in security, order and efficiency. The chapter explores the key political, legal and regulatory means for resolving conflicts between privacy rights and security methods to encourage convergence success.

Foreword

CONVERGENCE AND VARIETY IN EXPLORATION

In many contemporary information technology markets, exploration has high potential benefits. Yet, the market conditions do not always support a variety of firms who explore the unknown. This benefit from variety and the limits to its supply lies behind much of what we call convergence. That observation is not obvious, so it is worth explaining.

DISPERSION AND EXPLORATION

Less concentration has two benefits in a technology market with uncertain value. First, and most directly, more variety means there is a wider variance of firm experiments. A wider variety raises the probability that an unusually good experiment will exist and survive a market test.

Second, more variety increases the likelihood that a so-called contrarian reaches the marketplace sooner. Such a firm can commercialize a technology that otherwise might not have seen the light of day. That can spur innovative responses from established firms who otherwise would not have taken any action.

There are plenty of historical and contemporary examples to illustrate these two benefits.

Probably the best illustration occurred in 1993, just after the introduction of Internet access in the United States. The coming of pervasive Internet service was regarded as a pipedream. The first advertised services for commercial access appeared that year, but all of these came from non-mainstream firms except MCI and IBM, who, along with a few others, had operated the Internet for the National Science Foundation until that point.

While Netscape is often credited in popular portrayals as the "killer application" of the early commercial Internet, this characterization is incomplete. Many firms served as early catalysts before Netscape was founded–e.g., Netcom, BBN and PSINet and countless regional ISPs. These early entrants showed there was a market for commercial Internet services at a time when that was not at all apparent.

Another great illustration comes from events in 1998. This was a time of urgent investment in infrastructure to meet growing demand for Internet services. The dispersion of commercial leadership led to a thorough exploration of the commercial landscape. In fact, it appeared to be a frenzy to contemporaries: It involved both large and small and new and established enterprises from every major incumbent firm in computing and communications.

The contemporary situation for wireless Internet applications worldwide provides yet another illustration. For example, some wireless markets have to be explored at a large scale—e.g., worldwide distribution of cellular handsets inherently requires partnerships among large firms. Yet, it is also undeniable that some Wi-Fi applications can be explored by small innovative teams playing around with unlicensed spectra, as some of the mesh network groups do. Moreover, a few standards committees, such as those writing next generation Wi-Fi and Wi-Max, are looking into new technologies and these also could open up huge opportunities.

Moreover, a variety of approaches to wireless markets flourishes in quite a different sense, comparing firms across borders. Many factors produce such differences: prices for inputs, local regulatory restraints, demand for features and the viability of substitutes. Many of these experiments also involve businesses with local customer bases, shielding them from outside competition.

While the causes behind the variety are interesting, I want to emphasize their relevance to learning. The variety of experiments across countries yields a large number of lessons to the firms and consultants who are watching. In that sense, once again, variety facilitates learning.

Most interesting, perhaps, is that all these types of variety tend not to be stable in the long run. Exploratory behavior uncovers unknown sources of market value. These lessons accumulate as firms explore the market landscape. Indeed, in any active market the accumulation of such lessons is almost inexorable.

And there is the rub. Competitive pressures force firms to imitate each other in output markets or, if not, specialize in niche user markets. Moreover, either one firm or a small set will learn to execute with more efficiency, forcing out others.

Both such processes will look like convergence. That is, as all firms adopt each other's lessons it will lead to an almost inexorable decline in variety.

LIMITS ON DISPERSION

Do not misinterpret the discussion so far. Variety yields benefits, but this benefit comes at many costs. These costs place limits on a variety of experiments.

In fact, none of this is shocking because many limits are unglamorous.

For example, some opportunities need exploration but the market inherits the concentration of closely related predecessor markets. That can make it is too expensive for anyone to build the brand name, distribution network or product laboratory needed for large scale exploration.

IBM's dominance of the computer market in the 1970s illustrates the point. Its presence cast a huge shadow over the personal computer market just as it got off the ground. Once IBM succeeded with their initial design, the PC hardware market remained concentrated for the next half decade. That occurred even though exploration was valuable. Indeed, the exception proved the rule. Variety flourished in the parts of the market that IBM did not dominate, such as software applications.

A potential limit also can arise from a severe technical constraint. For example, it can be inefficient to frequently switch ownership and maintenance over databases just to nurture exploration. Hence, the management for Internet databases for each top level domain name does not change often–e.g., year after year, the same firms act as registries for .com, .net, .org, .bus, .info, .edu and so on. Though the Internet's operations are young enough to benefit from exploring a variety of norms for managing these databases, it is impractical to experiment with a different firm each year. Within each registry there will be a monopoly for the foreseeable future.

A different sort of limit arises from buyer habits in mainstream markets. For example, business users have limited capacity to integrate technologies from a variety of firms and, hence, prefer to limit their choices to a small number of vendors. In such a setting concentrated leadership can help organize technological transitions and upgrades, limiting exploration to the preferences of the few firms who dominate a market segment.

Microsoft, Cisco and Intel all play this role in their core markets. While each of them faces some competition, many of their users are quite hesitant to get new versions from anyone else. Their biggest competitors come from quite different types of organizations, such as open source projects or collections of firms pursuing activities around non-proprietary standards. None of these collections will put the leading firm out of business anytime soon.

Finally, even when exploration motivates many new entrants, technology markets stay concentrated because established firms have the ability to buy leadership from firms who are in the best position to be tomorrow's leadership. There are so many examples of this process at work, it is easier to illustrate it by its failures, which are rare.

Here is one recent failure. Many people forget that Microsoft tried to buy Netscape months prior to its IPO, a prospect that Netscape's VCs welcomed. Indeed, there was a price at which this sale would have occurred, but Microsoft only offered several hundred million dollars, undervaluing Netscape (and the commercial potential of the Internet).

In other words, Microsoft ended up competing with Netscape because of a poor forecast. That illustrates the main point: We do not hear about such errors often because leading firms, Microsoft included, do not make them often. Most leaders buy their future competitors before they ever blossom.

THE ROOTS OF CONVERGENCE

Where does that leave us? With a trite lesson and a subtle open question.

The trite lesson is this: There are many roads to convergence.

The subtle open question follows. It is also possible to define the ideal: All of the good roads explore the maximal variety of approaches, but are subject to the limits on number of firms. So one might reasonably wonder: How close does actual experience get to the ideal?

Shane M. Greenstein
Northwestern University, USA

Preface

In the past three decades, we have experienced unprecedented progresse in information and digital technologies. Until the early 1990s, the Internet was not a familiar term to many people. The introduction of the World Wide Web (WWW) indeed accelerated the growth of Internet usage. In 1990, there were only 10 million Internet users in the world, but worldwide Internet users have grown exponentially since 1996: 40 million users in 1996, 100 million in 1998 and 350 million users in 2000. The WWW, which began to take shape in 1989 stemming from a primary creator, Tim Berners-Lee, was designed specifically to allow easy linking (called hyperlinks) from any user to any set of data, demonstrating the importance of multimedia content (digitalized text, audio and video files) and user-friendly interfaces.

It is not a surprise that firms and governments began to explore the opportunities created by the development of the Internet and information technologies (IT). In the public sector, the operation and the organization of the government have been in transformation for e-government. In the private sector, firms first utilized the Internet and IT for more efficient management of inventories, information and knowledge. Soon, firms realized and began to explore the commercial opportunities generated by the Internet and the WWW, which led to the advent of e-commerce. Furthermore, the Internet began to change the nature of political campaigns, everyday lifestyle and the social structure. Korea, for instance, has recently experienced a new political campaign via the Internet, and the Internet community, which has had substantial influence on the way that people interact with each other.

As is well known, the Internet can be understood as a network of networks. What distinguishes the Internet is the way traffic is handled: A message is broken down into many chunks of data called *packets*, each of which contains necessary information such as an IP address, and then the packets are routed through many alternative routers to the destination. However, due to not only the growing Internet user population but also the emergence of home networks, new forms of media, and the convergence of fixed and wireless networks, the demand for IP addresses will outpace supply under the current IPv4 regime in the near future. Hence the Next Generation Network or Broadband convergence Network began to take shape, aiming to offer Internet security, enhanced quality of service (QoS) and mobility features along with the 128-bit IP system called IPv6.

Indeed, the innovations in VoIP (Voice over IP), digital TV and wireless communications lifted the Internet and IT revolution to digital convergence. VoIP and digital TV digitalized the voice information and TV contents in IP packets, causing not only service convergence in data, voice and video information, but also industry convergence, especially between the broadcast and the telephony sectors and the consumer electronics and computer industries. On the other hand, a deep penetration of the second-generation (2G) of mobile communications highlights demands for "mobility" in the digital age. It is widely believed that 3G and 4G mobile communications will enable users to enjoy a variety of wireless services including mobile Internet access and two-way multi-media services. The commercial DMB (Digital Multimedia Broadcast) services were already launched in 2005 in Korea, which made digital media contents mobile. Wi-Fi and Wi-Bro are expected to compete with 4G mobile communications in two-way multi-media services as well as mobile Internet access. The convergence in wired/wireless and data/voice/video services prods a convergence of IP, broadcast/cable and mobile communications networks into the Broadband convergence Network. The Broadband convergence Network is expected to be the key infrastructure of digital convergence over which Telematics, Home Networks and other convergence services can be provided.

Digital convergence which we witness now is only in the beginning stage and is expected to have deep and wide impacts on economies, politics and our daily lives. This convergence will foster new opportunities and challenges in private and public sectors. This book aims to address and position the issues in business strategies and public policies rising from digital convergence. This book is organized into three sections with twelve chapters.

Section I provides a comprehensive overview of the deployment of broadband technology and business strategies and public policy in the allocation of radio spectrum.

Chapter I views challenges and opportunities of broadband technology. The chapter discusses the control of transmission capacity with the coalition in favor of an open network (network neutrality) and its impacts on the future of the global Internet and implications for terrestrial networks, radio spectrum and satellite broadband.

Chapter II pays attention specifically to the social and cultural impacts of VoIP in the age of digital convergence. Through convergent systems and wireless means, VoIP is expected to alleviate economic or geographic restrictions, enabling individuals to communicate on a broader scale at a reasonable financial cost. This chapter explains the core components of VoIP and how it facilitates communication, and examines whether we are entering a truly "global village" through greater use of VoIP technologies.

Chapter III concerns public policy in the allocation of the radio spectrum. Digital convergence requires an efficient utilization of the radio spectrum. As one possibility, the paper proposes a modified lease auction (MLA) in which the government leases the spectrum competitively to business and public users and the process of transition from the current system to MLA. The chapter also discusses a provision of insurance as a way to protect incumbents from excessive risk of losing spectrum rights.

Chapter IV focuses on the Mobile Virtual Network Operators (MVNOs) as an alternative way to efficiently utilize the radio spectrum and to increase competition in the mobile communications industry. In many countries, the 3G licenses have been assigned to existing 2G operators, and the reserved 2G radio spectrum band is nearly saturated at least in the urban areas. Hence, not much room is left for new players to enter the 3G mobile communications market. The chapter considers MVNO as an alternative way for firms to enter the 3G mobile communications market, and presents quantitative figures such as net present value, pay-back period, investment cost, revenues and running cost under different MVNO business cases.

Section II takes on new business opportunities generated by digital convergence and related issues in business strategies and public policies.

Chapter V examines Internet auctions and provides some intuitive views on the evolution of e-commerce. The chapter finds the existence of the network effect between Web site usage and listings, which explains the dominance of eBay even with higher fees in the Internet auctions market. The first-mover's advantage of eBay established by network effects is suggestive of the possible evolution of e-commerce in which clicks generate some values.

Chapter VI analyzes mobile payment issues and policy implications in Korea. As digital convergence proceeds, m-commerce takes shape and mobile banking becomes a front runner of m-commerce. In the mobile payment system, mobile network operators are on the verge of turning into non-bank financial institutions. Hence, mobile banking services raise a serious public policy issue in financial and banking sectors, which will substantially affect the evolution of these new services in the future.

Chapter VII studies the innovation strategy of Nokia, a major telecom company, in the emerging digital home market. The chapter finds that on one hand, Nokia follows a niche creation strategy, relying on its existing technological competencies in the areas of handset design and open device architecture, and on the other hand, Nokia builds new market competencies either developed in house or through collaboration with its industry partners.

Chapter VIII directs our attention to the importance of a variety of systems in digital convergence, and precedes further to put an emphasis on open systems which assure variety and interoperability. Then the chapter explores the different meanings and criteria suggested by the term "open systems" and the many ways openness is viewed. However, it should be noted that open systems will affect firms' incentives for innovations and pricing behavior, and thus the welfare consequences of open systems are not definite.

Section III raises governance issues in digital convergence. Successful governance is a key element of the realization of digital convergence.

Chapter IX deals with issues in the governance of the Internet, which is the core of the infrastructure of digital convergence. Internet governance refers to the complex interaction of root servers, software, and public and private entities through which content is made available over the World Wide Web. This chapter discusses the outcome of largely libertarian origins of Internet management and the future structure of Internet governance, which will have significant geo-political repercussions in the process of digital convergence.

Chapter X takes on the major regulatory challenges for the development and the effective provision of audio-visual or other forms of digital content services in the continuing digital convergence. The paper details a more proactive and consistent regulatory approach of the European Union in the wider electronic (mainly Internet-based) communications areas, including a variety of modern broadcasting activities. These recent regulatory developments aim to promote those different forms of content should be legally available for use, treatment, storage and distribution in various technological platforms.

Chapter XI considers the challenges that the Internet and IT present to the traditional copyright legal system. This chapter reviews and compares the copyright history in the US and China, and explores major rationales behind copyright policies of these two countries as well as the main reasons why they were able to avert potential Intellectual Property trade wars in recent years. The author makes some specific suggestions on how to achieve a sound balance of Intellectual Property protection and social development in the digital age.

Chapter XII explains the public policy constraints on the deployment of most technology in digital convergence. Specifically, privacy and security are a balance between individual interests in secrecy/solitude and society's interests in security, order and efficiency. This chapter explores the key political, legal and regulatory means for resolving conflicts between privacy rights and security methods to encourage convergence success.

Digital convergence is only in the nascent stage. By nature, unexpected is expected in the parade of convergence. Business strategies and public policies will also play a substantial role in taking the forms and paths of digital convergence, a progress which, in turn, will bring new opportunities and challenges in private and public sectors. The book provides a critical overview of the issues in business strategies and public policies of digital convergence from the perspective of where we stand. It is my wish that this book can be a foothold for better understanding of many facets of digital convergence which are yet to come.

Sangin Park
Editor
Seoul, Korea
December 2006

Acknowledgments

I would first like to acknowledge the inspiring foreword written by Shane Greenstein and the excellent contributions of all the chapter authors to this book. Most of the authors also served as referees for articles written by others. I would like to express my gratitude to all those who provided constructive and comprehensive reviews. Some of the reviewers who are not chapter authors but gladly provided their professional comments include: Kiho Yun of Korea University, Minchul Kim of KISDI and Sungjin Cho of Hanyang University.

Support of the Graduate School of Public Administration at Seoul National University is acknowledged in the collation and review process of the book. I am particularly grateful to Jyun Kim and Yeon-Tae Choi for their editorial work and assistance in coordinating this year-long project.

Special thanks also go to the publishing team at Idea Group Inc., in particular to Kristin Roth, who continuously prodded me via e-mail to keep the project on schedule.

Finally, I want to thank my wife, Cecilia Hwangpo, for her love and support throughout this project.

Sangin Park
Editor
Seoul, Korea
December 2006

About the Editor

Sangin Park is associate professor of IT and Industrial Policy at the Graduate School of Public Administration at Seoul National University, Korea. Prior to that, he was Assistant Professor of Economics at the State University of New York at Stony Brook (1996-2003), and Visiting Assistant Professor of Economics at Yale University (Fall 2002), where he worked on Industrial Organization, Econometrics and Applied Microeconomics. His current research interests include standardization and network externalities, IP policies in digital convergence, competition policy, and structural economic policy. Dr. Park holds a Ph D in Economics from Yale University.

Section I
Deployment of Broadband Technology

Chapter I
Broadband Technology:
Challenges and Opportunities
for Digital Convergence

Meheroo Jussawalla
East West Center, USA

ABSTRACT

An important struggle for the control of the Internet is underway. It is fundamental in as much as it initiates control of the broadband network itself. It raises issues about what resources users will be able to reach, what content will be accessible, from whom and at what price and what functions application providers will be able to deliver. A core issue is control of transmission capacity. The chapter notes the struggles between carrier/content interests which desire to use Internet technologies for control of the global network and the global Internet. Implications for terrestrial networks, radio spectrum and satellite broadband are discussed. Finally the chapter concludes that access to broadband networks is a pre-condition for opening up opportunities for globalization and social integration and for making the power of the knowledge economy widespread. International organizations have a significant role to play in advancing this process.

INTRODUCTION

Even as telecommunications transmissions and investments have been revolutionized by the Internet and by Mobile connectivity, so also digitization and the use of broadband have completely altered the mode and models of voice and data transmissions along with streaming video, music and entertainment on demand. Every sector of economic activity, including education and health, has been affected by packet technologies, IP (Internet Protocol) applications and new business models. Traditional telephone revenues have been migrating to VOIP (Voice Over Internet Protocol) and high-speed broadband devices, which are versatile and faster and are leading industry growth.

Alternative access technologies, including 3G, broadband using electric power and WIMAX have disrupted conventional assumptions about convergence, market demand and operations risk. Mobile is moving from traditional cellular to a universe of portable Internet and entertainment devices, and location-based advertising services are targeting them. Video markets are in readiness for the arrival of IPTV, broadcast over mobile, podcasting, and DSL's response to cable. Next generation soft switch networks threaten the dominance of circuit-switched communications. The transition from IP based communications and media services spells opportunities for some and challenges for others.

Broadband has brought a seismic shift, which is dramatic in introducing a transformation toward services delivered using Internet Protocol. Service providers have to devise new business models for these innovations while, simultaneously, Internet providers will have to ensure network security, content management and real-time delivery.

Convergence and transformation in the global telecom industry is dependent on a robust infrastructure able to deliver and support a changing broadband network. This structural change affords enormous opportunities for equipment manufacturers and vendors to develop long-term relationships with their customers, operators and carriers. However, the challenge is to design, deploy and manage the huge changes that depend on the IP network within the framework of broadband systems and the commercial transformation that is challenging the Asian operator community. Even with the opportunities afforded by high bandwidth, we still find that globally 77 % of subscribers never use mobile data, making the outlook for 3G grim (*Telecom TV Review,* May 2005, p. 7). Under the circumstances, is the future of broadband assured?

Voice over broadband is considered a disruptive technology because it threatens the traditional wire line carriers. For most incumbent telecommunication companies in Asia, the U.S., and globally, revenues have been declining because local loops are competing. With VOIP becoming a mass market, incumbent carriers in Europe and Asia are being forced to change.

Among the challenges to this growing trend of broadband IP transit is that it is not sustainable, and in Europe it is almost declining (Gary Kim, *Fat Pipe,* June 15, 2005, p. 21). The prediction is that high bandwidth, cross-border traffic could face a meltdown similar to the one that IP transit is expected to face. There is a migration toward Ethernet and customers are buying 10 Gbps Ethernet ports.

This chapter will examine the possibilities that broadband holds for industry players. What should consumers in the digital, mobile, networked nano world of today expect from their network providers? What will be the role of public interest in the multimedia opportunities available to consumers? How will regulators protect the public interest and assure commercial success? In a new converged world, will the traditional big players be forced to give ground to better equipped small scale entrepreneurs? These issues will be the objectives this chapter discusses.

THE BACKGROUND FOR THIS CHAPTER FOCUSES ON THE ADVANCES MADE IN SOUTH KOREA

The use of Broadband technology has gained strategic importance around the globe with Korea having a vast majority of households and businesses using Broadband for WCDMA (Wireless Code Division Multiple Access) for messaging. The growth of broadband technology applications in Korea has enhanced opportunities for commercial applications providing Internet access for not just movies on demand but for access in rural areas for health and education. Even though the USA started providing Broadband Internet one year before South Korea, there are twice as many broadband lines per head of population in Korea as any other country as of July 1998 when Thrunet of Korea introduced cable modem service. In the same year, DACOM (Data Communications a leading Korean Company) entered the cable modem sector and in 1999 Hanaro Telecom(also of Korea) launched ADSL (Asynchronous Digital Subscriber Line) services. Korea Telecom also entered the same market with both ISDN (Integrated Services Digital Network) and ADSL services to compete in the domestic market. According to Lee and Chan (2004) three companies commanded 93% of the domestic market in 2000: KT, Hanaro and Thrunet. By June 2002, 60% of South Korean households were connected to broadband service, making Korea the world leader in broadband.

There are 10 million users, projected to increase to 13.5 million by 2007 in Korea. Most Asian countries, using the Korean model, are waging spectrum wars, with service technology competition directed to wireless access. Debate continues on whether this success was caused by genuine competition which drove down prices, the absence of flat rate dial-up services in Korea helped the competition between suppliers or if there was vigorous infrastructure competition between ADSL and cable modem networks (Kiedrowski, 2002). Backed by the Government, KT was able to dominate the market in 2000, but the incumbent soon lost to Thrunet and Hanaro. This happened because there was an oversupply of optical fiber infrastructure laid by Powercomm, who entered into a revenue sharing agreement with Thrunet and Hanaro to provide broadband services to residential and business consumers. The result is that such private infrastructure suppliers reduced prices in most high rise buildings in Seoul where 49% of the population of the country lives. Buildings are designed with built-in fiber conduits which render last mile access easier and high broadband penetration less costly.

In its educational policy, the government was able to provide all schools with high speed Internet free of charge by the year 2000. Demand for

e-services led to training programs in IT literacy for the elderly, housewives and the military under the government- promulgated program to reduce the digital divide. In addition to these advantages, Korean children are skilful in playing online games and Internet cafes encouraged teenagers in playing these games, which helped the rapid rollout of broadband services. According to a Korean Government white paper in May 2003, the government aimed at providing 20Mbps to all households by 2005.

If we look at broadband penetration in Europe we find that in OECD countries (Organization for Economic Cooperation and Development) per 100 persons we find that Korea has 9.2 compared with Canada's 4.54, USA's 2.25 and Australia's 1.70.

The U.S. Federal Communications Commission Chairman, Kevin Martin, claims that regulations for broadband will boost high-speed Internet service in the United States. His theory is that phone and cable companies will be more inclined to expand broadband connections for consumers if they do not have to share marginal network costs with their competitors. In 2004, President Bush called for all Americans to have universal affordable access to high-speed Internet by 2007, yet the country still ranks 16th among developed nations in broadband availability (Amy Scahtz, *The Wall Street Journal,* July 19, 2005, pA4) The causes for the lead that Korea has over other countries is attributed by the ITU (International Telecommunications Union, 2003) to a miracle of culture and the development of an IT infrastructure, as the contributing factors . In the U.S., cable dominates DSL and has 28% of the broadband market in 2003 as per the *Cyber Atlas*, 2003. The Internet has been   the major technological innovation at the turn of the century, providing connectivity between networks, people and businesses and overcomes the limitations of time and space (Jussawalla, 1989). Porter (1990) determined that a country's advantage in trade may be determined by an analysis of industrial performance at the national level based on the theory of competitive rather than comparative advantage.

The importance of broadband lies in the fact that the Internet's future is closely related to its 0 growth; yet even today most Internet users in the developed world use low-speed dial-up connections because of the cost advantage. However, without broadband, the last mile bottleneck cannot be solved in order to provide a platform for supplying interactive multimedia services.

TeleGeography's recent survey dated June 15, 2005 shows that 30% of U.S. broadband subscribers have never heard of VOIP. This is a crucial point for providers, because there is a connection between VOIP and broadband subscribers. Approximately 76% of US households will subscribe to VOIP only if they are assured of having 911 (Emergency) facilities within the package and if they can get wireless substitution. Only then will they prefer to replace their landline connections.

Korea has made large investments in improving the supply structure for convergence but was unable to introduce the Direct Broadcast Service because of the conflict of interest between the government regulators and the private sector. Even though Koreasat satellites were launched in 1995, they were not used for over six years, similar to the case of Digital TV service in representing the slow progress of convergence. The Ministry of Information and Communication in Korea selected the American standard for transmission for Digital TV in 1997, but it came under attack from the broadcasting industry for several years. It was in 2004 that the issue was finally resolved but another such problem occurred for the introduction of the Digital Multimedia Broadcasting service which was to be commercialized for the first time in the world. In 2004, Dr. Jaechun Park of Inha University proposed a Subscribers' Network for Convergence in Korea.

CONTROVERSIES SURROUNDING THE COMPETITIVE ADVANTAGE OF BROADBAND USAGE

While the economic impacts of Broadband have been identified, the social and personal benefits are left debatable, according to Firth and Mellor (2005). Innovative business models, as well as organizational efficiency, are associated with the introduction of broadband. There is a dearth of data about the controversies surrounding the impact of broadband, which makes it difficult to assess the public policy implications for the economy and business organizations. In 2002, FCC Commissioner Michael Copps declared that "broadband is the front and center of America's 21st century transformation. Those who have access to advanced communications like broadband will win and those who don't will lose."

The applications of broadband are touted as its major advantages, such as video on demand, gaming, streaming video and VOIP. Also e-learning, e-health, e-commerce and e-government are all benefits of broadband applications. However, in this debate the public interest aspect seems to get overlooked. Furthermore, the benefits have not been accurately measured, which makes Bauer, et al. (2002) claim that while it may be possible to achieve high rates of broadband access, it is not known how far these rates benefit the economy or society. However, it is recognized that computer assisted learning systems become more efficient with broadband by reducing the time gap and by greater participation in interactive programs.

One area in which broadband is of greater benefit to society is in telemedicine, provided it is available to the poorer sections of society and to senior citizens at affordable prices. This is particularly true for those who may not have the finances to meet the practitioners on a face-to-face basis for every medical need. This is especially a concern for the Koreans because the consistent use of cyber cafes has an adverse impact on health and leads to a sedentary lifestyle which is especially harmful for youth in need of medical assistance.

It is to be noted that broadband deployment is not uniform either in terms of geographical or demographic spread. This is applicable to both voice and data. It is found that DSL modems or cable provide an improvement by a factor of ten over dial-up services, which offer 50kbps; whereas consumer broadband services in the U.S. provide one Mbps downstream and a few hundred kbps upstream(Gillett, et al., 2004). The main roadblock to a uniform policy for broadband deployment is the lack of data and its evaluation so that policy-makers are unable to receive guidance for local government policies. The proliferation of wireless technologies and FTTH (Fiber to the Home) and FTTC(Fiber to the Curb) wire line connections provide higher bandwidth services which entail new investments and may not be economically viable for all communities.

If we look at the historical trends, we find that since the early nineties convergence of data and voice along with digital telephony Voice Over IP and cellular technology have all been the ruling trends. This was followed by convergence of data and broadcasting with digital cable, interactive television and satellite TV. With the emergence of broadband, Internet built on Open Standards; connection technologies using broadband connectivity became commodities. This meant that all network devices were always on. This became true of all applications such as airline reservations, retail banking, stock brokering, insurance and even retail sales. This implies that as universal broadband access evolves in more countries, the geographical constraints of doing business will disappear and VOIP telephones will overtake landlines and that wireless along with VOIP will replace current mobile technologies. Most services will become virtualized except television. Local Exchange carriers will be bypassed by providers of VOIP carriers. Users' choices will

be enhanced, leading to group video conferencing and even the deployment of proprietary network architectures.

SUGGESTED SOLUTIONS

The question of how to create a service bundle of voice, video, data, content and gaming makes the future of broadband services more attractive if the bundle is well defined and properly targeted. Applications will cover information and communications up to pure entertainment. This means that far more players will be competing in the game of Broadband Internet access and services. Movie, gaming and broadcast TV content providers will assume significant roles in making broadband ubiquitous, so as to become a mass residential service that will reach every home. Such a scenario will call for a migration of incumbent operators from legacy to next-generation networks. Therefore, the challenge will be to design an organic infrastructure which will ensure a real offer of new services which must be novel, useful and accessible for all.

As end user demand for bandwidth grows, suppliers may have to move to optical access, including FTTC and FTTH. TeleGeography forecasts that bandwidth demand will outpace price declines (Jason Kowal, *TelegeographyUpdate*, April 7, 2005). According to this report, after a five year decline, the international bandwidth market is showing renewed signs of life. Steady traffic growth and a freeze in network construction have been reducing the excess capacity. Aggregate global demand for international bandwidth grew 42% in 2004, with the largest gains coming from Asian countries. The growth in demand may not require immediate additional network construction if suppliers can respond by lighting wavelengths and fiber pairs on an as-needed basis. This type of incremental approach will balance the increase in demand for bandwidth.

Another controversy surrounding broadband usage is with regard to termination costs which represent 70% of the total cost of providing long distance voice services, especially on international routes. When a carrier owns several switches over which lots of traffic flows, there will be the threat of changes in the underlying cost structure. This means that the way the carrier routes its traffic will determine how the carrier makes its margin. The market has moved to an optimized routing approach so that the least cost factor is not an important determinant any more (Gary Kim, *Fat Pipe,* April 15, 2004, p. 34). There are many exponential options for routing and termination points, which makes it difficult for carriers to balance the costs. The carrier has to have an automated system for deciding on an optimal instead of a least-cost routing. Automated systems provide value in helping network engineers predict how much additional capacity might have to be purchased from trading partners. The carrier has to monitor the traffic on a regular basis when broadband supplies the speed for transmission.

In a world of Broadband Internet surfing, the user will be at ease with interactive television and can install webcams at home and much more as a consequence of the Broadband revolution. Broadband does not only supply the user with fast speeds for the Internet, but can render the user's television set an information and entertainment hub, supplying pay-per-view and video on demand. Several kinds of set top boxes are available to provide a host of value-added services. Audio and video conferences also become easily accessible.

In the era of broadband convergence, there comes a time when a convergence node is established, as in Korea in the 1990s. Convergence is the technology which uses one fat pipe through which all voice, video, Internet, data music and television flow, using either a DSL with fiber optic cable or an optical cable which may be more powerful for transmission. If the suppliers own this node, they will build their own fiber network and allow the carriers and CATV to interconnect to their network. In such a case, they will try to grab as many services connected to their networks as possible and drive out competition. It is therefore essential to let the convergence node become a bottleneck facility for which there is competition between suppliers.

The demand side of the equation puts power in the hands of the subscribers who have the incentive to interconnect. As was shown previously, this happened in the case of Korea when companies like Hanaro planned DSL services for large apartment complexes where population density was high and the owners of the apartments owned the DSL connections.

GLOBAL GRAB FOR BROADBAND

Globally speaking, telephone companies that are in the VOIP segment of the market are ebullient. The largest ILECS (Incumbent Local Exchange Carriers) are optimistic, based on their projections of the regulatory climate. Rural telephone companies have been historically protected due to regulations and Universal Service payments, access charges, and inter-carrier compensation. But with bandwidth demand growing, they face competition with cable and wireless segments of the industry. According to *Telegeography* (as quoted by Gary Kim in *Fat Pipe,* May 15, 2005), there is rapid decline in prices of bandwidth which is ruining the Internet Bandwidth industry along with brutal competition. In Asia, the monthly prices per Mbps have declined from $200 in 2003 to $110 in 2004. In Europe, they have declined form $125 to $74 over the same period. This decline in prices is matched by the growth in demand for IP transit VOIP. Ethernet, frame relay and ATM (Asynchronous Transfer Mode) and are not geography dependent. Legacy pricing models are no longer used in a global context. Most carriers are pricing on a market basis rather than a cost basis, even below the level of operating costs. The demand for Ethernet is growing faster than any other wavelength. The regulations are not in favor of UNE-P (Unbundled Network Element), hence they have to concentrate on building cost structures around the fact that prices will continue to drop. All services supported by Moore's law will continue to drop in prices, so that suppliers will have to find ways to keep embedded costs as low as possible. Gordon Moore, who founded Intel, predicted that as size of a semiconductor decreases, its power increases geometrically.

The prognosis is that IPTV is becoming a reality because telecom companies are betting on it (*The Economist,* "War of the Wires," July 30 2005, p. 53). This is because cable companies are luring customers away from telephone companies for entertainment programs because they can supply telephone, TV and broadband services. At the same time, mobile phone operators are getting young subscribers to abandon the fixed line suppliers. There is also the attack from VOIP providers like Vonage, whose subscribers in America alone number four million currently. The world's largest supplier of VOIP is SKYPE, which is a simple software application that lets users make free calls between computers. It is headquartered in Luxembourg and was bought by E-Bay for over $2.6 billion (September 6, 2005).

Traditional telephone companies are meeting the challenge by adopting Internet technologies themselves, like VSNL (Videsh Sanchar Nigam Ltd.), the top operator in India, who is buying Tele-globe, the world's largest international wholesale VOIP carrier. British Telecom is also moving its customers to VOIP to neutralize the threat. With IPTV, telecom companies will be able to catch up with their cable rivals for broadband services. Set top boxes will then meet the demands for IPTV.

REGULATORY IMPLICATIONS OF BROADBAND CONVERGENCE

Leading broadband markets of the world are making policies that will allow price competition within different broadband platforms. Therefore, several policy challenges arise, such as the scope and authority of the regulators on problems of network access ownership issues and content as related to convergence (Irene Wu, *Telecommunications Policy,* Vol 28,1, 2004, pp. 79-96). Several countries like Canada, South Korea, Netherlands and Sweden are facing regulatory challenges with the convergence between broadband telecommunications, broadcasting and Internet services.

In Canada, the federal department of industry is responsible for telecommunications while the Minister for Canadian Heritage is responsible for broadcasting. For both these services there is a Commission on Radio-Television and Telecommunications. The house of Commons reviews the Broadcast Law.

In Korea, the Broadcast Act went into operation in 2000 and established the Korean Broadcasting Commission, which licenses operators and regulates program content. However, the Ministry of Communication is responsible for planning and regulating all multimedia industries. It has control over broadcasters' use of the Internet so that Korean Broadcast Commission and citizen groups believe that some clarification of the mandate is needed (Irene Wu, *Ibid,* 2004).

With a different set of regulations, the Netherlands Office of Post and Telecommunications is in charge of competition policy, and since 1998 is also responsible for dispute settlement between program providers and cable network operators. By contrast, the Swedish Post and Telecommunication Agency grants licenses and also allocates radio frequencies, whereas the Ministry of Culture issues licenses for TV and broadcast services and guarantees the independence of the mass media in the public interest.

Access to the telecommunications infrastructure involves unbundling the local loop. All four countries have as their objective the regulation of effective competition. Such regulations went into effect in Canada in 1998, in the Netherlands in 2000, in Sweden in 2001 and in Korea in 2002.

In Korea, state ownership of companies, such as Korea Telecom and Powercomm, were not allowed to provide services over the network. In 2002, Korea Telecom's cable services were sold to other providers. On the whole, network access rules have created problems for providers. This makes it incumbent on regulators to resolve some issues of conflict. The most significant problem is that as bandwidth demand grows and multimedia applications become more popular, the Next Generation Convergence Network makes it difficult for providers to meet the demand from tens of megabits per second to hundreds of megabits per second depending on the number of multimedia streams. In Japan these services are based on Passive Optical Network technology.

RADIO SPECTRUM DEMAND

Most emerging economies are waging spectrum wars with service technology competition directed to wireless access. While the ITU has propagated the IMT 2000 as the acceptable standard, experts are debating whether service suppliers will accept 3G or 4G or if WiFi will prevail. China has devised its own standard called the SCDMA and is now moving towards 3G. For the time being, their SMS (Short Messaging System) is most popular with subscribers for wireless use of the Internet. Globally, there is a scramble for the 700 MHZ and 800 MHZ bands, described as the worst examples of wireless politics (Caroline Gabriel, ARC Chart Blueprint, October 1, 2004). The problem is that the microelectronic spectrum is a valuable commodity which is required for broadband transmissions within and across countries. Control of the spectrum is being held by major cellular companies and broadcasters, either in the government or the private sector. Liberalizing the use of the spectrum is the challenge for new wireless services as they are introduced. In the United States, the auction of the 1.9GHz band is one of the bases of the spectrum wars. Broadcast-

ers are not willing to return the spectrum in the 700 MHZ band as they move to Digital TV. The current law requires broadcasters to surrender the spectrum when 85% of the viewers in their area can receive a digital signal. There is an attempt in Congress to free up the spectrum by 2009 for the public interest and for use in emergency response and law enforcement. Nextel is able to swap its holding of the spectrum in the 700 and 800 GHZ bands in exchange for the 1.9GHz block without its being auctioned. In the U.S,, broadcasters have been granted free spectrum for transition to Digital TV. The purpose of this subsidy is to hasten the return of the spectrum in the 108 MHZ band which the FCC has whittled from the 200MHZ band in 1995. In Britain, on the other hand, the subsidies are much less for broadcasters and they are not required to multicast or meet a "must carry" provision for transition to DTV. Despite this liberal regulation, the transition total to DTV in the UK is 50% compared to the U.S. with 41% (J.H. Snider, Working Paper, *New America Foundation Spectrum Policy Program*, May 2005). It is estimated that if there is a hard deadline for the return of the spectrum in the U.S., the auction revenue will range from $10 billion to $20 billion.

Europe's troubled attempts to auction the spectrum in 2000 for the use of 3G networks reached a critical stage when operators paid $125 billion for licenses to operate and became victims of their own hype (*The Economist,* "Vision Meets Reality," September 4, 2004, p. 63). This was the time that stock markets plunged and operators abandoned their purchases of the auctioned spectrum. In 2003, the UMTS(W-CDMA) networks started again in Europe, with many countries starting their own broadband technologies. Vodafone, the world's largest mobile operator, went ahead with operating 2.5 and 3G connections. This led to the patchwork of WiFi to link laptop computers to the Internet. Qualcomm, which pioneered the W-CDMA, was having trouble meeting the demand for the chips which gave optimism to what

3G can deliver. Japan, however, provided the IMT 2000 band for its users at no cost, whereas Korea is also providing the same standard at a cost of $2000 for the use of the IMT standard. This is because Korea is near saturation point in the use of the broadband spectrum.

India also is launching into broadband by giving the spectrum free to users, while Milton Freidman, in the *New York Times*, is advising India to sell its broadband spectrum. Metamorphosis via technology is speeding up the convergence process in India, bringing in mobile solutions for the banking and financial markets. Technological advances have led to convergence of multiple financial services due to which banks have been converted to financial super bazaars. Since the universal access regime of 2003 in India, the potential for efficiency gains in the economy rose tremendously. Currently, GSM operators work within the 1800 to 1880 MHZ bands and CDMA operators like Tata and Reliance use their specified bands also at a downlink of 1800 to 1880 MHZ frequencies. The IMT 2000 frequencies are 1920 to 1980 MHZ, currently used by 2G mobile services. In India, the Telecom Regulatory Authority (TRAI) is allowing depreciation benefits for equipment and the broadband policy defines service as an "always on" 256 kbps data connection available to all subscribers from a service provider. The Department of Telecom (DOT) in India anticipates one million users by the end of 2005. Another broadband initiative in the country is a projected international consortium, including Indian and American companies as well as the World Bank to establish thousands of rural Internet centers to bring banking, government and education services to isolated villages. This is a policy initiative to bridge the digital divide with the use of broadband technology. The policy in India is to supply a broadband connection without investing in a PC. VSNL(Vijay Sanchar Nigam Ltd.), a company owned by Tata TeleServices, is offering a personal Internet Communicator. Several types of set top boxes are being made available to offer

broadcast facilities and make webcam surveillance possible. Prices of fiber have crashed and have become virtually similar to those of copper. The price of electronic transmission equipment has also dropped so that fixed wire and wireless broadband solutions are now possible.

Policymakers are still grappling with competing demand for bandwidth and there is evidence of interfering emissions and confusion over the public interest. The controversy rages over whether the spectrum is underutilized or if the airwaves are overcrowded(Hazlett, Editorial, *Telecommunications Policy*, 27, 2003, p. 479). The rights to the radio spectrum continue to be ill defined and without market allocation; regulators have to evaluate competing uses, technologies and market structures. Law does not allow the market to determine the price of the resource unlike other economic resources.

SATELLITE-BASED BROADBAND

Satellites have a better infrastructure than land-based and wireless networks because of a more cost effective solution to high speed Internet, based on satellites being insensitive to distance. This implies that there will be price wars with operators inducing narrowband users to migrate to broadband. Inmarsat 4 is bringing Mobile Broadband globally. This satellite is rolling out Broadband Global Area Network service to provide data and voice simultaneously through a single device anywhere in the world. Based on IP technology, it will deliver data rates up to 432kbps and the satellite terminal will be as small as a notebook PC (*Via Satellite,* April 2005, p. 12). Broadcasters will be able to use this facility from disaster hit areas, war zones and remote regions. Despite high bandwidth prices and cost of ground equipment, operators, especially in Asia, are investing in next generation satellites(Jussawalla, Paper, "Satellite-Based Broadband in Asia," Proceedings of Pacific Telecommunications Conference,

Honolulu 2004). Among them is Shin satellite Company of Nonthaburi, Thailand, which has invested $250 million in its iPSTAR satellite to deliver high speed Internet access across Asia. Its goal is to deliver high speed Internet at prices comparable to terrestrial solutions like DSL or cable modems. It is a subsidiary of Shinawatra, which has three Thaicom satellites already in orbit. Four Asian firms have signed agreements with Shin Satellite Company to become resellers of broadband data services on the iPSTAR. These are Shanghai VSAT network Systems of China, VSNL of India, Siamsat and Samarat Telecom, both of Thailand. The current plan for iPSTAR is to carry 87 Ku band spot beams and 10 KA band spot beams, which makes it a high-powered system for broadband convergence for multimedia services.

Another broadband-based satellite is New Skies, which is a spinoff of Intelsat's privatization under the Orbit Act and is located in the Hague in the Netherlands. Its NSS6 satellite provides KA band for satellite services, Internet and other data rich content directly to users equipped with small antennas. New Skies is also supporting the International Broadcasting Bureau's expansion into the Indian Ocean Region. It is used for broadcasts such as the Voice of America, Radio and TV Marti, Radio Free Asia, and now Radio Free Afghanistan using DAMA (Demand Assigned Multiple Access) technology. Internet data transmission at high speeds is also done by New Sat USA, which sells transponders to link Internet companies in Asia to providers in Europe

using the refurbished Palapa B2R satellite and a teleport in Ottobrunn in Germany. It is providing benefits to a portion of the satellite market which is price sensitive and provides broadband service at low cost.

Asiasat has been, by far, the most successful operator in Asia, and its footprint covers not only Asia but also the Middle East and enables over a billion television viewers to access programs in a variety of languages. Disputed orbital allocation due to the proximity in orbit of iPSTAR caused some delays in launching the Asiasat 4, but its investments in Speedcast of Hong Kong allows it to be a leading enabler of broadband-based services in the Asia Pacific region. It offers online multimedia services such as NetTV, Biz TV and delivers content to ISP networks and end user PCs. These services are currently provided via Asiasat 3S which serves two thirds of the world population.

India's first privately owned satellite is Agrani, owned by Subash Chandra, the head of the Essel Group. It was built by Alcatel and launched by Arian Space with 14 Ku band transponders for broadband pan Asian transmission. India's own Edusat is designed to provide education to the remote and rural areas of the country.

The marketplace for transponder capacity is created by brokers and resellers who have created a secondary market and have fuelled competition between satellite-based and terrestrial wireless companies. In order to make secondary markets more efficient, regulators have to recognize usage rights to the spectrum, which can be transferable

Table 1. Region subscribers in millions 2003-2008 (Source: Northern Sky Research Via Satellite May 2004)

	2003	2005	2007	2008	CAGR
North America	0.190	0.352	0.731	0.948	37.9%
Western Europe	0.035	0.051	0.166	0.266	50.8%
Latin America	0.005	0.008	0.042	0.102	82.9%
Asia	0.013	0.038	0.124	0.194	73%
Middle East/Africa	0.003	0.010	0.044	0.065	91.9%
Global Total	0.255	0.476	1.156	1.675	45.7%

and visible. Demand for the Internet has revived the resale of satellite capacity much faster in recent years, and regulators must refrain from interfering with the principle of spectrum sharing between services. If we look at consumer and Small Office and Home Office (SOHO) satellite subscribers for broadband by region, the strategic benefits become clear.

The current version of the Internet Protocol, IPv4, was designed to be used by a small network of engineers and scientists for file transfers and e-mail. As the growth of the Internet exploded, a new version of IP was developed and designated IPv6 to increase the size of addresses from 32 to 128 bits. The primary difference with this next generation version of IP is the increase in the source and destination addresses. The satellite industry works under a common misconception that IPv6 will overcome the limitations of TCP/IP over satellite which is incorrect, according to Palter (*Satellites and the Internet,* 2003, 72). It will not change the operation of satellite-delivered broadband.

KATRINA AND THE FAILURE OF BROADBAND SPECTRUM POLICY IN THE USA

A hurricane of the intensity of Katrina resulted in the total failure of IT technology and its ability to keep communications viable in New Orleans and Louisiana. Without communications, Katrina wreaked havoc in the southern states leaving dwellers without essentials for days till relief arrived. This has been avoided to some extent with Rita, which followed close on the heels of Katrina. At a Capitol Hill Forum organized by the new America Foundation, its Vice president, Michael Calabrese, pointed out that since it is not possible to lay fiber lines to all rural areas, wireless networks can provide broadband communications quickly and inexpensively. During this calamity, Wireless Internet Service Providers

(WISPS) used unlicensed spectrum to address this problem to link hurricane shelters (J.H. Snider, Media Backgrounder, Via Internet, September 9, 2005). Congress is moving toward digital TV legislation, which will free up broadcast spectrum for broadband use. The FCC has initiated a rule-making docket (04-186) to require broadcast channels to be opened up for unlicensed broadband use to reach rural areas and evacuee shelters in emergencies.

The failure of regular communication channels led to thousands of persons crowding shelters like the Superdome in New Orleans where there was a shortage of water and food. It was the satellites that were operating and transmitting information to the media and to the regulatory agencies. This lack of organization led to the charge that the Mayor of New Orleans was inefficient and did not convey the information about the impending storm to the networks on time. This also led to the resignation of the Director of FEMA (Federal Emergency Management Agency) for his inability to communicate the emergency requirements to the householders. As such, there was a failure of traditional communication channels like land lines and dependence had to be placed on wireless and mobile channels only. These mobile channels depended upon the free usage of spectrum available for broadband networks. People in the South of the United States are still suffering because of the destruction of their homes and property and the loss of jobs to replenish their incomes. Hence, the failure at the time of hurricanes has become a model for future usage of broadband through mobile networks and the use of free spectrum for such resources.

FUTURE TRENDS AND CONCLUSION

With the new wave of Convergence of media and telecommunications facilitated by the innovation of broadband and wider spectrum usage, global interconnectivity is advancing rapidly, bringing global markets into the sphere of domestic demand and supply. The inelasticity of demand for voice and data together with multimedia is likely to make an impossible dream of convergence through a single pipe come true. For over two decades, the issue of the Digital Divide has been haunting policymakers internationally. The Maitland Commission's Report, *The Missing Link* (1986), first alerted global policymakers that universal access was a fundamental human right and that all rural areas need to be linked with an Information Superhighway. The G8 Ministers in 2000 drafted an Okinawa Report setting up a Digital Opportunities Task Force under the UN to urge advanced countries to help developing ones provide access to telephones and the Internet in their deprived regions. As technology advances and more resources, both natural and human, are multiplying, greater information access for the remote sections of the world will become possible. This will be achieved through Digital Convergence using broadband technology that is either terrestrial, wireless mobile or satellite-based. It is anticipated that the next decade will witness the bridging of the Digital Divide.

Power to the people in rural areas will become possible with pioneering innovations like those of Iqbal Qadir in Bangladesh, who decided that a telephone is a weapon against poverty. He built upon the existence of the Grameen Bank, which supplies micro credit to the rural poor in Bangladesh. In 1997 he launched the Grameen Phone or Village Phone.

When culture and nature are translated into digital information, the commercial exploitation of this information becomes a source of extraordinary power(Pradip N.Thomas, *Media Development2/2003, 3-11)* In an era of convergence, the need to monitor new sources of global economic and political power becomes imperative. Digital convergence between broadcasting and telecommunications is considered a part of "meta technologies," which are flexible and can be adapted to handle different types of interoperable communication devices and production processes (S. Braman, cited by Thomas, *ibid).*

Access to the spectrum for digital convergence is becoming an essential part of communication policies globally, and even with several challenges, it opens up opportunities for globalization and social integration, making the power of the knowledge economy widespread.

REFERENCES

Bauer, J., Kim, J., & Wildman, S. (2003). *Broadband deployment: Toward a more fully integrated policy perspective.* Quello Center Working Paper 001-2003 http://quello.msu.edu/wp-01-03 pdf

The Economist. (2004). Special report: Vision meets reality. September 4, 63-64.

The Economist. (2005). War of the wires. July 30, 53.

Firth, L., & Mellor, D. (2005). Broadband benefits and problems. *Telecommunications Policy* 29:2/3 March/April, 223-225.

Gabriel, C. (2004). U.S. spectrum wars. *ARC Chart: Blue Print online 10-18-2004*, 1-3.

Gillett, S.E., Lehr, W.E., & Osorio, C., (2004). Local government broadband initiatives. *Telecommunications Policy,* 28, 2004, 537-558.

Hazlett, T.W. (2003). Practical steps to spectrum markets. *Telecommunications Policy, Special Issue,* 27, 479-481.

Jussawalla, M. (1998). *Telecommunications: A bridge to the 21ˢᵗ century*, pp. 189-208. Amsterdam: North Holland.

Jussawalla, M. (2004). Satellite-based broadband: Current status and future prospects in Asia. *Proceedings of the Pacific Telecommunications Conference*, January, Honolulu.

Jussawalla, M., & Taylor, R. (2003). *IT parks of the Asia Pacific: Lessons for the regional digital divide*, pp. 254-282. New York: M. E. Sharpe.

Keidrowski, T.(2002). A model for broadband success. *Intermedia,* December, 26-28.

Kim, G. (2004). Assessing least cost revenue. *Fat Pipe,* April 15, 32-42.

Kim, G. (2005). European IP transit is toast. *Fat Pipe,* June 15, 21.

Kowal, J.(2005). *Telegeography update: Bandwidth demand outpaces price declines.* Online April 7.

Kowal, J. (2005). *Telegeography US VOIP Report.* Online Survey, June 15.

Lee, C., & Chan-Olmsted, (2004). Competitive advantages of broadband Internet: A comparative study between South Korea and the United States. *Telecommunications Policy*, pp. 679-696.

Missing Link Report (1985). *Report of the Maitland international commission.* International Telecommunications Union Geneva.

Park, J.(2004). *Subscribers' network: A new approach for convergence in Korea.* Unpublished Paper.

Porter,M. (1990). *The competitive advantage of nations.* New York, Free Press, 89.

Schatz, A. (2005). Fighting a broadband battle. *The Wall Street Journal,* July 19.

Snider, J.H. (2005). Should DTV must-carry be expanded, sunset, or preserved as-is?

Working Paper 12, Spectrum Policy Program, New America Foundation, Washington D.C. 1-19.

Telecom TV Review. (2005). May 7, 2006.

Wu, Irene. (2004). Canada, South Korea, Netherlands and Sweden: Regulatory implications of telecommunications, broadcasting, and Internet services. *Telecommunications Policy,* 28, 79-96.

Chapter II
Is this the Global Village?:
VoIP and Wire/Wireless Convergence

Jarice Hanson
Temple University, USA

ABSTRACT

A long-held desire on the part of many concerned technologists and social scientists has been the creation of a system that would allow individuals in the remotest regions of the globe to have access to communications technologies. Today, Voice over Internet Protocol (VoIP) allows individuals in regions formerly restricted by economic, geographic or cultural reasons to communicate on a broader scale at a reasonable financial cost, through convergent systems and wireless means, for purposes defined by themselves. This analysis explains the core components of VoIP and how it facilitates communication, considers the social and cultural impact of VoIP on a global scale and examines whether we are entering a truly "global village" through greater use of VoIP technologies.

INTRODUCTION

In 1844, Samuel F. B. Morse, developer of Morse code and the entrepreneur who perfected a "language" that enabled the new technology of telegraph to be more effectively used, predicted that telegraphy would result in a truly "global village" in which all communities and nations would eventually be connected by wires to systems that would change global communication patterns. By the end of the 1800s, Guglielmo Marconi had successfully experimented with radio and had begun to construct plans for the Marconi Wireless Telegraph Company Ltd.'s expansion to ultimately become what he called a "global village"—connecting areas and regions of the globe through wireless means (Dunlap, 1927). Later, Marshall McLuhan (1964) predicted visual and aural electronic media would eventually create a "global village" in which all inhabitants of the world could see, hear and respond to instant messages, from anywhere, anytime. Each of these forecasters maintained an optimistic view that global communication would reduce inequities among cultures and societies, eliminate hunger and social problems and create a more harmonious world in which people would respect difference and care for each other, ideals that might be expected in a village where faces, names and kinship bound individuals to others.

While these visions of a "global village" never came to pass because of technical, economic and political barriers, developments in technologies that combine wired forms (i.e., the Internet and World Wide Web) and wireless forms (mobile telephones) have indeed come of age to suggest yet another image of a "global village" in which the ability to communicate over distances has begun to contribute to cultural change and global awareness in many regions of the world. This time, however, the village represents groups of people who maintain their distinctive indigenous values and cultures while interacting with others throughout the world to maintain and improve their survival at the local level. When these cultures interact through the global economy, the sense of "village" finds a broader meaning. The new global village involves both the way in which local cultures participate in the global economy, and the way information and knowledge can be accessed so that it can be made to work for the best interests of the local community. What makes it possible for these groups to interact with greater knowledge and efficiency is the growth of low-cost communications that extend their ability to communicate over distances. Voice over Internet Protocol (VoIP) is a system that facilitates interaction at relatively low cost that could lead toward a new vision of the global village.

Some of the past barriers to participating in the global economy have involved the cost of large-scale infrastructures necessary to support electronic communications, literacy and restriction to major power-broker access. But today, the lower cost of wireless communication, the ability to use local spoken languages rather than written

communication and greater access to knowledge, have aided in the ability of a larger number of nations and cultures to participate in the global information infrastructure.

Voice-over-Internet protocol (VoIP) is the result of the convergence of wired and wireless forms (i.e., Internet and mobile phone) to facilitate voice, data and text-based communication. It marks total convergence, in the sense that VoIP uses all of the same technologies necessary to make seamless interoperability available for voice, data and text.

This analysis focuses on examples of how VoIP technologies and policies have changed communication practices, thereby contributing to cultural change that is viewed through a global lens. By examining some of the situations, we can better understand how this type of convergence brings social and cultural consequences, and consider whether VoIP may indeed be one of the key technologies allowing nations and cultures to participate in the new global village.

There are three objectives for this chapter: to explain the basic core components of VoIP and discuss the phenomena of VoIP communications, to consider the social and cultural impact of VoIP technological convergence on a global scale and to examine whether the "global village" is now a reality, given the growing use of VoIP technology.

BACKGROUND

It is amazing to think of the extraordinary changes in the world in the last 60 years—particularly in terms of what we know about other nations, and how all nations have responded to contemporary technology. In post-World War II days, the general knowledge of national and cultural diversity was limited, and that which existed was often primarily parochial and colonial. The post-war years resulted in the organization of several groups that stimulated support of rural telecommunications projects and research around the world, including the International Telecommunications Union (ITU), the United Nations Educational, Scientific and Cultural Organization (UNESCO), the Development Centre of the Organization for Economic Cooperation and Development (OECD), the World Bank and the Inter-American Development Bank (IDB), as well as the U.S. Agency for International Development (AID). More than any other group, UNESCO funded research on the growing utility of media to help inhabitants of developing countries deal with immediate problems of illiteracy, nutrition and improving agriculture.

In the 1960s, a number of studies proposed using media for development purposes. Among some of the most well-known included work by Lerner (1958), Schramm (1964) and Pool (1977), all of which suggested that media systems would inevitably lead to modernization of groups and nations. A common attitude toward helping lesser-developed countries become participants in the global economy was to help each nation increase its gross national product (GNP). Many of the problems identified by researchers reflected what was then known as the "dominant paradigm," which viewed the growth of mass media as a necessary component of assuring economic growth. Very little attention was paid to quality of life factors. In 1976, Rogers published an influential treatise that identified the problems with this "dominant paradigm" and the harm it could do to a culture in the developing world because of its hegemonic result.

As the work of scholars from other cultures began to influence the development dialogue, greater emphasis fell to the perspective of allowing developing nations to determine their own needs and to maintain indigenous cultures and practices. And while many nations lacked the internal economy to support the high cost of many forms of media that might be used for development purposes, many experiments succeeded, while many more failed. A number of scholars attempted to determine how local cultures could

survive if and when their dependency on other nations, groups or businesses became a mainstay of their cultures (see for example, Diaz-Bordenave, 1976; Mowlana, 1985).

Telephony in particular constituted an extraordinary investment by international aid organizations as well as private corporations. "In 1945 there were 41 million phones worldwide; by 1982, the total expenditures were more than 494 million, an increase of more than 1,200% (Hudson, 1984, p. 8)." But the growth of telephone systems was limited by geography, expense and the large scale infrastructure necessary to support such systems. And, while the utility of telephones was evidenced by a number of scenarios indicating how telephones could aid in getting medical help, emergency warnings and other needs communicated over distances, telephones did little within rural environments when oral communication was sufficient for the local needs and economy of the individuals.

Fast-Forward

Since those naive days of searching for theories by investigating how and what role media and telecommunications could play in creating opportunities for cultures to use technology for development purposes, as well as others, the world of technology has virtually exploded. In particular, the extraordinary development of the World Wide Web and the development of wireless technologies have expanded rapidly—creating a situation in which the problems associated with large-scale infrastructure technologies and communicating over distances, have changed faster than the academics have been able to publish theories and ideas on technology's role in social change. Companies, corporations, and occasionally national ministries of post, telecommunications or information have joined forces in some controversial ways—but have resulted quite often in newly formed organizations that are truly international in their manufacture and implementation of telecommunications systems.

Digital technology has grown exponentially since the 1980s, and has introduced new concerns that describe countries that have and have not access to telecommunications in today's world. The development of digital transmission systems that result in wired and wireless convergence as a means of creating a more level playing field for a global telecommunication infrastructure is viewed as an antidote to what has been called the "digital divide." And while the technologies are constantly changing, as are the companies and corporations hoping to supply digital technology and systems for global communication, new theoretical perspectives are attempting to explain change in an environment in which the only constant is change.

ISSUES, EXAMPLES, CONTROVERSIES, AND PROBLEMS

Even though the problems associated with fixed-wire telephone services were myriad, growth of telephony in nations around the world has steadily increased since the 1950s (Curwen, 2002, p.11). What tipped the balance was the extraordinary growth of mobile phones that operate on a wireless platform, eliminating the need for expensive wiring across distances. With the aid of new, less expensive switching systems, service can be maintained at much lower cost than traditional fixed phones. Without the cumbersome, expensive process of running cables or fiber optics over great distances, mobile phones have freed many nations from the slow roll-out of expensive wired telephony. An important benchmark for the shift from traditional fixed-wire telephony to mobile phones occurred in 2004, when in that year alone, 90% of the world's new telecommunications connections were mobile (Gartner, 2005). Since the early days of mobile phones, many countries

have embraced the new technology and many of the new consumers have found the mobile phone superior to the fixed-wire service.

While the origin of VoIP can be traced to the early days of the Internet, when, in the U.S., it was referred to as "Voice Funnel" as part of an ARPA project involving packetized audio, it did not become a reliable method of voiced communications until 1995 when digital-signal processing (DSP) and microprocessors became sophisticated enough for mainstream use. Generically referred to as IP-telephony, the first generation technology required that users log on to the Internet to access other phoneware users through a directory service. Public directories, or e-mail addresses routed calls to other IP-telephone users. Each party had a microphone connected to a soundcard in their computer; the phone software would then digitize and compress the audio signal and route it through TCP/IP connections over the Internet, where it would be modulated to an audio sound at the other end. In the early days, the modem speed often had to be adjusted for particular speech styles. Silence, for example, would send the modem into a "search" mode for frequency; once it was found, the levels again had to be re-balanced. Once higher speed modems began to be used, many of the problems inherent in voiced communication were corrected electronically. Since that time, a number of hardware and software vendors have emerged to improve various VoIP components. And while the sound quality has improved, some of the commercial VoIP providers have yet to be totally successful with connecting one of their VoIP users with conventional telephones, though progress toward this end is rapidly taking place. When this is effectively accomplished, the potential for the new global village will expand dramatically because, as Greenblatt has written, "VoIP will change peoples lives through increasingly personalized services (2003, p. 66)."

The great benefit of VoIP is that it costs significantly less than traditional phone calls, and, distance no longer seems to be a cost-prohibitive feature for telephone service. For example, in 2001, even though VoIP technology was not as widely available as it is today, on Mother's Day, ITXC, a VoIP carrier, announced that the U.S. used 5.7 million minutes on its networks. In Mexico, on the same day, over 4.2 million minutes were used. And in the U.S., 96% of the calls made on that day were international calls, sent to over 200 countries (Archer, 2001, p.1).

In short, VoIP routes voice, data and text over the Internet of any other IP-based network, rather than over traditional circuit-switched voice transmission lines. What makes VoIP such an exciting possibility for connecting the growing number of mobile telephones, world-wide, with the growing number of Internet connections in a low-cost format, has to do with the flexibility afforded by VoIP architecture. In addition to facilitating communication among broadband (wired or wireless), and handheld devices, like those used for a mobile phone, VoIP drives convergence of other technologies and can be used for a number of value-added services, including speech recognition and virtual private networks. The system is reliable, and interoperable—meaning it can operate over a variety of different platforms and networks in a seamless manner. The growth of mobile phones, particularly 3G phones, provides the necessary hardware for user-friendly services that thrive on VoIP services.

Figure 1 compares the growth of the Internet and the growth of mobile communications in countries around the world (World Summit on the Information Society, 2005).

It could be said that the global diffusion of the Internet was initially a natural evolution of the large-scale infrastructural developments that retarded growth of greater equality of access to communication and information such as those referred to in an earlier section of this chapter, but what made both the Internet and mobile phones more practical technologies for social and cultural change within formerly lesser-developed countries, was the ability to "connect" these technologies through wireless means. Without a doubt, the user-friendly features of mobile phones provided the necessary final link to making distributed communications more possible for a greater number of people.

Figure 1. Comparison of mobile subscribers and Internet penetration (Source: ITU. [2005]. World Summit on the Information Society)

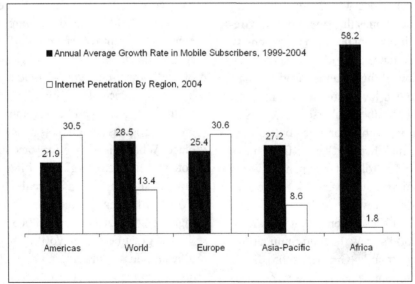

The Mobile Phone Connection

Different countries took different routes toward mobile telephony. In Nordic countries, analog mobile phones were introduced as early as 1981, but when digital services became possible in 1982, voice, text and data could be packet-switched with little loss of signal. Europe was in position to use GSM technology, which resulted in a much more rapid diffusion of mobile phones. Soon 3-G phones became the standard.

The United States began to see analog mobile phones in 1983, but the ubiquity of wired services made the new phones seem experimental, rather than fully functional. In the U.S., the Federal Communications Commission (FCC) was slow to approve any particular standard of transmissions, so by 2005 approximately 75% of the adults in the U.S. had a mobile phone (Levinson, 2004, p. 32) but those phones did not have the technical sophistication of 3G phones.

Consider some of the countries in which mobile handsets now outnumber fixed-wire handsets: Finland, the world's most heavily saturated mobile phone culture, exceeded the number of fixed-handset phones in 1998; by 1999, Austria, Hong Kong, Israel, South Korea, Japan, Uganda and Venezuela exceeded fixed-wire handsets with mobiles. By the year 2000, the worldwide growth of mobile phones was so great that Bahrain, Chile, Greece, Mexico, the Netherlands, Philippines, Rwanda, South Africa and the UK all joined a "more mobile" telephone infrastructure (Curwen, p. 12).

THE SOCIAL AND CULTURAL IMPACT

There is no doubt that the concept of the "digital divide" still exists among the regions of the world, but due to the recent growth of the Internet, mobile phones and VoIP, we could see very dramatic changes in the near future. Once the architecture and end-user technologies are available, VoIP will reduce the cost of transmission while still offering more services.   According to International Telecommunications Union data, Africa still remains the most "underdeveloped" developing nation with less than 3 out of every 100 Africans using the Internet, but at the same time, Africa has greater growth in mobile communications than any other region of the world (World Summit on the Information Society, pp. 1-2). Europe by contrast, has more mobile subscribers now than fixed line telephone users, with a 70% penetration in the western countries, while there are a growing number in central and eastern Europe. Internet capability throughout Europe mirrors the penetration rates of mobile telephony (p. 5).

The United States and Canada have about twice the mobile penetration and twice the Internet availability than do South America and the Caribbean (p. 3). On a regional basis, the Asia-Pacific region has the greatest number of inequities in mobile/Internet technologies, with less than 1% Internet penetration in some of the smaller countries, to 90% Internet penetration in Hong Kong and Singapore, and a growing number of mobile phones. Australia and The Republic of Korea each have 65% Internet access, but India has the greatest mobile growth with a 90% per annum growth rate in recent years (p. 4).

The VoIP Providers

Traditional concepts of development and the "global village" warned of the problems of colonization and the political influence wielded by many of the former telecom providers. Greenblatt (2003, p. 147) has identified some of the most powerful convergence companies, based upon their 2001 sales (in billions of U.S. dollars) in Table 1.

What is noticeable when considering the major companies involved in VoIP technology is the partnerships that make the companies truly international in nature. In addition to the above-named companies, Verizon, the largest

Table 1.

3Com	Avaya	Alcatel	Cisco	Deltathree	IBasics	ITXC	Nortel	Lucent	Juniper
2.8	6.8	22.6	22.3	.016	.134	.173	.17.5	21.3	.887

U.S. telephone company, has shifted much of its traditional business to wireless—and uses the growing availability of VoIP. Verizon is 55% owned by the Verizon Corporation in America, but 45% owned by the British Vodafone Group, PLC (Mohammed, 2005).

Global growth of consumer VoIP services have begun to accelerate. In the U.S., for example, there are several competing companies, such as Skype, Google Talk, and Vonage. Even Microsoft has been gearing up to enter the U.S. market. In one particularly important U.S. city, New Orleans, which had all domestic telecommunications destroyed by Hurricane Katrina on September 30, 2005, plans have been developed to introduce VoIP services over 200 wireless nodes by the end of 2006, as that city attempts to rebuild with low cost, reliable telephone services that will continue to operate even in the wake of another natural disaster that could wipe out land lines.

In other parts of the world, the growth of VoIP is no less impressive. According to the *Kenya Times*, eight firms have been licensed to offer new VoIP services for businesses and consumers (Kiphagei, 2005). Malaysia, too, has doubled its efforts to introduce VoIP services, as has Burma, and Bahrain. South Korea, which had only one fixed-line phone for every 300 residents in 1960, now has a 90% penetration rate for fixed-line services, and three-quarters of the population have mobile phones that can access bank accounts and be used for a variety of additional services including on-line gaming (Man's best friend, 2005, pp. 8-9). The Singapore airport, the busiest in the world, now provides travelers in the international lounge with VoIP connections.

THE NEW GLOBAL VILLAGE

The remarkable changes in the development of technologies, the international nature of manufacturers, service providers and vendors, require new theories to help explain the impact of global communications change. The new global economy dictates the relationships of regions in the world, but issues of access to affordable, user-friendly technology are no longer the problem they once were. One of the newer theories that helps explain social change in the contemporary world comes from Barabasi (2002) and network theory that can explain how technological systems and social systems *together* act as agents of change in today's world. The basis of network theory is that it is impossible to isolate change agents in a dynamic infrastructure—a method far removed from the linear theoretical approaches in the last half of the twentieth century. What is particularly useful to Barabasi's interpretation is the idea that it is no longer possible to isolate every issue of national identity from the more common multinational corporation—and it is no longer possible to separate the local from the global in today's economic marketplace.

If we examine the impact of mobile phones and VoIP services only in the industrialized world, it would be possible to start with data on traditional, fixed-wire services and the new, value added services of the mobiles. Pricing structures would be fairly easy to comprehend because wireless technologies could be balanced against traditional legacy media. In these countries, the range of value added services through VoIP are many, but the most notable feature is the portability factor of the mobile phone for easy access anywhere, as long as the user is in a wireless range. When a call can be transferred through the Internet, the mobile phone becomes almost like an extension of the computer—and can access financial records, entertainment, data, voice and much more, including voiced services for directions, clarification of information and passive instruction. While the mobile phone may not do anything that a number of other technologies could not do—the phone does it with the help of the one, portable unit. When connected through the Internet for transmission, the cost goes down, but the number of services go up.

The greater impact by far is on the nations of the world that never had sufficient fixed-line services. When we consider the early research on development and consider the plight of lesser developed nations in particular, we see that attempts to engineer social change required access to affordable technology while considering the culture's literacy rate as an indicator of individuals' learning how to use new technology. In oral societies in particular, this impediment prevented effective roll-out of many communications technologies.

As Goody and Watt (1968, pp. 31-4) reminded us, oral societies have a strong connection to homeostasis, which grounds cultural action in the present. The pace of change is expected to be slow. So how, then, do individuals in oral societies now use mobile services?

The extraordinary cultural impact of using mobile phones and VoIP technologies has provided a number of interesting images of social and cultural change, but in most cases, the mobile technologies are, in part, used to facilitate traditional beliefs. Spirituality is one example of how mobile technology has facilitated traditional beliefs.Today, Muslims in more than 500 cities around the world can use mobile phones to remind them of prayer times, and with 3G phones, they can use the features of the handset to orient themselves toward Mecca at times of prayer (A spiritual connection, 2005, pp. 12 and 15).

Even some of the poorest regions of the world have had individuals who have used mobile telephones in very creative ways that extend social relationships. In some regions, collectives of fishermen or farmers pool funds to use a mobile phone to find the best prices for their goods. When VoIP is used, meager pools of money go much farther.

Even though the number of phones per 100 people in poor countries is much lower than in the developed world, they can have a dramatic impact: reducing transaction costs, broadening trade networks and reducing the need to travel, which is of particular value for people looking for work. Little wonder that people in poor countries spend a larger proportion of their income on telecommunications than those in rich ones (Calling across the divide, 205, p. 74).

While we cannot discount the efforts of international aid agencies in bringing telecommunications to different regions, we may well have crossed over to a time in which the aid agencies and the corporations have found a new working model. As cited in *The Economist* (Calling across the divide), mobile telephony does not require intervention of funding from the UN; mobile phones do not rely on electricity supply and can be used by people who cannot read or write. While the UN has set goals to help increase the number of mobile phones in developing nations by 2015, a new report from the World Bank noted that as of 2005, 77% of the world's population already lives within a range of a mobile network.

Ironically, but perhaps most importantly, mobile telephony and VoIP services have allowed cultures that have a strong base in village life to continue to live in communities in which the indigenous values predominate and support continuity.What mobile telephones and VoIP services do, however, is support the need for orality and control of one's cultural values. Even in regions where phones are shared and rented out by the call, such as those operated by "telephone ladies" in Bangladeshi villages, the new telecommunica-

Figure 2. Elements of the new Global Village with indigenous values at the center

tions allow villagers to access and receive needed information and reduce travel—all elements that strengthen local ties, rather than stress local values by external needs.

The new global village is linked through low-cost wireless means that privilege local values. Change may come more slowly, but it may come at a more culturally relevant pace.   In the new global village, the world has become the market-place, and at least the communication capabilities of individuals within their own cultures have become a little more equitable. Is the global village a place of harmony and understanding? Not yet, but we have moved toward a village in which different voices can now be heard.

The global village today is in a constant state of change, accelerating because of low cost telecommunication developments and distribution forms. Social relations and discourses have changed, and will continue to change. Physical location no longer restricts someone from interaction with others, or access to information.

FUTURE TRENDS: TOWARD TRUE CONVERGENCE

Many cities and regions throughout the world look forward to wireless access for all within their borders. VoIP will be the conduit by which this convergence takes place. Access will no longer remain the problem it once was for any society, or culture. But no matter where enhanced communications possibilities exist, there are drawbacks to greater reliance on these services too.

It would be naïve to say that the global village would be perfect. There are many more advances that need to be made on the technological/cost sides before we safely cross the digital divide. But at the same time, what once seemed like an insurmountable problem of attempting to equalize communications around the world, has begun to change. In the future, further development of 3G mobile telephones and low-cost computational devices, such as "hundred dollar laptops" (HDLs) could continue to aid information access to even some of the poorest citizens of the world (Pontin, 2005, p. 14).

Both China and India, two of the world's most populous regions, have also begun to make mobile telephony and VoIP more available to a wider variety of individuals within their own borders. Within a few years, China may have its own domestic industry and telecommunications infrastructure that would truly help the Chinese take their place as one of the world's leaders is mobile manufacturing. And, though India already has major urban areas that use VoIP technologies to provide global services, a domestic market in mobile manufacture, as part of other multinational corporations' efforts to reach the large population, is already being developed.

The Controversies

While access to mobile telecommunications is indeed growing rapidly, VoIP is not a panacea for local and global communications. Like many digital technologies, new problems seem to emerge at an alarming rate. In particular, spam and unlawful monitoring, or "packet snooping" and eavesdropping, have emerged as problems associated with the growth of VoIP. The vulnerabilities of data networking often bring to the fore issues of security and national sovereignty regarding the privacy of citizens.

In the U.S., the VOIP Security Alliance has attempted to press for regulatory and policy efforts to control threats ranging from spam to denial of service attacks and unlawful monitoring of calls (Carlson, 2005, p. 22), and on the global front, NGOs and international agencies alike have called for protocols and penalties for those who misuse the networks. One great fear is that the packet-switching protocol could lead toward a surveillance society because of the vulnerability of packet-switching to be intercepted and manipulated.

The new global village may not reflect the same values and ideas as identified by Morse, Marconi or McLuhan, but may reflect the importance of localism and local cultural values as integrally important to maintaining a sense of local identity, despite the growth and pressure of surviving in a global economy. The global villages may also not have absolute equality among other villages, cities and regions of the world—but as information access becomes more prevalent, the individuals involved will have the ability to make better, more locally informed decisions. The idea that local growth could not occur until literacy was adopted, and the problems associated with long-term development strategies are not as important as they once seemed. The technologies that draw on orality and oral maintenance of culture have found the type of voiced communication medium that still values, and actually needs the ability to communicate through a voiced message system.

As we experience these changes, our traditional concepts and definitions will be challenged. How we once defined "village" has changed, as have traditional concepts of what *social* and *cultural* mean. The *social* is no longer circumscribed by interpersonal, face-to-face communication, or defined by persons in groups. Rather, it may involve voiced transmission, or voice and data, over greater distances, with the purpose of utilizing technologies to reach others (persons, databases and information repositories) for the benefit of the user, or his/her constituencies. The term "cultural" has expanded too, from strictly identifying indigenous beliefs, practices and values,to that of sharing some form of partnership in interaction. As evidenced by the examples in this chapter, "cultural" can also mean participation in a technological culture—such as telecommunications.

While it is often said, "hindsight is 20-20," what earlier development theories lacked was the idea that media or telecommunications could be viewed as an entire system. Of course, in the days in which corporations were far more closed entities, it was simpler to point an accusatory finger at an agency or corporation and identify hegemonic practices that ended in at the bottom line. Today capitalism has been triumphant on a global scale, and while this author prefers not to comment on how that model serves humanity, to overlook the role of the contemporary global economy would be irresponsible and naïve. What has emerged, however, is a different playing field that can be examined on alternative criteria, and that may well be in the form of access to information that can no longer be separated from its sponsor, or source.

VoIP is the means toward creating a more equitable communications infrastructure for the world. With the convergence of technologies, VoIP will stand as a leader in uniting people while privileging traditional values and behaviors. As a result, it may truly be the quintessential form of creating equality toward purposes of communication.

REFERENCES

Agar, J. (2003). *Constant touch: A global history of the mobile phone.* Cambridge, UK: Icon Books.

Archer, R. (2001, May 14). U.S. and Mexico mother's days set all-time VoIP traffic records. *IP Telephony News.*

Barabasi, A. (2002). *Linked: How everything is connected to everything else and what it means for business, science, and everyday life.* NY: Plume.

Beck, J., & Wade, M. (2003). *DoCoMo: Japan's wireless tsunami.* NY: American Management Association.

Carlson, C. (2005, October 24). Alliance tackles VoIP threats. *eWeek,* 22.

Curwen, P. (2002). *The future of mobile communications: Awaiting third generation.* NY: Palgrave/Macmillan.

Diaz-Bordenave, J. (1976). Communication of agricultural innovations. In E. Rogers (Ed.), *Communication and development: Critical perspectives.* Beverly Hills, CA: Sage, 43-62.

Dunlap, O. E., Jr. (1927). *The story of radio.* NY: The Dial Press.

The Economist (2005). A spiritual connection, March 12-18, 374, 12 & 15.

The Economist (2005). Behind the digital divide, March 12-18, 374, 22 & 25.

The Economist (2005). Calling across the divide, March 12-18, 374, 74. *The Economist* (2005). The device that ate everything? March 12-18, 374.

The Economist (2005). Man's best friend: Not a dog, but a mobile phone, April 2-5, 374, 8-10.

The Economist (2005). The real digital divide, March 12-18, 374, 11.

Galambos, L., & Abrahamson, E. J. (2002). *Anytime, anywhere: Entrepreneurship and the creation of a wireless world.* Cambridge, UK: Cambridge University Press.

Gartner Report (South Africa). (2005, Nov. 30). *Gartner identifies six trends for the future.* Accessed at: http://www.moneyweb.co.za/business_today/64126.htm

Goody, J., & Watt, I. (1968). The consequences of literacy. In J. Goody (Ed.), *Literacy in traditional societies.* Cambridge, UK: Cambridge University Press.

Greenblatt, D. (2003) *The call heard 'round the world'.* NY: American Management Association.

Hudson, H. E. (1984). *When telephones reach the village.* Norwood, NJ: Ablex Publications.

International Telecommunications Union (2005). *World summit on the information society,* Geneva 2003-Tunis, 2005. Accessed at www.itu.int/wsis/tunis/newsroom/stats

Kiphagei, N. (2005, November 30). Eight firms licensed to offer VoIP Services. Accessed at http://www.timesnews.co.k/30nov05/mainnews.html

Krug, G. (2005). *Communication, technology and cultural change.* London and Thousand Oaks, CA: Sage.

Lerner, D. (1958). *The passing of traditional society.* Glencoe, IL: Free Press.

Levinson, P. (2004). *Cellphone: The story of the world's most mobile medium and how it transformed everything!* NY: Palmgrave/Macmillan.

McLuhan, M. (1964). *Understanding media: The extensions of man.* NY: McGraw-Hill.

Mohammed, A. (2005, July 27). Telecom plugs into wireless. Accessed at http://www.washingtonpost.com/wp-dyn/content/article/2005/07/26/AR2005072601756-p.htm

Mowlana, H. (1985). *Global information and world communication.* NY: Longman.

Muller, N. J. (2002). *Desktop encyclopedia of telecommunications* (Vol. 2). NY: McGraw-Hill.

Organization for Economic Co-operation and Development (2002). *Mobile phones: Pricing structures and trends.* Paris: OECD Publications.

Pontin, J. (2005, August). Mediating poverty. *Technology Review, 108,* 14.

Pool, I. de Sola. (1977). *The social impact of the telephone.* Cambridge, MA: MIT Press.

Rogers, E. M. (1976). Communication and development: The passing of the dominant paradigm. *Communiction Research 3,* 213-240.

Schramm, W. (1964). *Mass media and national development.* Stanford, Ca: Stanford University Press.

Steinbock, D. (2003). *Wireless horizon: Strategy and competition in the worldwide mobile marketplace.* NY: American Management Association.

Chapter III
Modified Lease Auction:
Proposal of a New System for Efficient Assignment of Radio-Spectrum Resources

Hajime Oniki
Osaka-Gakuin University, Japan

ABSTRACT

This paper proposes a system by means of which the utilization of radio spectrum may be improved from extreme inefficiency at present to equilibrium and efficiency in the future. It introduces a system which takes advantage of market mechanism with regard to spectrum assignment as distinct from spectrum allocation. It is composed of two parts. The first part proposes a system called "modified lease auction (MLA)," in which the government leases (rents) spectrum competitively to business and public users. To protect incumbents from excessive risk of losing spectrum rights, it proposes a number of ways including a provision of insurance. The second part considers the transition from the current system to MLA. It proposes a process in which the spectrum price be increased gradually from the current zero level to the target equilibrium level. Further, in order to reconcile to oppositions by incumbents to MLA, a scheme is proposed for compensating income to incumbents without hurting the incentive to save spectrum.

INTRODUCTION AND BACKGROUND

The objective of this paper is to propose a system by means of which the utilization of radio spectrum may be improved from the state of extreme inefficiency at the present time to a state of efficiency and equilibrium in the future.

We will propose a system to be called "modified lease auction (MLA)," in which the government retains the ownership of radio spectrum but leases it to users according to auction on lease prices. In order to remedy shortcomings of the lease system, a number of modifications will be introduced to it, hence the naming of *modified* lease auction. Lease prices may be used by the government for making adjustments in the allocation of spectrum bands in the long run as well as for assigning spectrum blocks to users in the short run.

In the second part of this paper, a scheme will be proposed for gradual transition from the present state of spectrum utilization with zero price to a state in which the market price prevails. In addition, in order to reconcile political oppositions to the introduction of MLA by incumbent spectrum users, a provision for income compensation will be introduced so as to protect incumbent income on the one hand, but not to lower the efficiency of spectrum utilization on the other. Radio spectrum in Japan, as in other countries, was first used about 100 years ago for navigational safety and navy operations. Since that time, the utilization of spectrum has expanded steadily and greatly. In the 1920s, voice radio broadcasting became popular, and in the 1940s, during the War, radar was invented. After the War, in the 1950s, television receivers, first black and white and then color, became a major household good. Meanwhile, the use of spectrum for military, police and other public activities has increased. Today, in many countries, mobile telephony shows a penetration exceeding one-half of the population, and spectrum is used widely for many other purposes, including remote sensing by satellites.

Such remarkable development of the utilization of radio spectrum was achieved, needless to say, by a succession of technological advances. Typically, a new technology was introduced by making use of a new "band" of radio frequencies which had so far been unused; that is to say, the development process was an expansion of the frontier of spectrum utilization. The issue to be dealt with in this paper arises from the fact that such frontiers are nearly exhausted today.

During the course of this process, the administration of of radio spectrum use was under the direct command and control of the central government in almost every country. For one thing, the major concern was how to prevent interference between spectrum users; thus calling for public regulation. For another, spectrum was first used for safety and security; it was natural for the government to play a management role. Furthermore, since new utilization of spectrum was made possible by the expansion of spectrum frontier, spectrum scarcity was not a major concern; the government was able to award the right to use spectrum without trouble.

Thus, until recently, the principle of command and control by the government prevailed in spectrum utilization. The government first determines that a particular band of frequencies be used for a specified purpose, and then assigns it to users on a first-come basis or by discretion. In Japan, as in many other countries, there has been no rent charged by the government from spectrum users except nominal fees for the cost of administration. In short, the world of radio spectrum has been a socialistic island under the governmental command and control in an ocean of economic activities under market mechanism.

This situation, however, changed in the 1990s. As the speed of technological progress was increased, the demand for radio spectrum grew exponentially in envisioning new services such as mobile telephony and wireless Internet access. Roughly speaking, at the beginning of the 21st century, the frontier of economically usable spectrum was nearly exhausted. The present situation is such that we are unable to find a frequency band for new services in the same way as we were able in the past.

It should be noted, however, that, while the frontier may have been exhausted, it does not mean that there is no way to find additional spectrum for new services. There still remains a great many opportunities of increasing the supply of spectrum by means of spectrum adjustments such as *reallocation* and *reassignment*. A large portion of the spectrum bands which have been allocated and assigned to users (particularly military and corporate users) remains unused or used very inefficiently. During the time of frontier expansion, it was of little concern to the government to have spectrum used efficiently. Furthermore, it was not a concern of users either to save spectrum use since the price was near zero, except with such users as mobile telephone operators, for which the supply of spectrum was insufficient relative to their need. As a consequence, the state of utilization of radio spectrum at the present time is in extreme disequilibrium; some spectrum is used efficiently with a large amount of expenditure on new equipment, but other spectrum is used inefficiently with old and obsolete equipment. This situation may be compared to a case in which large farmland is found within the City of London or next to the Empire State Building in New York. Such a case in the use of land would be precluded by the market power. For radio spectrum, we have extremely unbalanced utilization, since the market power is not working there.

The challenge we face today is to find a way to get out of such inefficient disequilibrium. Since the frontier has been exhausted and the utilization remains unbalanced, some reallocation or reassignment of radio spectrum between incumbent and new users is unavoidable. There are, however, several factors which make such adjustments of spectrum use under the governmental command and control extremely difficult.

First of all, the need for adjustments depends on technological progress which increases the efficiency of spectrum utilization. Since, however, the speed and the cost of technological progress cannot be predicted precisely, there will always be uncertainly as to what would be a desirable extent of reallocation or reassignment.

Second, there will be strong opposition to spectrum adjustments by incumbents, who have been using spectrum free of charge for years and have vested interest in it in the form of equipment, devices and other investment. A consequence would be irresolvable disputes on an adjustment proposal between incumbent and new users.

On top of these, the presence of technical and other regulations on the use of spectrum increases the difficulty of spectrum adjustments. The regulations are complicated and many of them are outdated because of the rapid progress of technology in the past. It would be difficult to evaluate an adjustment plan in the presence of a complicated regulatory environment. It would be more difficult to do so if the *issue of improving regulations itself* needed to be taken into consideration. Because of these factors, spectrum adjustments in many countries tend to become not only a regulatory issue but also a political conflict on which it is difficult to reach an agreement.

The objective of this paper is to propose a system for improving the efficiency of spectrum utilization by means of reassignments. In view of the above observations, we will adopt the following strategy for the presentation in this paper:First, we concentrate on economic aspects of spectrum utilization and adjustments. By this we mean that we do not deal with the issue of improving technical regulations; we take them as given in our discussion. This does not mean, however, that there is no need for improving technical regulations; on the contrary, we think there is a strong need for it. We only try to separate economic considerations from technical ones.

Next, it will be one of our main concerns to propose a system in which the benefit of technological progress be fully materialized and the incentive to promote technological progress be maximized. This paper, however, is not concerned with evaluating or recommending a particular technology for spectrum utilization. The author of this paper agrees that new technologies for sharing spectrum (such as spread spectrum, ultra-wide band and software-defined radio) may greatly improve the efficiency of spectrum utilization in the near future. The objective of this paper is to propose an economic system in which superior technology, regardless whether such technology is for shared or other use, be adopted through competition, not through the governmental command and control.

In the followingSection, a summary will be given of the economic properties of spectrum resource and of spectrum utilization at the present time. In the thirdSection, the system of modified lease auction (MLA) will be presented. It is noted that MLA can accommodate various modes of spectrum utilization such as exclusive , club and commons use. The fourthSection presents a scheme for transition from the present system to MLA. It is composed of two procedures. One is a stepwise increase in the lease price from the present level of zero price to the equilibrium market price. The other is a scheme for income compensation. The Appendix gives a list of acronyms used in this paper.

THE PRESENT SYSTEM OF SPECTRUM UTILIZATION

Outline

In this section, we first summarize the economic properties of radio spectrum, which will be considered as one of space resources. We then proceed to explain the present system of spectrum utilization. The proposal to be made in this paper would greatly change, on the one hand, the substance of spectrum utilization in that it introduces lease auction and other market elements to replace command-and-control decisions by the government. On the other hand, as explained in the preceding section, the proposal will be presented in such a way not to change much the formality of spectrum utilization given by technical regulations. Therefore, it will be useful to give a perspective of the formality in which radio spectrum is utilized at the present time and then to make clear at which points within this formality the proposal of this paper intends to introduce changes.

Spectrum as an Economic Resource

Radio spectrum is a non-reproducible natural resource. It is different from oil or mineral deposits in that it does not deplete. It is different from produced capital in that it does not depreciate. Radio spectrum, however, is not a resource of unlimited supply. As such, radio spectrum in many respects resembles "land" as real estate. In fact, radio spectrum as an economic resource may be classified into a category of *space resources*, of which examples are land space, water space, air space and the space of satellite orbits, to name a few. The term "spectrum" means, in many cases, the *space* for having radiowaves of designated frequencies propagate through.[1, 2]

Radio spectrum is used for many purposes and communication is a major, but not the only, one. In order to use radio spectrum, we always need to prepare some capital stock such as equipment, devices, software and others.

Technology plays an important role in using spectrum. Technological progress makes it possible to improve or invent capital stock (e.g., communications devices), thereby increasing the *capacity* of spectrum utilization (e.g., the capacity for data transmission). For example, spread spectrum (such as CDMA used for the third generation of mobile telephony) or code compression (such as MPEG formats used, among others, for digital television broadcasting), both being technology to increase the communications capacity

Figure 1. Tradeoff between capital stock (K) and spectrum bandwidth (B) in the use of spectrum with given technology

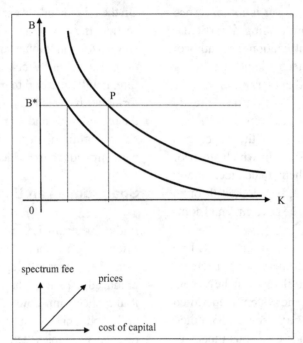

of spectrum, may be compared with skyscraper buildings, a product of technology to increase the capacity of land for office and other use.

In fact, using radio spectrum can be viewed as an activity for producing a service such as mobile telephony and Internet access. In this activity, spectrum and capital stock are substitutable inputs; a given quantity of service can be produced with different quantities of spectrum and capital stock as represented by a curve in Figure 1; the shape and the location of a curve is determined by the technology being used for production.

Suppose, for example, that a mobile-phone provider with old technology operates at point P by using up the assigned spectrum at B*. With the introduction of new technology, the curve may be shifted toward the origin, and the provider could save spectrum by operating at Q. At the present time, however, the price of using spectrum is zero, and the operator would choose point R to save

capital investment instead (or to increase service production with given capital investment). Thus, there is no incentive for the provider to save spectrum under the present system of zero price.

It may be convenient to summarize briefly some of the economic characteristics common to land and spectrum (and to space resources in general). First, both land and spectrum can be used in various modes, including exclusive use, club use and commons use. A land space for residence is used exclusively, while streets and city parks are examples of commons. We will consider different modes of spectrum utilization in detail in the third subsection of the second section.

Second, space resources exhibit economies of scale; that is, there are cases in which doubling the size of land or spectrum returns more-than-doubled outcome. For the case of land, an example of economies of scale may be seen in the traffic capacity of highways; the capacity of a two-lane highway is greater than twice that of a single-lane one, and the capacity of a three-lane highway is greater than one-and-half times of that of a two-lane one. Similar examples may be found with land space used for buildings. The benefit obtained by sharing spectrum by means of spread technology is an example of economies of scale in spectrum utilization.

Third, space resources have external diseconomies in that excessive use of a space lowers the return; such a case is called "congestion" in the use of land and "interferences" in the use of spectrum.

Fourth, we note that, in general, a space resource may be in the state of short supply or of excess supply. For example, there are excess supplies of land in rural areas, whereas the supply is tight in cities. Similarly, spectrum is scarce in urban areas, but not so scarce in rural areas. The state of a space resource with regard to "supply tightness" depends on the demand for it, the size of the space as given by Mother Nature and the technology for using it. Spectrum utilization has become an important issue, since the demand for spectrum grew faster than the advancement of technology, which can increase the efficiency of spectrum utilization.

Lastly, a major difference between land and spectrum at the present time is that a large portion of land is used under market mechanism in most countries, whereas the use of spectrum is under the command and control by the government. The command and control worked well at the time when the supply of spectrum resources was abundant relative to the demand. It is obsolete at the time of spectrum scarcity, as agreed upon widely (e.g., FCC (2002)). The objective of this paper is to propose a system dealing with spectrum scarcity by using the power of market mechanism.

Allocation of Spectrum Bands

The utilization of radio spectrum at the present time is administered by the government in two stages; the first stage is the allocation of spectrum bands for specific purposes (to be called *ALLOC* in this paper), and the second stage is the assignment of spectrum blocks to users (*ASSGN*).

The ALLOC stage specifies *spectrum bands* and the ASSGN stage subdivides a band into *spectrum blocks*, both frequency-wise and area-wise. A band is a range of radio frequencies given one or more objectives for which it is to be used. An example of ALLOC and ASSGN is given in Figure 2.[3] As the objective for spectrum usage, it gives "Broadcast" for band A, "Commercial Mobile" for band B and so on. An overall specification of spectrum bands is determined by the World Administrative Radio Conferences (WARC) under the International Telecommunications Union (ITU) in order to facilitate international coordination of spectrum utilization. The WARC is held periodically; it designates the use of spectrum bands for each of the three regions of the world: Regions One (Europe and Africa), Two (Americas) and Three (Asia and Oceania). The government of each country may specify a band and its objective in more detail within the framework determined by the WARC.

Occasionally, we introduce a secondary objective for using a band; in that case, the right to use the band is divided, according to *priority*, into two, the right on a primary basis and the right on secondary basis. A primary user has the same right as given in the absence of a a secondary user. A secondary user can use it within the restriction not to disturb the primary user and to accept any possible disturbances from the primary user.[4] In Figure 2, all users are given primary rights.

Figure 2. Example of spectrum usage (current system)

	Spectrum Band (Frequencies)	Band A		Band B			Band C	Band D	Band E	Band F
ALLOC	Objective	Broadcast		Commercial Mobile			Security	Air Transportation	Internet Access	Unspecified (ISM)
	Priority	Primary		Primary			Primary	Primary	Primary	Primary
	Usage mode specified by government (Mode-G)	Exclusive		Exclusive			Exclusive	Club	Commons ("unlicensed")	Commons ("unlicensed")
ASSGN	Spectrum Block (Area, Time) with License	A1	A2	B1	B2	B3	C	D	(E)	(F)
	Duration	10yrs		5yrs			5yrs	(indefinite)	(indefinite)	(indefinite)
	Spectrum User (Licensee)	Broadcast Stations		Mobile-phone Providers			Police, Fire Stations	Airlines	(NA)	(NA)
	Usage mode specified by user (Mode-L)	Club/ commons		Club			Exclusive	Club	(NA)	(NA)
	Final user	Consumers, etc., of Services using Spectrum								

In addition to the objective and the priority of using spectrum bands, this paper considers an additional attribute of spectrum, *usage mode*, systematically. Three usage modes are introduced; exclusive use, club use and commons use[5]. Further, the paper proposes to consider usage mode in two levels: usage mode specified by the government (*Mode-G*) and usage mode specified by users, i.e., licensees (*Mode-L*).

In the exclusive use, there is only one spectrum user who is allowed to use a band/block exclusively. For the club use, there are two or more users of the same spectrum band/block; the way in which the users are admitted and requested to coordinate is specified by the government for Mode-G or by the licensee for Mode-L. The commons mode, as the naming indicates, is an open and free use by unspecified users, as in the case of a city park or streets used by many people. We consider usage mode more in detail in the fifth subsection of the second section.

In addition to the specifications at the ALLOC level as explained above, there are many technical regulations including power emission, prevention of interferences, protection from interferences, data transmission method, standardization, etc. This paper, as stated previously, takes such technical regulations as given.

Assignment of Spectrum Blocks (Licensing)

The second stage of specifying spectrum utilization, ASSGN, first divides each spectrum band into one or more spectrum *blocks*. The block is the actual unit of spectrum to be assigned to users. A license is issued to each user.. In the present-day system of spectrum utilization in Japan, the licensee is selected by the government on a first-come basis or by discretion, and recently by comparative hearings. In the U.S., UK and other countries, as is widely known, attempts have been made to select initial licensees by auction.[6] In the proposal of this paper, licenses are to be issued solely on the outcome of lease auction.

In Figure 2, we see that band A is divided into two blocks with licenses A1 and A2. Band B is divided into three blocks, B1, B2 and B3. Further, bands C and D are not divided; bands E and F, being unlicensed ones, have no licensee.

Each license has its duration indicated by the date it becomes effective and the date it is terminated. In Figure 2, each of the two broadcast licenses in band A has a duration of 10 years, whereas each of the three blocks of band B for commercial mobile services and license C have a duration of five years. The duration of license D is indefinite.

In the present-day system in Japan and in other countries, the duration of a license is established formally by law, but its actual effect is unclear, since in most cases a license is renewed repeatedly. As a consequence, a license is often considered to represent a semi-permanent right of using the spectrum block free of charge. This did not bring in problems at the time that the supply of spectrum was abundant and its effective price was zero. However, once the supply became tight and the effective price was no longer zero, such semi-automatic renewal of a license gave its holder an economic advantage and vested interests.

Attempts to reallocate or reassign spectrum from low-efficiency to high-efficiency use have been made under the governmental command and control in Japan and in other countries. Outcome from such attempts, however, is limited and is far from solving the problem of the extreme inefficiency in spectrum utilization, because of opposition by incumbent license holders.[7]

In the system to be proposed in this paper, the duration of a license is to be observed strictly. The holder of a license must win an auction in order to continue to use a license beyond the termination for the same block of spectrum that the holder used previously.

Usage Mode

In this subsection, we consider spectrum utilization at the present time with regard to Mode-G and Mode-L. The row of Mode-G in Figure 2 shows that bands A through C are of exclusive mode, band D of club mode and bands E and F of commons mode.

The exclusive mode of spectrum utilization is typical in the current system. The club mode is also seen with many spectrum bands, such as those for navigation and aviation. The spectrum band for commons use in the present-day system is known under the name of "unlicensed band." It is an open and free use without a license, hence the word "unlicensed."

The choice at the level of Mode G, especially the choice between the exclusive mode (combined with a property system) and the commons mode, has been in the center of debates on the use of spectrum. We note that there are strong advocates for introducing the commons use widely, emphasizing the benefits of technological progress such as UWB, overlay and SDR.[8] As such, it is a demand to change ALLOC specifications, and, under the present-day system, the only way to meet such demand is through the governmental command and control. We point out, however, that it is possible to accommodate commons use in Mode-L under MLA, i.e., to realize commons as a choice of spectrum users. We also point out that it is possible to accommodate commons use in Mode-G under MLA with certain arrangements on public budgeting to supply commons as a public good (see the following subsection).[9] This paper attempts to introduce a system in which the demand for spectrum for commons may be realized under market principle, not through direct command and control by the government.[10]

To explain further, observe that usage mode specified by licensees (Mode-L), as shown in Figure 2, simply reflects the fact that the licensee of exclusive use in Mode-G may introduce club or commons mode to final users of the spectrum. Users in band A, broadcast stations, provide consumers with broadcast services in commons mode (free-to-air broadcast) or in club mode (pay-per-station or pay-per-view). Band B is used by mobile-phone operators, who provide their subscribers with mobile-phone services in the club mode. The licensee of block C, e.g., a fire station, has an exclusive right to use it (exclusive use in Mode-G); we state, just for a formality, that the fire station provides the service produced with spectrum C to itself exclusively (exclusive use in Mode-L), and block D likewise (club use in Mode-L). Band E is an example in which Internet access providers and their customers are given the right to use the band in commons mode (unlicensed use) by the government. Likewise, band F, an ISM band, is used freely by consumers (final users) without licenses. For these cases, there is no need to consider the duration of a license or a Mode-L specification.

Thus, it is seen that a spectrum block can be used in the club or in the commons mode at the level of Mode-L as well as at the level of Mode-G. In addition, Mode-L club or commons may be introduced by an exclusive user at Mode-G. This paper proposes a system in which the choice of mode be made preferably at Mode-L, not at Mode-G, i.e., competitively under market principle.[11]

Provision for Spectrum Commons as a Public Good

In the following sections, we will see that a lease auction system (MLA) can accommodate various usage modes both in Mode-G and in Mode-L. This subsection explains how spectrum commons can be realized as a public good within the system of MLA.

In general, we state that it is desirable to "privatize" the use (not the ownership) of spectrum resources whenever possible. In order to realize a club or commons mode, the first choice should be Mode-L, not Mode-G. Further, we propose

that Mode-G club and commons be realized as public goods, as explained below.

First, we propose that a public agent be established as the "user (licensee)" of a block for Mode-G commons. The objective of this agent is to secure a spectrum block at a lowest possible cost for the use by the public in the same way that unlicensed band is used today. In order to bid for this under MLA, the agent is given a certain amount of budget by the government administering the general public budget (e.g., Ministry of Treasury, to be denoted as *GPB* in this subsection only). The size of this budget should be equal to the greatest amount of money that GPB would approve in view of the "utility" of securing the block for the public. Thus, this block is a public good; it will be supplied by the agent to final users (consumers) free of charge.

This may seem a redundant way to secure a spectrum block as Mode-G commons for the reason that the public agent for commons could bid arbitrarily high as long as a budget is provided by GPB, the receiver of the auction income. Observe, however, that, in the proposed system, GPB should give a budget to the public agent in such an amount as to represent the demand price of the block to the society. It is possible for GPB to give "an unlimited budget" to the agent on its decision that the spectrum block "must be secured at any cost (e.g., for security)." Such a case should be an exception, though. Further, after an auction, the agent would end up with a (finite) price for leasing the block.

The following are some of the advantages of providing Mode-G commons as a public good through auction, as explained above, instead of providing by the governmental command and control. Observe that this arrangement makes explicit the opportunity cost of securing a Mode-G commons. Thus, when a new technology fitting to a new Mode-G commons emerges and obtains support by the public, it is possible to secure a spectrum block for it by having GPB allocate some budget for this purpose. Conversely, when the usefulness of a commons decreases (e.g., by a new technology superseding it), GPB can make an adjustment by trimming the public budget given to it. Of course, there should be a political or other process to change the public budget for such a purpose, and conflicts of interests would have to be solved. This arrangement, however, is better than the direct command and control process, since the latter generates direct confrontation between new and incumbent users, whereas the former can solve the issue in the framework of the allocation of GPB.

The foregoing discussion suggests that, whenever possible, spectrum commons or clubs should be realized in Mode-L than in Mode-G. The reason is simply that Mode-L commons can be realized without a political process on the public budget. An example of this may be a group of manufacturers producing devices on new technology for communication services (such as a broadband Internet access) using a block of spectrum; the group may win an auction and pay the bid price from the revenue of selling the new devices; the block may be used in Mode-L commons or in a Mode-L club as chosen by the manufacturers.

To summarize, this paper proposes that spectrum utilization under auction be as follows:. Club or commons use in Mode-G can be realized by the government, if desired, through a public-good provision as stated above. Alternatively and preferably, club or commons use can be realized in Mode-L through a (private) arrangement made by a user of an exclusive block. Thus, this paper proposes to let users of spectrum blocks choose a mode of use freely by considering the technology and the demand-supply conditions. Users, including public agents responsible for Mode-G club or commons, would be in competition each other. This would be beneficial to the consumers (final users of the spectrum).

To facilitate our understanding, we will explain, in terms of Figure 3, an example of spectrum usage with the system proposed in this paper. Figure 3 is an extension of Figure 2; the items new or changed from Figure 2 are denoted by italics in Figure 3.

Let us first consider an example of government-arranged club use, the primary use of band C in Figure 3. In this case, the primary right would be won through auction by a public agent, and then given to public users such as police, coast guards, fire stations and others in a Mode-L club. If such a band is very important and must be secured for the security agents, then a very high amount of budget should be given by GPB to the agent.

With regard to commons use, note that there are two types. The first type of commons is like the unlicensed one at the present time. It is for the use within a small area such as a household; examples are wireless telephones, home wireless LAN and electric ovens. In Figure 3, band F is designated for the use of such commons; the objective of this band is unspecified and license F is to be won by a public agent responsible for this block, which lets the public use it free of charge (within the ALLOC and the ASSGN specifications). In the future, if an expansion of this block becomes necessary, this agent would be given an additional budget to win an auction for additional blocks. Further, if the price (lease fee) of this block increases, then the government may consider increasing the size of Band F through some reallocation.

Examples of the second type of commons are what is called UWB (Ultra Wide Band) and overlay. They are for a secondary right to exploit the vacant portion of a spectrum band both timewise and areawise, thanks to newly developed technology. UWB utilizes widely spread frequencies so as not to interfere with the primary use in any band. Overlay uses software-defined radio (SDR); the device for SDR can detect unused segments of spectrum (with regard to frequencies, location and time) and exploit them so as not to interfere the primary use of the same band.

In Figure 3, the secondary right to use band B is obtained by a public agent through auction; the secondary right would then be released for

Figure 3. Example of spectrum usage (MLA). Note: Entries in italics are introduced anew in this example.

	Spectrum Band	Band A		Band B			Band C		Band D	Band E	Band F
ALLOC	Objective	Broadcast		Commercial Mobile		Unspecified	Security	Internet Access	Air Transportation	Internet Access	Unspecified (ISM)
	Priority	Primary		Primary		Secondary	Primary	Secondary	Primary	Primary	Primary
	Mode-G	Exclusive		Exclusive		(Exclusive)	Exclusive	(Exclusive)	Club	Exclusive	Commons
ASSGN	License (Spectrum Block)	A1	A2	B1	B2	B3 / BB		C	CC	D	E	F
	Duration	10yrs		5yrs		5yrs	5yrs	5yrs	(Indefinite)	5yrs	5yrs
	Spectrum User (Licensee)	Broadcast Stations		Mobile-phone Providers		Public Agent	Police, Fire Stations	Union of Internet Access Providers	Airlines	Union of Internet Access Providers	Public Agent
	Mode-L	Club/commons		Club		Commons (UWB)	Club	Club (Overlay)	Club	Commons	Commons
	Lease price			*(Determined by auction)*							
Final user		Consumers, etc., of Services using Spectrum									

UWB. The lease price for this is to be paid by GPB so that, in effect, the UWB service becomes a public good.

Further, in Figure 3, band E is designated to be used for Internet access and the license E is obtained exclusively by a union of Internet access providers. The union uses this block as a Mode-L commons of the second type. In this case, the government may impose a regulation so that union membership be open and the members of the union share the payment of the lease price according to a predetermined scheme. In effect, such a union would become a half-public, half-private entity.

The secondary use of band C in Figure 3 is specified to be Mode-G exclusive. In this example, too, the union of Internet access providers possesses an exclusive license CC; the block is also devoted to Internet access services. Since license CC is of the secondary right in this example, the block might be preoccupied by public security users from time to time. In that case, of course, the secondary rights to use band C must be conceded to the primary users; to Internet users, such a case would appear that the Internet were busy because of an emergency.

SPECTRUM REASSIGNMENT BY MEANS OF MODIFIED LEASE AUCTION (MLA)—COMPETITVE ASSIGNMENT OF SPECTRUM BLOCKS

Outline

ThisSection proposes *modified lease auction (MLA);* it is a means for ASSGN.

First of all, observe that the present-day system under the governmental command and control is, in effect, a zero-price lease with high probability of repeated renewals. The system to be proposed in this section, MLA, is under the control of market power (auctions); further, it is a lease with clearly stated duration. The difference between the two systems is quite large; the cost of jumping from the present-day system to MLA would be very high. We need a scheme for gradual transition, which will be presented later in the last section. The system of MLA to be presented in this section, therefore, is a long-term target; it is for the case in which systems of spectrum utilization were designed from scratch.

In the following subsection, the system of (simple) lease auction is explained together with its merits and shortcomings. The two subsections following it together will introduce modified lease auction (MLA), an improvement of simple lease auction with regard to the risk that the incumbent spectrum user (lessee) faces. In the last subsection of this section, we compare MLA with other systems for spectrum utilization, including the property system, and conclude that MLA is a system with balanced properties.

The System of (Simple) Lease Auction (LA)

Let us first explain (simple) lease auction (LA) for spectrum assignment. It means the following; The ownership of radio spectrum is in the hands of the government, which leases a block of spectrum to a user by auction on the lease price. This paper proposes that, for a reason to be explained later in the two subsections following this one, the lease be applied to all users including private, public and government users; there should be no exception to this principle. Further, once a user obtains a license for a particular block of spectrum through an auction, the licensee will be allowed to use it, sell it or sublease it within the ALLOC and the ASSGN specifications.

Typically, an assignment of a spectrum block with LA would proceed as follows: First, the government establishes terms of a license including its duration. Before the start of a license, an auc-

tion would be held on its lease price; the winner would obtain the license upon paying the bid price. When the termination of the license approaches, another auction would be held to determine who would obtain the license for the following term. And so on.

The obvious advantage of introducing lease auction (LA) in the assignment of spectrum lies in its *flexibility*. That is to say, in comparison with the command-and-control system or with the property system, LA makes it easy for a block of spectrum to be reassigned from old to new users according to the need arising from technological and economic changes. This will increase the efficiency of spectrum utilization, and the society as a whole will benefit from it. Further, the amount of money involved in LA (or MLA for this mater) would be far less than auctions for initial assignments or those in a property system as proposed in Faulhaber and Farber (2002) and Kwerel and Williams (2002). Incentives for hoarding, speculations and "winner's curse" would be limited in LA and MLA.

There is a serious disadvantage, however, in the system of LA. From the standpoint of a spectrum user, it would be desirable to be able to use it in the future indefinitely, since such would protect investment of the user made in the past. In other words, LA would impose the risk on the spectrum user that the license might not be renewable. We call it the *risk of losing spectrum rights*.

Two categories of the risk may be distinguished. The first category arises when newcomers outbid incumbents in the auction to be held for the lease following the current one. It is always possible that, because of a change in technological or economic conditions, a new service or a new method for providing the same service as the incumbent did may emerge so that a newcomer can offer a higher price for using the spectrum than the incumbent can. Under the property system, the incumbent could continue to use it at least until the investment made in the past was fully recovered. Under the system of LA, the incumbent user might not be able to do this. This is the risk of first category.

The second category arises from an ALLOC decision by the government. When the government (or WARC of ITU for this matter) decides to change the objective for the spectrum band that the incumbent has been using, the incumbent must give up using it beyond the expiation of the current license. This is the risk of second category.

It is possible that the spectrum user is exposed to such a risk to an excessive extent; as a consequence, the investment made under such risk might be less than the level optimum to the society as a whole. We will discuss implications of risk more in detail later in the last subsection of this Section. In the following subsection, we will propose modifications of LA so that the shortcomings arising from the risk of first category may be remedied. The subsection following it will discuss a way to deal with the risk of second category.

Protecting Incumbents from the Risk of First Category

In order to protect incumbents from the risk of first category, we may employ one or more of the following modifications of LA:

a. First of all, when a spectrum band is composed of more than one block, incumbents may be protected if the government holds a (lease) auction for each of the blocks in the band simultaneously and, at the same time, designates the object of the auction to be *some* block in the band, not a particular block. Let us explain by taking a case of mobile phones as an example.

Suppose that there are six blocks in the band for mobile phones. It is desirable, but not imperative, that the band be consecutive and each block be of the same size. Suppose further that an incumbent operator of mobile phones has been using the second block of the band. The (lease) auction for the six blocks is to be held simultaneously, and auction participants including the incumbents are to bid for a yet-to-be-designated block in the band. (If the size of the blocks differs, the bid price should be set for a unit of spectrum (such as 1 MHz) instead of for an entire block.) If the incumbent operator wins, i.e., finishes the auction within the top six bidders, then the operator will be entitled to lease the same block that the operator used previously. Thus, an incumbent operator would lose a license only when the incumbent cannot outbid the lowest wining bid for the six blocks of the band. Such an arrangement would reduce the risk greatly.

(The following can be used regardless of the number of blocks in a band.)

b. To give a discount of the lease price to incumbents: This would protect incumbents by letting them save the amount of money to be paid for lease. In other words, newcomers would be able to access a spectrum block only if they could offer a significantly higher price than the incumbent did; the discount may be justified in view of the investment that the incumbent made in the past. To find an appropriate percentage of discount, trials and errors may be needed. To begin with, a discount of 40% for a five-year lease and a discount of 20% for a 10-year lease might be suggested.

c. To hold an auction for lease several years prior to the beginning of the lease period: This would favor incumbents against newcomers in terms of the timing of decision. Because of the investment made in the past, it is easier for incumbents to make a decision on the demand price for a license in the future than for newcomers starting from scratch. Further, this would lower the burden imposed on the incumbents in the maintenance of the carried-over capital stock and others, thus letting the incumbents bid higher than otherwise.

d. To use what may be called a "pre-auction," in which the winner obtains a discount of lease price in exchange for the amount bid. A pre-auction might be held on the percentage of discount or on the amount of discount; it is like auctioning on a "reservation fee" for a theater ticket, or more precisely, like auctioning on a "fee for partial reservation." This, in effect, is a combination of (b) and (c) above, since this would protect incumbents in terms of both the amount of money to be paid for lease and the timing of decision.

e. To create futures and/or options markets for the right of leasing spectrum. This is an extension of (d) above. Auction for a lease would be held some periods before the actual lease starts, say, 10 or 15 years prior to the start of a five-year lease. Then, futures and/or options markets for the lease might develop, and incumbents might be able to purchase the right to continue to use the same spectrum block in the future as the one used previously.

We can think of other ways for protecting incumbents from excessive risk of first category. This may be a possible research subject in the future. We will discuss why incumbents need to be protected at all later in the last subsection of this Section.

Protecting Incumbents from the Risk of Second Category

This risk of losing spectrum rights arises from the government decision to change the objective for using spectrum. The government should change ALLOC in such a way that, roughly speaking, the size of spectrum bands with low lease prices is decreased and the size of spectrum bands with high prices is increased. In order to do this, the government must terminate the current specifica-

tion of the objective of a (low-priced) spectrum band. This means that there would be no auction in the future for the spectrum band with the terminated objective. A new objective would be established and initial licenses for the band would be assigned in new auctions.

Therefore, the old user of the spectrum with the objective to be terminated must give up using it at the end of the current lease, even if the user could bid sufficiently high enough to win an auction over competitors under the old objective. In other words, it is a risk arising not from the insufficient competition capability of the user, but from the insufficient competition capability of the group of the users with the old objective.

We propose to create a *spectrum insurance* to protect the user from the risk. The decision by the government to discontinue an ALLOC specification may be justified from the standpoint of the demand and the supply of all spectrum resources. However, to an individual user, it is like a natural disaster or a fire for which the user has no direct responsibility. Insurance is the best way to deal with such risk.

Under the spectrum insurance proposed, a spectrum user would declare an amount to be compensated in case such a termination of the lease took place. This amount might reflect the part of the investment having been made for using the spectrum and not having been recovered through depreciation allowances and other means. Roughly speaking, the amount insured would be determined by the spectrum user in such a way that the outcome to the user in the case of lease termination be indifferent to the outcome from the case of no termination.

The user should pay an *insurance fee* for this, since, without an insurance fee, there would be a strong incentive for a licensee to declare an extremely high amount to be compensated in case of lease termination. It is proposed that the amount of insurance fee be equal to the product of an *insurance-fee rate* and the amount of money insured. It is further proposed that this spectrum insurance program be run by the government as an actuarially fair insurance; that is to say, the insurance-fee rate should be determined so as to balance the fee revenues and the payments of insurance money in the long run. Further, the government should choose spectrum bands to be reclaimed so as to minimize the sum of insurance payments.[12]

Economic Meanings of the Risk of Losing Spectrum Rights and Comparison of MLA with Other Systems

Let us consider here economic meanings of the risk of losing spectrum rights. In this subsection we also compare MLA with other systems for managing spectrum resources, including the governmental command and control and a property system.[13]

First of all, the risk arises when the spectrum user is forced to give up using a spectrum block because of a decision made by other spectrum users (the risk of first category) or by the government (of second category). It is observed that

the risk is a consequence of economic growth and changes; there would be no such risk if the whole economy remained stationary (stagnant) so that the economic activities each year were the same as the economic activities in the preceding years. In other words, the risk is a price which incumbent spectrum users have to bear in order for the whole economy to achieve flexibility in spectrum utilization.

Thus, we can state that the degree of the risk determines the balance between the security to incumbents and the flexibility for entry by newcomers; that is, we face a tradeoff between security and flexibility in using spectrum. Figure 4 illustrates this tradeoff. To choose a system for spectrum utilization is to choose a point on a curve representing the tradeoff.

We first observe that the level of the risk is near zero but the flexibility is nil in the current system (command and control with automatic renewal by the government), which is represented by the origin O in Figure 4. In the property system, the risk is low but not zero, and the flexibility is higher; it is represented by point A in the tradeoff. In (simple) LA, the flexibility is high, but the level

Figure 4. Tradeoff between security (risk) and flexibility in alternative systems for using spectrum

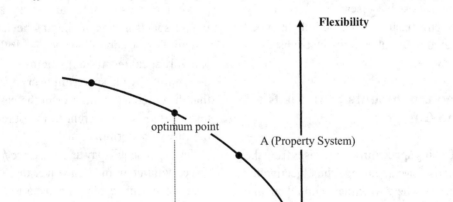

of the risk is also high, since incumbents are not protected at all; LA is represented by point C. We can conclude that MLA provides a medium level for both the risk and the flexibility; given a preference over the risk and flexibility, a point such as B in Figure 4 may represent an optimum.[14] An important question is which point between A and C on the tradeoff is to be chosen; it is for future research to establish a solid theory on this issue. Meanwhile, in the reality, actual choice may be made by the government through successive adjustments (i.e., by trial and error).

The remainder of this subsection is devoted to comparing the property system (to be abbreviated as *PS* in this subsection only) and MLA with regard to flexibility and security.

On the one hand, it is clear that the security of PS is greater than that of MLA (i.e., the risk is higher with MLA than with PS), since, in PS, the user of spectrum is its owner and can always make a decision whether to continue using it or not.

On the other hand, the flexibility of MLA, in general, is greater than that of PS, since the chance for newcomers to be able to lease spectrum is greater with MLA than PS. In this regard, it is sometimes stated that, under an ideal condition, the flexibility of PS may be as great as that of MLA. This is correct, but, in the reality, the market mechanism is far from being complete and this assertion does not hold.

In the Arrow-Debreu world in which complete contingency markets existed, a high flexibility might be achieved with PS. In reality, of course, the transaction cost of having such complete markets is prohibitively high; we have to live with a system of incomplete markets and to simplify a large number of contingencies into the reality of decision-making under uncertainty.

There are at least two sources which lower the flexibility of PS. One is the presence of economies of scale in the use of radio spectrum. Spectrum resources, as other space resources (see the second Section), exhibit economies of scale in the sense that, if more than one spectrum band

or block were put together and placed under an integrated use, the outcome from the integrated spectrum would be higher than the sum of the outcomes from the spectrum used separately. For the case of radio spectrum, an example of positive externalities may be the case of CDMA for distributed transmission of signals. Further, one can simply recall that the spectrum blocks for TV channels are put together in a small number of bands so as to save the cost of manufacturing TV devices.

Note that the range of spectrum bands or blocks which exhibit significant scale economies depends on the technology for using them; hence, the range may vary (usually it expands) depending on technological progress. If the range is expanded significantly, then it may become advantageous to integrate some number of spectrum bands or blocks into one.

Now, under PS, when such an integration is attempted through spectrum trade, it is possible that the owner of a small piece of spectrum who happened to be located at a strategic position charges an excessively high price for it, as we see in the case of land from time to time (the case of *holding-up*). Spectrum trade would be obstructed, then. The consequence, as experiences show, is that the cost of reaching even near to an equilibrium in a holding-up case is high in time and money; the parties, after long and wasteful negotiations, would be forced to settle at a contract which is far from optimum. Thus, the flexibility of PS is actually lower than that of MLA, in which any holding-up would be eliminated at the time of auction.[15]

The other source which lowers the flexibility of PS is the presence of capital stock and other investment for using spectrum. The cost of spectrum adjustment to the user (i.e., the least amount of money that the user would accept for giving up using a spectrum block) depends upon the size and the content of investment made in the past on capital stock (devices, equipment, etc.) and others for the use of spectrum. To realize an adjustment of spectrum desirable to the whole society, this cost must be revealed in some way. In PS, the only way to reveal it is through the course of negotiations; the transactions cost (the negotiation cost) for this would be high. As explained in the preceding subsection, each user's adjustment cost may be revealed through spectrum insurance. Thus, we can assert that the flexibility of PS is lower than that of MLA at least when the latter is combined with spectrum insurance.

At this point, let us summarize the system for spectrum assignment (MLA) as proposed in this paper. The following are the basic principles of the system:

1. The government is the sole owner of the spectrum resources.
2. Spectrum blocks are assigned (and reassigned) competitively under lease auction (MLA).
3. Spectrum bands are allocated (and reallocated) by the government.[16]
4. Mode-G commons are treated as a public good and run by a public agent with a given (public) budget for its lease and insurance fees.

GRADUAL TRANSITION FROM THE CURRENT SYSTEM TO THE LONG-RUN TARGET, MLA

Outline

In this section, we deal with the issue of transition from the current system to the long-run target, MLA. As discussed in the preceding sections, MLA has a number of desirable characteristics over the current system (command and control by the government). The difference between the two systems, however, is so large that it is extremely costly to jump from the current system to MLA. The spectrum users under the current system, with the expectation that free use of spectrum would

continue, have made a large amount of investment in the form of equipment and devices, human skills, business organizations, etc., which could not be recovered within a short period of time. We cannot simply discard such sunk investment by jumping to a new system. What is needed is a gradual, as distinct from sudden and once-and-for-all, transition, in which the current users of spectrum can make adjustments over years by using depreciation allowances on investment and other means.

We note that all users of spectrum would be affected by the introduction of MLA in the ASSGN stage, which would impose spectrum fees uniformly, whereas only a small number of users would be affected by the introduction of reallocation in the ALLOC stage, and those affected would be protected by spectrum insurance. For this reason, the proposal in this section is directed mainly to the introduction of MLA.

Next, in addition to the above, we emphasize the need for informed transition. The number of spectrum users, even excluding those of mobile phones, is of the scale of 100,000 in Japan. In order to minimize the cost of transition, every user should be informed fully of the process of transition so as to be able to plan well ahead of the adjustments needed. This means that the government should spell out in detail the process of transition, including plans for major contingencies.

The transition process proposed in this paper is composed of three elements: (a) the formation of benchmark lease prices (BLP) during the preparation period, (b) the gradual implementation of spectrum usage fees during the execution period and (c) a provision for income compensation.

To propose a process for transition, let us first define three periods: *the preparation period, the execution period* and *the income compensation period.* Let M, N and T be the length of the preparation, the execution and the income compensation periods, respectively. Furthermore, let the beginning of the preparation period be set at

Figure 5. Example of transition (case of M=5, M=10, M=20)

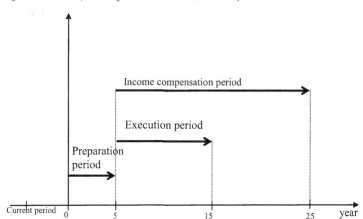

the beginning of the entire transition process, and let the beginning of the execution and the income compensation periods be set at the end of the preparation period. Figure 5 illustrates this arrangement for the case of *M=5, N=10* and *T=20* (years). In the following, we spell out the proposed activities for each of these three periods.

Formation of Benchmark Lease Prices (BLP) during the Preparation Period

The main objective during the M-year preparation period is to form *benchmark lease prices (BLP)*. BLP will be used as a proxy for market lease prices during the execution and the income compensation periods.

In order to do this, the government would first define the spectrum blocks by specifying a range of frequencies and a geographical area with, if necessary, a time of use and a priority. Figure 6 gives an illustration with a simple case in which the frequencies and the areas are represented by a vertical axis and a horizontal axis, respectively. In Figure 6, spectrum band D may be a broadcast band or an unlicensed band; there is no geographical division for that band. Further, bands A through C are not divided in area III.

Gradual formation of BLP would proceed as follows. During the preparation period, any new assignment of spectrum blocks must be done by auction (MLA). It would not be difficult to do this, since the auction would be held for new assignments and no incumbent user would be involved. Suppose in Figure 6, the gray rectangles were assigned by auctions, and white rectangles were used by incumbents. The BLP for each rectangle would be determined in the following way. First, for the gray rectangle, the BLP would simply be the price determined by auction. Second, for the white rectangle, the BLP would be the value obtained by linear interpolation of the prices with the gray rectangle nearest to it. If two or more linear interpolations existed, the average would be taken. If no interpolation were available, simply apply an extrapolation. In those rectangles of extremely low or high, or those rectangles located in an area in which the supply of spectrum clearly exceeded the demand, the BLP would simply be set to zero. Further, BLP should be revised regularly, say, monthly or quarterly.

Whereas this process, at the outset, might not be so accurate as desired, we would obtain at least a first approximation of BLP. As time goes on during the preparation period through the execution period, the number of gray rectangles would be increased so that the BLP would be closer to market prices.

During the preparation period and thereafter, new users of spectrum would be under MLA to its full extent; thus, they would pay lease fees as determined by auction and be subject to reallocation with the protection of spectrum insurance. The incumbents, however, would be outside of MLA and pay nothing except that they would be informed of the BLP of the spectrum blocks they were using. However, there seems to be no reason to exclude them from subscribing to the spectrum insurance by accepting the possibility of ALLOC reallocation on a voluntary basis. It may be expected that those blocks with very low efficiency would be reallocated; reclaimed bands should be put to auction for newcomers, increasing the number of gray rectangles in Figure 6.

Finally, by the end of the preparation period, for each block used in Mode-G club or commons, a public agent should be established as explained previously.

Gradual Increase in Lease Fees during the Execution Period

The execution period is a period in which the incumbents would start paying *partial lease prices (PLP)* as follows. The PLP in the nth year of the execution period would be equal to n/N times the BLP of the block being used:

$$PLP(n) = (n/N)* BLP(n), \quad n=1,2,...,N.$$

Thus if $N=10$, PLP would start from zero, and would then increase by 10 percent annually; in the 10th year, i.e., at the end of the execution period, the PLP would be equal to BLP, *the full lease price (FLP)*.

The status of incumbents during the execution period would be the same as in the preparation period except that (a) they must pay PLP, and (b) they should be allowed to "return" to the government a potion of the spectrum they were using in order to avoid payment of PLP. (But note that

Figure 6. Establishing "benchmark lease prices (BLP)"

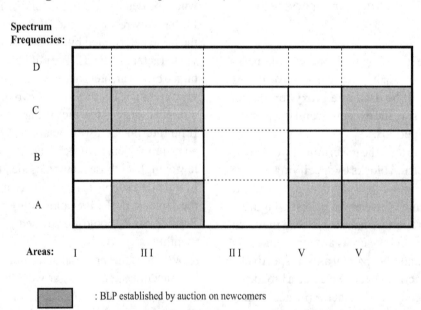

this is not reallocation; the incumbents returning spectrum cannot claim insurance payment even in the case they subscribe to it.)

Thus, the incumbents could adjust their use of spectrum gradually during the execution period. They might return to the government a portion of the spectrum blocks they were using; in this case, they might employ more efficient equipment to save spectrum or they might shift to other means for communication such as optical fibers.

At the end of the execution period, the incumbents would start paying FLP. Thus, it would be straightforward to move to a full-scale MLA at the end of the execution period. In particular, all licenses would have to be issued under MLA upon expiration, and the incumbents, as well as newcomers, would face the risk of losing spectrum rights. Furthermore, once the execution period is over, the users of spectrum should be allowed to sell or sublease licenses as desired but within the ALLOC and the ASSIGN specifications.

Income Compensation

An obvious difficulty in an attempt to implement MLA with the transition process as proposed above would be political opposition by incumbents. They have been using spectrum for years free of charge, and now they are asked to pay PLP and eventually FLP; it is natural for incumbents to oppose strongly the introduction of MLA. This is, after all, an issue of income distribution between the incumbent spectrum users and the rest of the society. In the case where spectrum is used by a branch of the government (e.g., by the Ministry of Defense), the issue is essentially of the allocation of public budget to that branch. When spectrum is used for a security or safety purpose, opposition to MLA would be strong and might sound justifiable.

In this section, we propose a scheme for income compensation for incumbents; this scheme might be used in order to make an implementation of MLA and the transition plan easy to be accepted

by incumbent users, particularly by government users (military users). This scheme for income compensation would change the distribution of income, to an extent chosen, in favor of the incumbents at the burden on the rest of the society. However, it would not affect the incentives for the incumbents to save spectrum at all. Thus, the scheme is independent of the non-distributive effects of MLA with the transition process as proposed previously.[17]

Let us begin with a reminder of the definition of the compensation period; Figure 5 shows an example of a period starting at the end of the preparation period and continuing for 20 years. During the compensation period, incumbent users might receive compensation, whereas once the income compensation period is over, there would be no compensation at all. This is a sunset scheme.

In order to specify an amount of money to be returned to an incumbent for compensation, let us define *the base amount of payment* in period t, *BAP(t)*, to be the value of the spectrum *held by the incumbent at t=0* evaluated in terms of PLP or FLP, whichever is prevailing, in period t. Observe that *BAP(t)* would vary over time depending on PLP or FLP, but the spectrum base used for calculating *BAP(t)* would not change over time.

Next, we introduce *the degree of compensation* for period t to be $d(t)$ in such a way that,

$$0 \leq d(t) \leq 1 \text{ for } 0 \leq t \leq T; \; d(t) = 0 \text{ for } t > T.$$

An example of $d(t)$ is a linear sunset:

$$d(t)=(T-t)/T, \text{ for } t \leq T, \text{ and } d(t)=0, \text{ for } t > T.$$

Other examples are conceivable.

Further, we define g ($0 \leq g \leq 1$) to denote *the ratio of compensation*, which may differ depending on the group to which the incumbent belongs. For example, in a simple setting, we might set a near-full compensation for military and security users ($g=1$), partial compensation for government users, public utilities, public transportation operators, welfare agents, etc. ($g=0.5$) and no compensation for profit-seeking entities and individual users ($g=0$).

The *actual amount of compensation* in period t, $AAC(t)$, may be set by:

$$AAC(t) = g*d(t)*BAP(t), \quad t = 1,2,...,T.$$

Note that,

$$0 \leq AAC(t) \leq BAP(t), \text{ for all } t,$$

so that the actual amount of compensation is always within $BAP(t)$ and the government's budget for income compensation will never be in deficit.

The actual amount of compensation, $AAC(t)$, would vary as $BAP(t)$; it would typically decrease as time goes on. If the incumbent continued to use the spectrum blocks which were held at the beginning of the income compensation period, then the net payment by the incumbent would be $BAP(t)$ minus $AAC(t)$. If $d(t)=1$ and $g=1$, the incumbent would be fully compensated; the spectrum blocks would be used free of charge. If not, the incumbent would be compensated partially.

Observe that if, in the middle of the income compensation period, the incumbent returned a portion of the spectrum which was held in the beginning of the period, then the incumbent would not need to pay PLP or FLP for the returned spectrum, i.e., the incumbent would be paying less than $BAP(t)$, but would still continue to receive $AAC(t)$. In other words, by returning the spectrum, the incumbent would be excused from paying the lease fees for it *without losing the compensation*. It is possible that the incumbent receives a net positive amount (i.e., a subsidy) from the government. But note that the government would never be in deficit even with such compensation, since $BAP(t)$ is calculated on $BLP(t)$, which, in this case, would

be fully paid by a newcomer winning the auction on the returned spectrum. Thus, this scheme would provide a strong incentive for the incumbent to save and return spectrum, which would be beneficial to the society as a whole (a win-win case). In other words, the income compensation scheme as proposed here is independent of the non-income effects of MLA in the transition process.

To conclude, the overall effects of the transition process with regard to lease prices would be something like the following: In the beginning of the transition period, the average lease price (PLP or FLP) might stay at a high level because of the scarcity of the spectrum created with inefficient use. Newcomers might bid aggressively to obtain the right to use a spectrum block, since the spectrum would likely promise high returns from the service using it. However, as time goes on, incumbents would start returning spectrum to the government; the returned spectrum would be assigned to newcomers by auction, increasing the supply. Thus, the average lease price would gradually fall. At the end of the execution period, it is possible that reallocation of spectrum would proceed to lower significantly the average lease price of the spectrum so that the spectrum might be close to a free good once again, if only temporarily.[18] Such process may be accelerated if the government arranges incentives for incumbents to return spectrum. An example would be to give discounts of PLP to incumbents releasing spectrum voluntarily during the preparation and the execution periods.

APPENDIX: LIST OF ACRONYMS

Note: Box 1 is a list of acronyms used in this paper together with the number of a Section in which the acronym is defined. An asterisk (*) indicates that the acronym is used only in the section defining it.

Box 1.

MLA (modified lease auction)	First and third sections
ALLOC (allocation)	Third subsection of second section
ASSGN (assignment)	Fourth subsection of second section
Mode-G (government level)	Third and fifth subsections of second section
Mode-L (non-government level)	Third and fifth subsections of second section
GPB (general public budget) *	Sixth subsection of second section
LA (simple lease auction)	Second subsection of third section
PS (property system)*	Sixth subsection of third section
BLP (benchmark lease price)	Second subsection of fourth section
PLP (partial lease price) *	Third subsection of fourth section
FLP (full lease price) *	Third subsection of fourth section
BAP (base amount of payment)*	Fourth subsection of fourth section
AAC (actual amount of compensation)*	Fourth subsection of fourth section

REFERENCES

Baran, P. (1995). *Is the UHF frequency shortage a self-made problem?* Speech at the Marconi Centennial Symposium, Belogna, Italy, June 23, 1995. Retrieved December 27, 2001 from http://wireless.oldcolo.com/course/baran2.txt

Benkler, Y. (1998). Overcoming agoraphobia. *Harvard Journal of Law and Technology,*11.

Cave, M. (2002). *Review of radio spectrum management: An independent review for Department of Trade and Industry and HM Treasury.* Retrieved October 12, 2002 from http://www.spectrumreview.radio.gov.uk

Coase, R.H. (1959). The federal communications commissions. *The Journal of Law and Economics, 2*

Cramton, P., Kwerel, E., & Williams, J. (1998). Efficient relocation of spectrum incumbents. *The Journal of Law and Economics, 41, 647-675.*

Faulhaber, G.R., & Farber, D. (2002). *Spectrum management: Property rights, markets, and the common.* Retrieved October 26, 2002 from http://bpp.wharton.upenn.edu/Acrobat/ Faulhaber_AEW_paper_6_19_02.pdf

Federal Communications Commission (2002). *Spectrum policy task force report.* ET Docket No.02-135. Retrieved on March 25, 2003 from, http://www.fcc.gov/Daily_Releases/Daily_Business/2002/db1115/DOC-228542A1.pdf

Federal Communications Commission (2003). *Report and order and further notice of proposed rulemaking in the matter of promoting efficient use of spectrum through elimination of barriers to the development of secondary markets.* Retrieved on December 19, 2005 from http://hraunfoss.fcc.gov/edocs_public/attachmatch/FCC-03-113A1.pdf

Federal Communications Commission (2004). *Second report and order: Order on reconsideration, and second further notice of proposed rulemaking in the matter of promoting efficient use of spectrum through elimination of barriers to the development of secondary markets.* Retrieved December 19, 2005 from http://hraunfoss.fcc.gov/edocs_public/attachmatch/FCC-04-167A1.pdf

Gilder, G. (1994). Auctioning the airwaves. *Forbes*, April 11, 1994. Retrieved December 27, 2001 from http://www.seas.upenn.edu/~gaj1/auctngg.html

Hazlett, T.W. (1998). Assigning property rights to radio spectrum users: Why did FCC license auctions take 67 years? *Journal of Law and Economics,* 529-576.

Ikeda, N. (2002). The spectrum as commons: Digital wireless technologies and the radio policy. *RIETI Discussion Paper Series*. Retrieved October 26, 2002 from http://www.rieti.go.jp/jp/publications/summary/02030001.html

Kwerel, E., & Rosston G. (2000). An insiders' view of FCC spectrum auctions. *Journal of Regulatory Economics, 17*(3), 253-289.

Kwerel, E., & Williams, J. (2002). *A proposal for a rapid transition to market allocation of spectrum.* Federal Communications Commission, OPP Working Paper Series, No. 38, November 2002. Retrieved March 25, 2003 from http://hraunfoss.fcc.gov/edocs_public/attachmatch/DOC-228552A1.pdf

Milgrom, P. (2004). *Putting auction theory to work.* Cambridge: Cambridge University Press.

Noam, E.M. (1998). Spectrum auctions: Yesterday's heresy, today's orthodoxy, tomorrow's anachronism. Taking the next step to open spectrum access. *Journal of Law and Economics,* October 1998, 765-790.

Oniki, H. (2004). *Reallocation of radiowave spectrum with a price mechanism: Proposal of a system of insurance and compensation.* Paper presented at the 32nd Research Conference on Communication, Information anolding-up may be avoided even with PS.

Sugaya M. & Yukuchi, K. (2002). Broadcasting Regulation in the age of Media Convergence (draft). Paper presented for *International Conference on Convergence in Communications Industries.* Warwick University, November 2-4, 2002. Retrieved from http://users.wbs.warwick.ac.uk/cmur/conference_publication/sugaya_yuguch.pdf (as seen on March 25, 2003).

ENDNOTES

[1] It is sometimes stated that the government has no right to regulate the use of radio spectrum for the same reason that the government has no right to regulate the use of red or green light, both being a range of electro-magnetic frequencies. This is correct but irrelevant. The actual object of regulation is not the right to use radiowave itself but the right to use a space for radiowave propagation.

[2] In general, a space has a dimension to represent the number of independent axes and a measure to represent its "size." Physical spaces such as land and water (surface) spaces have two dimensions and air space three dimensions. The satellite orbit is a one-dimensional space. Terrestrial spectrum spaces may be considered to be of three dimensions, since, to the two dimensions used to designate an area on the earth, we add one dimension for frequencies.

[3] ALLOC as a regulation on spectrum space resembles with "zoning" as a regulation on land use.

[4] The right on the secondary basis, roughly speaking, corresponds to "easement" discussed in Faulhaber and Farber (2002).

[5] The term "club" was used by Sugaya and Yukuchi (2002).

[6] See, e.g., Chapter 1 of Milgram (2004), Kwerel and Rosston (2000) for U.S., and Cave (2002) for UK. New Zealand was the first country to use auction for initial assignment of spectrum blocks (in 1990), followed by Australia (in 1991). It was in 1994 that U.S. conducted its first auction of spectrum assignment; since then, there have been more than fifty auctions held in U.S. until today. In 2000, 3G auctions were held in Europe with an outcome of excessively high bids for spectrum.

7   In 2003, FCC of U.S., in order to facilitate more efficient use of spectrum quickly, introduced a provision of secondary markets, in which licensees may sublease spectrum blocks at a market price (FCC, 2003 and 2004). Whereas this system does achieve allocative efficiency in spectrum utilization, it may bring in undesirable redistribution of income in that it may give windfall profits to incumbent licensees. It is noted that the system to be introduced in the fourth subsection of the last section of this paper has a scheme to control redistribution of income to an extent chosen by the government.

8   See, e.g., Gilder (1994), Baran (1995), Noam (1998), Benkler (1998), and Ikeda (2002) among many others.

9   Fauhlhaber and Farber (2002) stated that a use in commons mode could be accommodated in the property system.

10   It would take more than ten years to implement the proposal of this paper to a full extent (see the last section). The author of this paper, therefore, does not oppose to assigning some spectrum bands for commons use under the governmental command and control to urgent needs at the present time such as wireless Internet access.

11   FCC has established a set of rules to implement "private commons," which is the same as Mode-L commons in the terminology of this paper (FCC, 2004).

12   See Oniki (2004) for a more systematic proposal of an insurance system for spectrum reallocation.

13   Note that this paper considers "spectrum commons" as a mode of using spectrum which can be realized under command and control, under a property system, or under MLA (fifth and sixth subsections of second section). Thus, this paper proposes MLA as an alternative to command and control or a property system, not as an alternative to commons.

14   Observe that the property system is a special case of LA in which the duration of a license is infinitely long; thus, the position of LA (and of MLA for this matter) on the curve of Figure 4 also depends on the length of its duration.

15   There is a case in which it is possible to bring the benefit of positive externalities even in the presence of spectrum holding-up; it is the case in which the user can bypass held-up spectrum by means of new technology such as software-defined radio (SDR) at a cost far lower than the cost of realizing the intended integration. Therefore, once SDR becomes not only an engineering goal but also economic reality, the harm from holding-up may be avoided even with PS.

16   See Oniki (2004), which proposes a system for the government to allocate (and reallocate) spectrum bands.

17   The effects of the scheme for income compensation proposed here are similar to those of a scheme for levying a charge on public (e.g., military) users of spectrum and at the same time letting them to sell or lease spectrum, as proposed by Cave (2002).

18   Faulhaber and Farber (2002) discusses on this point in detail.

Chapter IV
3G Mobile Virtual Network Operators (MVNOs):
Business Strategies, Regulation, and Policy Issues

Dimitris Katsianis
National and Kapodistrian University of Athens, Greece

Theodoros Rokkas
National and Kapodistrian University of Athens, Greece

Dimitris Varoutas
National and Kapodistrian University of Athens, Greece

Thomas Sphicopoulos
National and Kapodistrian University of Athens, Greece

Jarmo Harno
Nokia Research Center, Finland

Ilary Welling
Nokia Research Center, Finland

ABSTRACT

Digital convergence brings new players in the telecom market and the Mobile Virtual Network Opera-tors (MVNO) are an alternative way for companies to enter the 3G telecom market and start offering services. This chapter aims to contribute to the assessment of the market conditions, architectures and potential for profitable business cases of MVNOs aiming to operate in the mature and competitive markets. The results and conclusions provide guidelines for the wide audience of mobile market players and media companies, spanning telecom operators to regulators and academia. In the following, the necessary background information is presented, quantitative figures such as Net Present Value, pay-back period, investment cost, revenues and running cost for different MVNO business cases are estimated and compared. The MVNO's impacts on a MNO operator and the effects of MVNO collaboration with a WLAN operator are analyzed with the same method and figures.

INTRODUCTION

The traditional barriers between separate sectors (so far) like telecom and broadcast companies, as well as fixed and mobile operators, are no longer so distinct.

Digital convergence will appear at different levels, such as user terminal, backbone network technology, tariffs and even at business or commercial levels. It seems that in few years the separation between mobile and fixed markets and between telecom and broadcast companies will disappear, allowing many agents to compete in a single telecom market.

As the licensing phase of 3G networks reaches a more mature level and the telecommunications operators are investigating the business perspectives of 4G networks, there is an increased interest worldwide from enterprises, active or not in the telecommunications sector without a 3G license, to become part of the 3G value chain, as it is considered a business opportunity with exceptional or acceptable profit margins. However, the economic and technical requirements imposed upon 3G licensees act as an economic burden to 3G developments and therefore the questions of better and more rapid market exploitation of licenses have already arisen and business collaborations are sought after. This situation encourages solutions without a radio access network via the network operations or service provision market channel. Especially for those without a 3G license, a new channel of entering and participating into the mobile business is the Mobile Virtual Network Operator (MVNO) channel. MVNOs initially appeared in the 2G market reflecting the self-evident interest of companies to enter the telecom market and start offering services.

Companies from different sectors, working or not in the mobile sector, as a first step to enter the market and start offering services can use the channel of MVNO, which is complementary either to service provision channel or to operator channel.

According to their origination, companies can be classified into three categories (Lillehagen, et al., 2001). First, those who already have business in the communication sector, second, those with business outside the communication sector and last, companies with business inside the Information and Communication Technology (ICT) sector but not as telecommunication operators (media and broadcast companies).

The interest from the companies that are already activated in the telecom sector is originated from their need to enter new markets and to increase their total market share. Operators with only fixed networks want to expand into the mobile sector because they experienced a substitution from fixed to mobile telephony and a reduction of their traffic while the total mobile traffic increased. Mobile operators already want to expand in order to increase their geographical coverage (domestic or international) in areas where they don't own a license. In this case main business sectors such as marketing, billing and customer care are shared by both networks in order to reduce the operational cost of the overall network. Furthermore, some network elements that the company already owns reduce the cost of the initial investment.

Companies inside the ICT but not in the communications sector, e.g., Internet Service Providers (ISPs), content providers and media companies, seek to increase their sales by introducing new services to the customers. ISPs foresee that users want to have access everywhere, and that means that beside the fixed broadband Internet, they must develop wireless broadband Internet solutions as well. Content providers want to be able to offer richer content through the broadband 3G mobile networks. Companies from the broadcast sector discern that the transmission of media content is no longer their exclusive right. So in order to gain back their market power, these companies must find a way to enter the new convergence scenery.

There are also companies outside the ICT sector that want to become MVNOs because they want to be able to provide mobile services to their customers (e.g., financial institutions, automotive industry, etc.) or want an extra sales channel to promote their brand names or products (e.g., consumer electronics companies) (OMSYC, 2004).

Between these three groups, large differences concerning their drivers to become an MVNO exist, since they have different business models, different characteristics and positions in the market. Early studies regarding both the Mobile Network Operators (MNOs) (Katsianis, et al., 2001) and the MVNOs (Varoutas, et al., 2006), have shown that market factors such as population density, customers type, timing of entry and penetration levels by new entrants will determine which strategy can be used in different areas and at different stages of market development.

But, in spite of MVNOs abilities and strategies, their competitiveness in the 3G mobile business will be severely limited if MNOs, which effectively control the available frequencies, the network infrastructure and the operation facilities, charge monopoly prices for their services. Due to the fact that in many cases MNOs are vertically integrated in the 3G market, they may also

have incentives to restrict access to the facilities required by MVNOs through the imposition of prices, which will make the MVNO business case totally unprofitable for enterprises wishing to enter the market and effectively compete for 3G customers.

Of course, as the mobile market becomes more competitive and the regulatory framework more mature for such cases, the cost-based approach to charge MVNOs for their access to a 3G network would become less necessary, but it could circumscribe MNOs' incentives to invest in infrastructure. These arguments should be assessed within the context of the overall objective of promoting and strengthening the competitive framework for mobile services, which is the prime rationale for allowing MVNOs to operate in the market in the first place (ITU, 2001).

This chapter aims to contribute to the assessment of the market conditions, the architecture and the potential for profitable business cases of MVNOs aiming to operate in the mature and competitive European markets focusing on either wide market or lucrative market segments. Starting in Section 2 with the necessary background information regarding the existing and foreseeable business models for MVNOs, as well as the regulatory and access issues worldwide, the chapter in Section 3 addresses interesting questions regarding the market potential, the critical factors affecting the profitability of MVNOs, such as access prices, but also the impact of MVNOs on the associated MNOs trying to identify the win-win situations. The business opportunities of WLAN as an access technology for MVNOs' users are also presented and discussed. Section 4 outlines future trends and research questions aiming to contribute to further development of issues addressed in this Chapter. Finally, Section 5 summarizes the results and conclusions to provide guidelines for the wide audience of mobile market players, spanning telecom operators to regulators and academia.

BACKGROUND

MVNO Business Models

In many countries, the reserved 2G frequency band is nearly saturated, at least in the urban areas, so not much room is left for new players to enter the telecom market. The existence of a market for mobile services is more than confirmed today and there are always more people who see in 3G the opportunity to take part in a big game.

In the cellular world there are two main routes in order to provide cellular services: network operation & service provision channels. In order to supply services through an owned network, radio spectrum is required; a resource that is limited in supply.

So, one of the possible ways to enter the world of 3G services, which have drawn considerable attention, is that of the MVNO model, meaning the reach of commercial agreements with already existing MNOs.

There is a lot of discussion and an obvious doubt over the degree to which an operator is considered to be virtual in comparison with actual network operators. The definition of the term "virtual operator" varies from each point of view. For example, certain analysts affirm that

an MVNO must necessarily have a network code and SIM cards of its own (OVUM). On the other hand, the UK Regulator (OFCOM) considers as an MVNO those without a SIM card, which can be also considered as Enhanced Service Providers (ESPs) (OFCOM, 1999). A general definition may be that an MVNO is an operator that provides cellular services (data or voice) without owning spectrum access rights. From the customers' point of view, there is no distinction between the two operators, since an MVNO looks like any MNO, but a MVNO does not imply ownership or operation of base station infrastructure. Figure 1 illustrates the MVNO idea compared to other mobile business schemes.

There are different scenarios for an MVNO approach and consequently different architectures for the MVNO such as (Table 1):

- A full MVNO, with its own SIM card, network selection code and switching capabilities as well as service center but without ownership of any radio spectrum (OVUM). The main difference from the other business models is the ability to operate independently from the MNOs network facilities and the full control over the design of services and

Figure 1. MVNO types and value chain

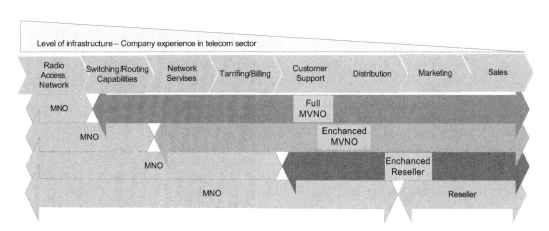

tariff structures. Furthermore, the possibility to select the host network (MNO) could be an option in the foreseeable future.

- Enhanced Service Provider ESP or Indirect Access MVNO (IA-MVNO) with its own SIM card, core network (circuit switched and/or packet) and service facilities, e.g., with its own IN or IP application servers (OFCOM, 1999). Some independence from the host MNO exists and under some constraints the provider can design services and differentiate its products.
- Wireless Service Provider (SP) without own core network and SIM card, basically an Internet portal providing wireless IP services based on the MNOs access and core network.
- Resellers just offering pre-packed cellular services to end users.

It is foreseen that MVNOs can act as an important driver for the emerging 3G market since potentially they would offer customers additional service baskets. In addition, since users are rather indifferent about the network infrastructure but put their emphasis on user interfaces and services, an operator with carefully selected content and good marketing strategy could drive forward the market if specific target groups, such as family users, are addressed.

The mobile market is, without doubt, considered important, especially the 3G, and very promising by a lot of firms; but in view of the surrounding uncertainty, "big" new entrants will be content with taking the opportunity of the virtual model, at least for the time being.

In many countries, the 3G licenses have been assigned to existing 2G operators, so there is enough place for new players, although in 3G the emergence of just one or two new operators can be witnessed. The new entrants, who in many cases will be quite well known brand names with considerable experience in the marketing, distribution and management of customer relations, will focus prevailingly on services of great added value and, above all, on m-commerce.

The new virtual operators can be a threat for new entrants in the 3G markets. In a mass market environment, where social, emotional and cultural criteria often prevail, each new entrant will attract a lot of attention. It is nonetheless reminded that the network operator, following an agreement such as that of the Virgin model (which according to OFCOM is an ESP (OFCOM, 1999)), obtains new clients and new earnings without investing actually anything additional in infrastructure and in the management of new services.

In the 3G world, it could become clearer that the above described prospect can bring to 3G MNOs immediate revenues so as to recover at least a

Table 1. Types of MVNOs

	Reseller	Service Provider	Enhanced Service Provider	Full MVNO
SIM Card	No	No/Yes	Yes	Yes
Interconnection/Roaming	No	No	No	Yes
Value Added Services	No	No/Yes	Yes	Yes
independence from Host MNO	High	High	Medium	Low
Control over tariffs	No	No	Medium	High
Size of own network infrastructure	None	None	Medium	High

part of the investment made as soon as possible. Furthermore, the MVNO offers prospects of expansion at an international level in markets that, up to now, have been closed to the participation of operators from different areas. For example, the European 2G operators could become virtual operators on the CDMA networks in U.S. and vice versa. In reality, both in the long and short run, the MVNO model represents a profitable option for all parties involved. The fear of losing customers to a virtual operator could in fact make mobile network operators lose an opportunity for development.

Regulatory Framework

Whether, and to what extent, regulatory intervention is necessary is still under discussion as national regulators in different countries have initiated discussions and consultation about the MVNO regulation. In the European Union (EU), until now there is no directive that obliges MNOs to grand access to MVNOs to use their 3G networks. Currently, while there is a tendency in favor of MVNOs, no major regulation actions have been undertaken. The ones in favour of the regulation believe that no MNO will provide access to MVNOs unless there is a regulators intervention. On the other hand, MNOs have very high profit margins and in some cases significantly over costs. The current regulation, as already interpreted by some national regulatory authorities, gives them the power to enforce an access obligation on existing operators following the paradigm of "local loop unbundling."

Regulatory intervention, especially in terms of pricing and access rights, is an important factor for MVNO success. Without it, the MVNO model depends only on the commercial negotiations and agreements between the MVNO and the network operators. Since MNOs are the owners of the desired radio spectrum, they will refuse to negotiate and so it may be difficult for companies, especially those originating outside the telecom sector, to enter the market, because traditional MNOs see the MVNO idea as a possible threat capable to shrink their market share and therefore their revenues. Regulators in general show little sign of intervention and hope that the market itself will achieve the desired agreements between the two parts.

In the EU, the National Regulatory Authority (NRA) in each member country is responsible for the determination of the framework that allows (or doesn't) an MVNO to enter the market. The EU defines an operator with market share over 40 percent as a Significant Market Player (SMP) and forces them to provide access to other minor network providers. Each NRA decides if an SMP exists but the EU can always intervene and take the final decision. If the local NRA determines that a MVNO is truly a network operator and a SMP status exists, then it is possible for the MVNO to enter the market although the appropriate regulatory framework does not exist.

Issues surrounding the MVNO concept have not been discussed in great detail, and hence most regulators are not yet in a position to provide statements of policy.

OFCOM recently assessed the state of policy development on MVNOs in other European countries and found that, with a few exceptions, it is premature for European regulators. In 2004, OFCOM decided that all the licensed operators in UK are SMP but the market is competitive, so there are no requirements for operators to grant access to their networks to MVNOs. The German NRA (Bundesnetzagentur) also determined than no operator is a SMP. In Italy, although the NRA (AGCOM) has adopted a decision at 2000 that permitted MVNOs to enter the mobile market, it afterwards decided that the conditions to amend the regulatory framework will not occur until the end of 2009. In Sweden, PTS forced 3G operators to allow MVNOs to access their networks (Analysys, 2002), while in Norway, the regulator (NPT) decided that MNOs are not obliged to give access to virtual network operators (MVNO pricing in Finland, 2005). On the hand, the French Telecommunications Regulator (ART) in 2002, decided that it had no power to force a licensed mobile operator to sign MVNO agreements. In 2005, the Spanish regulator (CMT) issued a license to launch services as long as the MVNO reaches an agreement with Spain's mobile network operators and in Ireland, the NRA (ODTR) has issued a 3G license to an operator who will host MVNOs.

The regulator of Hong Kong, the Office of the Telecommunications Authority (OFTA), has indicated that 3G networks should be opened up to MVNOs. In an analysis paper based on an industry-wide consultation (OFTA, 2001), OFTA proposed a 3G licensing framework based on an "open network" requirement. Under this requirement, 3G service provision would be separated from network operation in order to enhance competition in services and provide customers with more choices and price packages. Successful bidders of 3G licenses have been required to make at least 30 percent of their network capacity available to unaffiliated MVNOs and content and service providers but the term capacity is not defined. Furthermore, any successful bidder that currently operates a 2G network must agree to offer domestic roaming service to all new entrants. OFTA requires each MVNO to have its own Mobile Switching Centers (MSCs) and gateways, billing and customer care sections, to provide SIM cards and to be able to offer interconnection with other networks as well as roaming services.

Access Charges

The basic key cost element affecting the profitability of this telecommunication business model is the structure of the interconnection cost models.

At immature markets, as 3G, or when the competition is ineffective, cost-based prices are desirable. Yet, the determination of costs is debatable (Leive, 1995; Melody, 1997) and it is not clear which is the best methodology or even if the

resulting prices are consistent with what happens in the competitive mobile market.

The additional costs associated with mobile network elements that do not exist in fixed-line networks are the main reason why termination costs are higher on mobile networks than on fixed-line (OECD, 2000). However the cost of fixed-mobile interconnection is similar to those of interconnection in general (fixed to fixed, termination fees included) with the only exception being the different investments needed and the rapid changes in the technology (possible interconnection with additional schemes, WiMAX or similar technology).

According to the ITU (ITU, 2001) the methodologies that may be applied to the determination of interconnection charges rates include:

- Different forms of long-run incremental cost methodologies, such as Long-Run Average Incremental Costs (LRAIC), Total Element Long-Run Incremental Costs; (TELRIC) and Total Service Long-Run Incremental Costs (TSLRIC);
- Different forms of Fully Distributed Costs (FDC);
- Efficient Component Pricing Rule (ECPR); and
- Hybrid forms, such as LRIC, subject to FDC-based caps.

A study of Europe-wide mobile costs for the European Competitive Telecommunications Association (ECTA) (Analysys, 2000), revealed the controversy and the sensitivity of costing methodologies in the rapid changing mobile market. The Long Run Incremental Costs (LRIC) methodology used in this analysis indicated that Mobile operators charge 40% to 70% above their LRIC costs. However, operators argue that LRIC methodology is not appropriate for dynamic and rapidly growing markets (Clark, 2002).

MVNOs, in order to enter the 3G market, have a choice of different strategies as already described in the previous sections. The nature of MVNO and the extent to which it is engaging in interconnection or pure resale of network capacity should be reflected in the pricing principles that apply to the provision of services. So, a full MVNO with an extensive network of its own, will only make minimum use of the MNO's infrastructure and should be granted to interconnection on the same basis as the MNO.

The ability and the attractiveness of MVNOs to offer competition will be severely limited if network providers, who effectively control facilities, are in a position to charge monopoly prices for their services. Because network providers are in many cases vertically integrated into the competitive 3G market, they may also have incentives to restrict access to the facilities required by competitors through the imposition of prices which make it unprofitable for MVNOs to enter the market and effectively compete for 3G customers.

It is widely agreed that cost-based charging for access to a 3G operator's network by MVNOs would become less necessary as the market becomes more competitive and mature. It has also been claimed that cost-based access charges for MVNOs could damage incentives to invest in infrastructure, particularly in the early stages of investment in 3G systems. These arguments should be assessed within the context of the overall objective of promoting and strengthening the competitive framework for mobile services, which is the prime rationale for allowing MVNOs to operate in the market in the first place.

Market factors such as population density, customer type, timing of entry and penetration levels by new entrants will determine which strategy is used in different areas and at different stages of market development. Relying solely on full facilities-based competition to deliver competing 3G services may not provide 3G service competition to all end users, given the costs involved in duplicating a full network deployment throughout all areas of a country. As such, service-based competition through the resale of network capacity

will be an important element of the overall state of competition in the 3G market.

Currently the EU obliges companies with a market share of over 50 percent to open their networks to other users at a cost-plus-margin-based price and for the moment, only KPN Mobile is in this position. Other licensed operators with market shares of more than 35 percent do not have to charge on a cost-plus-margin basis, so leasing from them could be more expensive.

OFCOM takes the view that the logical principle for MVNO charging would be retail-minus which sets an interconnection price by looking at foregone costs and deducting these from the retail price. The costs foregone would be those associated with customer care, billing, provision of value-added services, etc. OFCOM concludes that simple resale of 3G capacity can encourage entry of efficient service providers of retail 3G services.

EVALUATION OF 3G MVNO BUSINESS STRATEGIES

Business Cases, Technoeconomic Methodology and Assumptions

Based on market studies and associated reports about companies which have expressed their interest to enter the market, several MVNO business profiles can be foreseen. The existing similarities lead to the grouping of these profiles into two main business profiles: those focusing on network operations and those focusing on service provisioning. Different demand models and service penetration rates must be defined in order to take into account these two different cases for an MVNO. This business classification will lead to specific service packages offered by these potential MVNOs and will be attributed to MVNO business profiles.

The techno-economic modeling was carried out using the TONIC tool, which has been developed by the IST-TONIC project (IST-TONIC, 2000). This tool is an implementation of the techno-economic modeling methodology developed by a series of EU co-operation projects in this field. The tool has been extensively used in several techno-economic studies among major European telecom organizations and academic institutes (Katsianis, et al., 2001; Monath, et al., 2003; Varoutas, et al., 2003; Varoutas, et al., 2006).

The tool calculates revenues, investments, cash flows and other financial results for the network architectures for each year of the study period. It consists of a dimensioning model for different architectures that is linked to a database containing the cost figures of the various network elements and the cost evolution of them over time. An analytical description of the methodology and a similar tool can be found in Ims (1998), while a more detailed description of the tool used in this analysis is presented in Katsianis, et al. (2001).

Structure of the Tool for the Techno-Economic Evaluations

The main principles of the methodology used in the techno-economic tool are analyzed in Figure 2. The cost figures for the network components have been collected in an integrated cost database, which is the "heart" of the model. This database is frequently updated with data obtained from the major telecommunication operators, suppliers, standardisation bodies and other available sources. These data concern the initial prices for the future commercial networks components as well as a projection for the future production volume of them. The cost evolution of the different components derives from the cost in a given reference year and a set of parameters which characterises the basic principles of each component. The cost evolution of each component in the database, the estimations for the OA&M cost and the production volume of the component are incorporated in

Figure 2. Techno-economic methodology (Katsianis, et al., 2001)

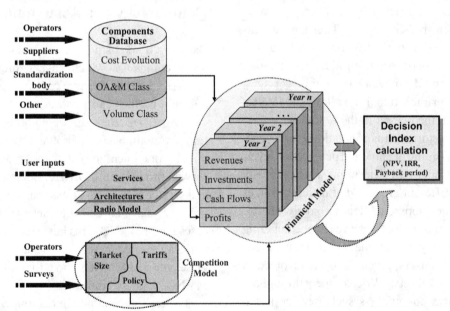

the database according to the model described in Appendix I. As a next step in the network evaluation, a specification of the services that will be provided to the consumers is needed. The network architectures for the selected set of services are defined, and a geometrical model (Olsen 1999) is used in order to calculate the length of the cables as well as the civil works for their installation (database data) for wireline access networks. In wireless networks, a radio model is incorporated in order to calculate the coverage used. The future market penetration of these services and the tariffs associated with them, according to each operator's policy, are used for the construction of the market evolution model as also defined in Appendix I. The operator tariff policy could be taken into account by modifying the tariff level in conjunction with the expected penetration of the offered services. Data from statistics or surveys can be easily integrated into the tool when formulas measuring the impact of tariff level to the saturation of the services are available.

The data are inserted into the financial model and the revenues, investments, cash flows and profits (or other financial results) for each year, during the project's study period, are calculated.

In this study, the full MVNO scenario has been analyzed, assuming that the MVNO owns exactly the same elements as the MNO, except the radio access part where the infrastructure of MNO is used. The dimensioning of the MNO UMTS network is performed starting from the coverage requirements set by the subscriber distribution information and WCDMA radio link characteristics. The obtained capacity for components and leased line is compared to the WCDMA radio interface capacity calculated from average busy hour need per subscriber. If the usage based capacity is higher than the coverage based, the additional components stations are added to the network build-out. The core network elements and their needed capacity are calculated from the base station distribution and traffic amount or number of served subscribers, depending on the limiting factor in the element capacity.

MVNO Business Cases

The MVNO business cases have exploited useful insights from previous 2G and 3G business cases (Varoutas, et al., 2003; Katsianis, et al., 2001). In order to compare the different scenarios and models, economic indicators such as NPV, IRR and payback period are presented (Appendix I).

A discount rate of 10% is selected in order to calculate discounted cash flows, which take into account the cost of capital and the expected risk-free return from investments in the telecom business. The value used reflects a mean value among the major European Telecommunication Operators.

The study period is ten years and the modelling focuses on two area scenarios: a large European country (population of 70 million) characterised, for example, by Germany and France and a small European country (population of 5 million) exemplified by Scandinavian countries like Norway or Finland. The models are not exactly representative of any defined country, but rather share typical demographic characteristics among these countries. The countries differ on several points in addition to their geographical and demographic features. The geographical approach been examined for full coverage in all areas icluding the rural ones. In Table 2 the charactersistics of the areas covered are illustrated. Note that the overall size of the surface area isn't the sum of all the sub-areas because certain areas (mountain tops, etc.) do not need to be covered.

The subscriber saturation level is estimated to be higher in the Nordic country type —95% versus 90% in the large country type. Second, usage differs in that the Scandinavian users are assumed to have 20% greater usage than their counterparts in the large country. Last, terminal subsidies are four times larger per new subscriber in the large country type than in the small country type. The

Table 2. Large and small countries demographics

CountryType	Large	Small	Description
Area size	370,000	330,000	Size of surface area of the country (km²)
Area dense	185	17	Size of dense urban area (km²)
Area urban	2,960	264	Size of urban area (km²)
Area suburban	37,000	3,300	Size of suburban area (km²)
Area rural	303,400	264,000	Size of rural area (km²)
Population dense	50,000	50,000	Number of inhabitants in dense urban area per km²
Population urban	4,000	4,000	Number of inhabitants in urban area per km²
Population suburban	1,000	1,000	Number of inhabitants in suburban area per km²
Population rural	40	3	Number of inhabitants in rural area per square km (during busy hour)
Total Population	65,000,000	5,500,000	Total population

country types differ in several points, in addition to their geographical and demographic features. The operator in the large country is assumed to have significant license costs and the two profiles for each type of country are differentiated in terms of greater usage and ARPU.

In the first case, it is considered the business profile of a telecom operator or a power company without a spectrum access license aiming to be a Full MVNO using the existing infrastructure in order to complement or expand its business to other market areas and services like B2 in Sweden, Kingston in UK, One.Tel in The Netherlands, etc. This will be the *Operator-like* MVNO business profile. This kind of MVNO takes advantage of issues such as initial market share, lower training costs, etc.

In the other profile, the MVNO has high brand-value with an existing large customer base aiming to expand its business in the mobile area and, therefore, aims to attract market share from the other MNOs. Consequently, the churn effects must be taken into account. In this case, several advantages (e.g., marketing costs) exist and disadvantages (e.g., leased lines costs and personnel costs) are the key elements. This is actually a *Service-oriented* MVNO business profile.

Evaluation of Business Cases

3G MVNO

Based on the previously described assumptions, an analysis for the profitability of the two full MVNO profiles, both in large and small countries, has been conducted and presented in Varoutas, et al. (2006). In Table 3 the main economic results for the different scenarios are presented.

In Varoutas, et al.(2006), it has been revealed that companies planning to provide 3G services can benefit from acceptable NPV and IRR figures. In more detail, operators investing in MVNO rollout benefit from more or less the same payback period and rather attractive economic figures. It has also been denoted that the investments are more or less proportional to the population for the large country but almost double for the small one. This difference is based on the necessity to offer coverage and, therefore, in the small country equipment that is not fully utilized is purchased. The figures are for rather pessimistic market shares (all are considered more or less new entrants) and surely MVNO can expect more optimistic results.

For the case of a small country, the initial position of the MVNO in the 2G world is mandatory for a successful business in the emerging 3G market. On the other hand, stronger service differentiation is followed by larger investments while the payback period remains the same.

The breakdown of total investments in the large country case confirms that the bulk of the OPEX is accounted for the interconnection costs. The running costs include leased lines, interconnection costs, terminal subsidies, employee and training cost, marketing and maintenance cost.

MVNO Impact to a MNO (UMTS) Operator

In this scenario, the impact of an Operator-like MVNO to its MNO is analysed and discussed. In this case, the MNO has increased costs since there are additional customers in the network but the benefit comes from the interconnection cost that the MVNO operator pays in order to use the UMTS network.

The selection of the appropriate value for the interconnection price between MVNO and MNO has been based on data from operators and reports. The situation where the interconnection cost is 50% increased yield to negative NPV and non-acceptable IRR and payback period for the MVNO case. This could be the turning point for this business case and the MVNO must have hard negotiation with the MNO in order to keep the interconnection costs as low as possible. On the other hand, the regulators should protect the new entrants as MVNOs and ensure that the interconnection price level will boost the

Table 3. Summary of the basic results (Varoutas, et al., 2006)

Country type	Large		Small	
MVNO type	**Operator – like**	**Service Oriented**	**Operator - like**	**Service Oriented**
NPV (M€)	111	332	259	28
IRR	12%	15%	40%	14%
Rest Value (M€)	48	39	5	2
Pay-back period (years)	8.2	7.7	5.0	7.6
Number of customers	4,800,000	3,600,000	640,000	210,000
Total mobile penetration - end	90%	90%	95%	95%
Total UMTS penetration - end	76%	76%	80%	80%
Investments (M€)	144	121	55	49

Table 4. Summary of the basic results (MVNO impact to MNO). (LC= Large country, High=High licenses fees, Wno=without WLAN, Impact=with a MVNO)

Country type	Large		Small	
	Higher license fees and MVNO	**High license fees without WLAN**	**Low license fees and MVNO**	**Low license fees without WLAN**
NPV (MEuros)	9,825	5,639	1,278	635
IRR	23.4%	18.8%	53.2%	38.6%
Rest Value (MEuros)	3,606	3,479	255	239
Payback period	6.8	7.1	6.0	6.3
Investments (MEuros)	7,432	7,308	381	363
Running costs (MEuros)	23,007	22,561	2,396	2,329
Revenues (MEuros)	55,682	46,475	5,602	4,182
Revenues-Running	32,675	23,914	3,206	1,853

Figure 3. Financial indexes for different cases

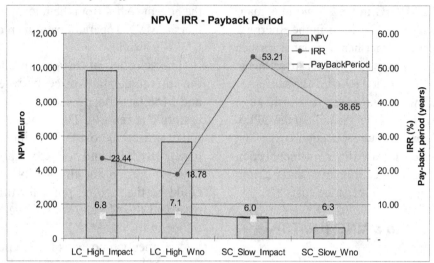

Figure 4. Basic financial indexes for a large country (including impact on MNO market share)

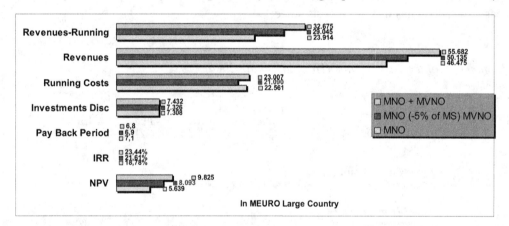

overall competition although it remains a good profit for the MNO.

The main economic results for the two basic scenarios are illustrated in Table 4 and Figure 3. These results show that companies that intend to provide UMTS services can have acceptable NPV and IRR figures when they support an additional MVNO in their network as well.

The economic figures (Figure 4) reveal that the revenues stream (for the MNO) from the MVNO operation exceeds the required investment and operation cost. The logical explanation for that

lies in the fact that the operators are going to build UMTS networks that are capable of serving more than the expected customers due to regulation implications. This obligation is based on the necessity to offer coverage, and therefore they purchase equipment that is not fully utilized.

In this business case it has been assumed that the MNO's market share remains 30%. It is logical to assume that the MVNO will gain some customers from its MNO. It has been calculated that 5% of MNO customers in the large country case will become MVNO customers in the future.

So a part of the MVNO's customers came from the potential MNO's share. Of course the MNO makes special agreements with its MVNO, so that as many as possible of the MVNO customers are out of the competitors share and not from its own potential customers. This market share's losses influence the running cost positively, since fewer customers must be served via the network. Furthermore, the revenues and NPV values are greater than in the basic case (without the MVNO) due to the interconnection cost.

Concluding, MVNO can have a positive impact to MNO even if it reduces its market share. MNOs have many benefits from their "marriage" with MVNOs and can overcome any strict coverage obligations or even pessimistic market forecasts.

MVNO as a WLAN Operator

In this case the MVNO deploys his own broadband wireless network (WiFi or WiMAX) in order to cut off the high connection costs that limit its ability to offer customers additional broadband services. An Operator-like MVNO and WLAN operator have been studied both in a large and a small European country. The case of a licensed UMTS+WLAN operator has been studied in Varoutas, et al. (2003).

The main economic results for the basic scenarios are illustrated in Table 5 and Figure 5. The WLAN MVNOs have a larger revenues stream since the WLAN operation will act as an additional service for its existing customers. This occurs due to better usage patterns of its customers and associated service consumption with only small additional investments needed. The WLAN operation could be the logical step for a MVNO since the investments are minimal and the additional potential revenues are in the scale of MEuros. In the large country, the NPV is almost three times more than in the basic case (without WLAN) whereas in the small country 30% greater. This occurs due to the larger number of potential customers that an operator can serve in a large country.

The main difference between running costs in both large and small country types are the marketing costs, because these are associated with the population. Furthermore, the additional running cost for the WLAN operation is negligible, especially in the small country.

The economic results reveal that investments are roughly proportional to population in the two country types. The population ratio is almost 14:1. It can be observed that the enhancement of the MVNOs' service basket due to the provision of broadband services via WLANs can act as a significant leverage to its business. The MVNO can almost double its economic figures with almost negligible investments. Taking into account the positive impact of MVNOs to a MNO, the additional revenues of MVNO due to broadband

Table 5. Summary of the basic results for an operator-like MVNO with and without WLAN operations

Country type	Large		Small	
	Without WLAN	*With WLAN*	*Without WLAN*	*With WLAN*
NPV (MEuros)	111	328	259	322
IRR	11.68%	14.18%	39.77%	38.22%
Rest Value (MEuros)	48	116	5	139
Pay-back period	8.2	8.1	5.0	5.7
Investments	144	194	55	141
Running Cost	23,070	24,042	3,080	3,092
Revenues	25,192	27,035	3,950	4,241
Revenues-Running	2,122	2,993	870	1,148

Figure 5. Basic financial indexes for all cases (OL=Operator-like).

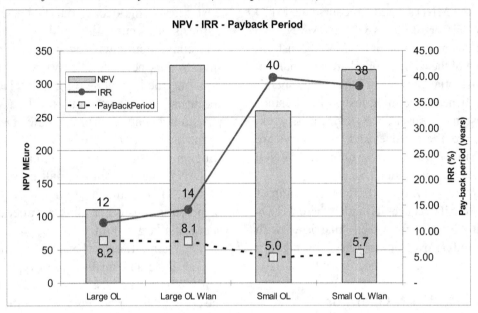

services can reverse the negative attitude of a MNO to MVNOs.

Regarding the other cost structures, analysis shows that usage and tariff levels have great impact. The tariff and usage levels are the most critical parameters for the economic criteria of NPV and IRR outside the interconnection related costs. The model links revenues to usage levels, which means that a 50% increase in revenue corresponds to a 50% increase in usage. Under these circumstances, it would be expected that network costs would increase accordingly. However, since network costs are essentially dictated by coverage constraints and not by capacity ones, an increase in usage leads only to greater revenues, while the corresponding increase in costs is minimal, and relates to core network elements.

FUTURE TRENDS

The future trends for MVNOs depend on several factors. First, the regulation continues to have an important role, as the market entry is in many cases dependent on protection against overcharged

radio network capacity. Once a virtual operator has reached a considerable share of subscribers, it has the bargaining power to approach several MNOs and does not need such protection.

Another aspect is the business model applied by the MVNO. The target may be the corporate market, where high IT competence and resources are needed, but, on the other hand, with deep co-operation, a large customer base can be won in one deal. In the future, MVNO business in the consumer market may be based more and more on bringing in large loyalty groups, whether relating to brand, lifestyle or other social of ethnic grouping.

The trend for many of the most important mobile service providers has led toward increasing infrastructure, and, in this way, strengthening their market power. Full MVNOs, with their own MSCs, can easily connect to several radio networks, and negotiate over termination fees. As more and more services are eventually being realized, through 2.5G, 3G and WLAN type of networks, MVNOs can start to compete not only with price but also with intelligent IP solutions. Integration of the traditional voice with the new services will definitely be crucial, whether VoIP or other solutions are used.

The MVNO business channel will be a viable financial path of digital convergence schemes. Several alternatives examined within this chapter, like pure 3G MVNO and MVNO with WLAN, will support digital convergence with the same technical approach as the traditional operators will implement.

This leads to the convergent service realm, where those owning certain type of access networks, whether fixed or mobile, or not owning any, can complement their access methods with the virtual mode to serve their customer base to the fullest. As the access means should be possible to select optimally for the particular situation and application, no player can any longer provide all possible networks physically everywhere; as a result, liaison is going to have increasing importance. Business opportunities are eventually going to migrate more and more from the network provisioning to the service provisioning and integration.

A trend toward market differentiation and service customization is taking place, and this gives opportunities for different kind of MVNOs. On the other hand, some smaller virtual operators can serve the niche groups, the virtual enablers (MVNEs) providing the technical platforms for them. Regional players would have more potential in the future world, as well as the pan-European and even international MVNOs. With international presence, the virtual operators would solve even the roaming conditions for their benefit, in the way towards a converging world.

After 3G licencing, especially in Europe, the case of a new entrant having its own 3G license in a small and large country market can be considered, in light of the new developments in regulation, technology, convergence and better understanding of the market demands. This business model is very important and follows the same rules as the model described in this chapter. Major effort should be expended in order to identify the hurdles

that have prevented entities from becoming new entrants. Understanding the cost structure of a new entrant and identifying parameters related to longer than seven years pay-back periods are issues for further study.

The possibility of building a CDMA450 network as a comparison scheme to the 3G MVNO could be also analyzed. This scenario could be pointed out since CDMA450 has been one of the skyrocketing sectors in the global wireless communication industry in the past few years. It has attracted keen interest in the industry because the initial driving force for CDMA450 was the urgent need to find a digital replacement for the ageing NMT450 analogue cellular systems that had been widely deployed, not just in the Nordic countries but also in many countries in Central and Eastern Europe. In addition, CDMA450 inherits all the technical and service advantages of the CDMA2000® system. This means that technology can become a 3G solution for some operators without UMTS licenses before becoming an MVNO player. A Greenfield CDMA450 operator could be entering the 2G and 3G mobile networks market. In this case study the economics for two build out strategies--a full country coverage case and a rural rollout case could also be studied.

Fixed line operators, in order to provide fixed-mobile convergence services, could also become MVNOs, using either their own infrastructure (and become a full MVNO) or just reach an agreement with a MNO to use the wireless access network (only service providers).

CONCLUSION

The interest of companies, either working in the mobile sector or not, entering this market is self-evident and many of them are looking for specific channels to start offering services under a Digital Convergence scheme. The channel of MVNO is either complementary to a service provision channel or operator channel but is still a ways off from taking part in this big game.

Acceptable business opportunities can be observed through calculations in terms of forecasted and actual mobile penetration across Europe. Agreements with MNOs for spectrum usage and interconnection give MVNOs enough space for business opportunities and acceptable profit margins. As the Digital Convergence path evolves, the MVNO channel will be more attractive for companies left out from the licencing.

Both infrastructure costs (which are high due to difficulties in obtaining volume discounts) and interconnection costs are too critical for the success of MVNOs. Interconnection costs, which could be the turning point for the business cases and the MVNO must have hard negotiation with the MNO in order to keep them as low as possible. On the other hand, the regulators should protect the new companies and ensure that the interconnection price level will boost the overall competition.

Marketing and entry costs in general can be a burden for a potential MVNO, but this can be overcome by means of a high brand firm or a company already operating. Although revenues from the provision of broadband services are missing from current MVNO business plans, this could be another opportunity for the MVNO to expand its business in the future. In reality, the MVNO way to 3G represents a profitable option for all parties involved and a key enabler for technology, network and services providers.

Future MVNOs should also benefit from WLAN if they complement their offer with WLAN services and in addition MNO profitability could be increased within the "financial" support of the concentrated to retail business MVNO.

Furthermore, different technology schemes and different business profiles could be studied in order to clearly achieve the optimal strategy and policies in the mobile era always including solutions for non regulated licensed operators offering even convergence applied services.

ACKNOWLEDGMENTS

This work has been partially supported from the European CELTIC/ECOSYS project, a PYTHAGORAS Grant from the Greek Ministry of Education and a PENED grant from the Greek Ministry of Development (General Secretariat for Research and Technology). Authors would like to acknowledge the fruitful comments and contributions from their colleagues from NOKIA Coorporation, Telenor AS R&D, France Télécom R&D, Helsinki University of Technology and University of Athens.

The authors would also like to thank the reviewers for their fruitful comments and suggestions.

REFERENCES

AGCOM. (2001). *Italian regulator of the telecommunication market*. Retrieved from http://www.agcom.it

Analysys. (2000). *Economic studies on the regulation of the mobile industry*. Final report for ECTA: Analysys.

Analysys. (2002). *The future of MVNOs*.

ART. *The French telecommunications regulator*. Retrieved from http://www.art-telecom.fr/eng/index.htm

Bundesnetzagentur. *German Federal network agency*. Retrieved from http://www.bundesnetzagentur.de/

Clark, V. (2002). Business & regulatory: Ecta pressures regulators on fixed-mobile access charges: Total Telecom.

CMT. *Spanish telecommunications market commission*. Retrieved from http://www.cmt.es

Ims, L. (1998). *Broadband access networks introduction strategies and techno-economic evaluation*. Chapman & Hall.

IST-TONIC. (2000). *Techno-economics of ip optimised networks and services*. IST: EU.

ITU. (2001). *Mobile virtual network operators*. ITU.

Katsianis, D., Welling, I., Ylonen, M., Varoutas, D., Sphicopoulos, T., & Elnegaard, N. K., et al. (2001). The financial perspective of the mobile networks in europe. *IEEE Personal Communications, 8*(6), 58-64.

Leive, D. M. (1995). *Interconnection: Regulatory issues*. Geneva: ITU.

Lillehagen, A., Armyr, L., Hauger, T., Masdal, V., & Skow, K.-A. (2001). An analysis of the MVNO business model. *Telektronikk, (4),* 7-14.

Melody, W. H. (1997). *Telecom reform: Principles, policies and regulatory practices,*Technical University of Denmark.

Monath, T., Elnegaard, N. K., Cadro, P., Katsianis, D., & Varoutas, D. (2003). Economics of fixed broadband access network strategies. *IEEE Communications Magazine. 41*(9), 132-139.

MVNO pricing in Finland. (2005). The Ministry of Transport and Communications of Finland.

NPT. *Norwegian NRA*. Retrieved from http://www.npt.no

ODTR. *Irish commission for communications regulation*. Retrieved from http://www.odtr.ie/

OECD. (2000). *Cellular mobile pricing structures and trends (No. DSTI/ICCP/TISP(99)11/FINAL).* OFCOM. *Ex OFTEL, the UK NRA*. Retrieved from http://www.ofcom.org.uk/

OFCOM. (1999). *Statement on mobile virtual network operators.*

OFTA. (2001). *Open network: Regulatory framework for third generation public mobile radio services in Hong kong* (Discussion Paper).

Olsen, B. T., Zaganiaris, A., Stordahl, K., Ims, L.A., Myhre, D., Overli, T., et al. (1996). Technoeconomic evaluation of narrowband and broadband access network alternatives and evolution scenario assessment. *IEEE Journal Selected Areas in Communications, 14*(8), 1203-1210.

Olsen, B. T. (1999). OPTIMUM – a techno-economic tool, *Telektronikk, 95*(2/3).

OMSYC. (2004). *MVNO in europe benefits and risks of co-opetition.*

OVUM. *Virtual mobile services: Strategies for fixed and mobile operators.*

PTS. *Swedish national post and telecom agency.* Retrieved from http://www.pts.se

Varoutas, D., Katsianis, D., Sphicopoulos, T., Loizillon, F., Kalhagen, K. O., Stordahl, K., et al. (2003). Business opportunities through umts-wlan networks. *Annales Des Telecommunications-Annals of Telecommunications, 58*(3-4), 553-575.

Varoutas, D., Katsianis, D., Sphicopoulos,T., Stordahl, K., & Welling, I. (2006). On the economics of 3G mobile virtual network operators (MVNOs). *Wireless Personal Communications, 36*(2), 129-142.

APPENDIX I

Cost Evolution of the Network Components

The cost prediction curve depends on a set of parameters such as reference cost at a given time, the learning curve coefficient that reflects the type of component, penetration at the starting time and penetration growth in the component's market. The cost database contains estimation on these parameters for all components and generates cost predictions based on the extended learning curve. The forecast function for the evolution of the relative accumulated volume $n_r(t)$ is illustrated in Equation (1) (Olsen 1996).

$$n_r(t) = \left(1 + e^{\left\{h\left[n_r(0)^{-1} - 1\right] - \left[\frac{2 \cdot h \cdot 9}{\Delta T}\right] \cdot t\right\}}\right)^{-1}$$

(1)

The expression for $n_r(t)$ can be substituted into a learning curve formula Equation (2) yielding the final expression for price versus time in the cost database.

$$P(t) = P(0) \cdot \left[n_r(0)^{-1} \cdot n_r(t)\right]^{\log_2 \cdot K}$$

(2)

where $n_r(0)$ is the relative accumulated volume in year 0. The value of $n_r(0)$ should be equal to 0.5 for components that exist in the market and their price is expected to be further reduced due to aging rather than due to the production volume (i.e., very old products--many years in the market). From estimations in industrial telecommunication network components, $n_r(0)$ could be 0.1 for mature products and 0.01 for new components in the market.

$P(0)$ is the price in the reference year 0, ΔT is the time for the accumulated volume to grow from 10% to 90%, and K is the learning curve coefficient. K is the factor that causes reduction in price when the production volume is doubled. The K factor can be obtained from the production industry, mainly the suppliers. For a component (with constant $nr(0)=0.1$) when the ΔT is equal to 10 years and K is equal to 0.98, Equation (2) gives almost 2% of reduction in the price of the component per year for the first 10 years. If ΔT is five years, this reduction is almost 4% per year for the first five years. All the above described values have been extensively used (Ims, 1998) for the evaluation of telecommunications investment projects.

OA&M Approach

The OA&M approach is divided into three separate components. Conceptually, the three components are defined as follows:

1. The cost of repair parts.
2. The cost of repair work.
3. The Operation and Administration cost for each service cross-related to the number of customers or to the number of critical network components.

The formula for calculating OA&M cost is given by Equation (3) (Olsen 1999).

$$(OA\&M)_i = \frac{V_{i-1} + V_i}{2} \cdot \left(P_i \cdot R_{class} + P_l \cdot \frac{MTTR}{MTBR}\right) + OA$$

(3)

The first term in the parenthesis represents the cost of repair parts, the second term is the cost of repair work while OA represents the Operation and Administration cost. V_i is the equipment volume in year i, P_i is the price of cost item in year i, Rclass is the maintenance cost percentage for every cost component, P_l is the cost of one working hour, MTTR is the mean time to repair for the cost item in question and MTBR is the mean time between failures for the cost item in question. In order to implement the calculation of the OA&M cost, classes for MTTR and MTBR are defined in the database of the Tool as well as cost for P_l and P_i.

DEMAND FORECASTS

A logistic model is used to perform demand forecasts. This model is recommended for long-term forecasts and for new services. To achieve a good fit, a four-parameter model, including the saturation level, is used.

The model is defined by the following expression:

$$Y_t = M / (1 + \exp(\alpha + \beta t))^\gamma$$

where the variables are as follows:

Y_t : Demand forecast at time t

M : Saturation level

t : Time

α, β, γ : Parameters

The parameters α, β, and γ cannot be estimated simultaneously by ordinary least-squares regression since the model is non-linear in the parameters. Instead, a stepwise procedure is used to find the optimal parameter estimates. The saturation level M is estimated, and is a fixed input to the forecasting model.

TECHNO-ECONOMIC TERMS

The objective of a business case for this network is to estimate investments, revenue, operating cost, general administration cost and taxes. The network is expected to generate revenue throughout the lifetime of the product. Depreciation, operating cost, general administration cost and taxes are deducted from the revenue stream. To assess the model, the cash flow is calculated by adding back the depreciation to the income (net). The business case is evaluated according to four conventional criteria: Net Present Value (NPV), Internal Rate of Return (IRR), cash balance and payback period.

The Net Present Value (NPV) is today's value of the sum of resultant discounted cash flows (annual investments and running costs), or the volume of money, which can be expected to receive over a given period of time. If the NPV is positive, the project earns money for the investor. It is a good indicator for the profitability of investment projects, taking into account the time value of money or opportunity cost, which is expressed in the discount rate (10 percent in most cases).

The Internal Rate of Return (IRR) is the interest rate calculated on an investment and income (resultant net cash flow) that occur over a period of time. If the IRR is greater than the discount rate used for the project, then the investment is judged to be profitable. This criterion is especially useful in comparing projects of different type and size. The Internal Rate of Return gives a good indication of "the value achieved" with respect to the money invested.

The Cash Balance curve (accumulated discounted Cash Flow) generally goes deeply negative because of high initial investments. Once revenues are generated, the cash flow turns positive and the Cash Balance curve starts to rise. The lowest point in the Cash Balance curve gives the maximum amount of funding required for the project. The point in time when the Cash Balance turns positive represents the Payback Period for the project.

Section II
New Business Opportunities

Chapter V
Network Effects and the Evolution of Internet Auctions

Sangin Park
Seoul National University, Republic of Korea

ABSTRACT

Based on the weekly data of listings and Web site usage of eBay and Yahoo!Auctions, as well as fee schedules and available auction mechanisms, this chapter provides empirical support of the network effect in Internet auctions: A seller's expected auction revenue increases with page views per listing on one hand and increased listings raise page views per listing on the other hand. The existence of the network effect between Web site usage and listings explains the first mover's advantage and the dominance of eBay even with higher fees in the Internet auctions market. Our empirical findings also highlight unique features of Internet auctions, especially in the entry behavior of potential bidders into specific auctions, inviting more theoretical studies of the market microstructure of Internet auctions.

INTRODUCTION

E-commerce has been hailed as a frictionless competitive market (Bakos, 1991; Bakos, 1997). It is widely believed that the Internet drastically reduces buyers' search costs (for prices, product offerings and shop locations) and lowers barriers to entry and exit. The low search costs and barriers to entry and exit induce strong price competition, leading to low profit margins and low deadweight losses. Consistently, some case studies have found that e-commerce has, on average, lower prices than the conventional retail market (Bailey, 1998; Brynjolfsson & Smith, 2000). However, as argued in Ellison and Ellison (2004), the overhead costs in e-commerce may not be as low as anticipated, and thus severe price competition may lead to the Bertrand paradox (with prices so low that firms cannot cover their overhead costs). Hence, the long-term viability of the e-commerce firms is often in question.

More recently, however, several empirical studies (Brynjolfsson & Smith, 2000; Clemons, et al., 2002; Johnson, et al., 2003; Loshe, et al., 2000) indicate some frictions in e-commerce: (i) compared to the conventional retail market, e-commerce has low prices on average but high market concentrations; (ii) an e-commerce firm with the highest market share does not charge the lowest price and often charges a price higher than the average; and (iii) the price dispersion is higher in e-commerce than in the conventional retail market. Hence, attentions have been directed to the possibility and sources of the first-mover's advantage which explains the reason that the pioneering firms, such as Amazon.com, Yahoo!, E*Trade and eBay, have dominant market shares despite their higher prices.

The network effect is widely considered a source of this first-mover's advantage, especially in Internet auctions. As is well known, eBay, the pioneer of the Internet auctions, has been very profitable and dominated the Internet auctions market. It is speculated that the positive feedback effect (or network effect) between buyers' Web site usage and sellers' listing behavior might be the reason for eBay's profitability and dominance. The idea of this network effect seems quite straightforward: More potential buyers will visit an Internet auctions site if there are more listed items for auctions, and more sellers will list their items on that site if more (potential) buyers visit the site. However, there are several *non-trivial* issues when we connect this (naïve) idea to the data and the auction theories.

First of all, it is not straightforward whether more potential buyers will visit an Internet auctions site with more listed items. Whether a potential bidder will log on to an Internet auctions site may depend on not only the probability that the buyer will find an item she/he wants but also the expected sale price of the item and the probability of winning the item in the auction. The transaction cost (the search cost for a potential buyer to find a wanted item) decreases with more listings in

an Internet auctions site. However, the buyer's expected trade surplus, which is determined by expected sale price and the probability of winning the auction, may depend on the number of substitutable (listed) items as well as the market microstructure of the Internet auctions and the number of potential bidders.

Second, there is no theoretical guarantee that more sellers will list their items on an auction site with more potential buyers. The literature of auction theory predicts that a seller's expected auction revenue is either decreasing or increasing with the number of the potential bidders, depending on whether potential bidders' entries into a specific auction are endogenous or exogenous (Levin & Smith, 1994; Bulow & Klemperer, 1996). As will be detailed in Sections 2 and 4, the Internet auction model (including the entry behavior of potential bidders into a specific auction) may not be appropriately specified by the market microstructure of traditional auctions.

Lastly, the number of *potential bidders* faced by a specific seller on an Internet auctions site may not be exactly measured by the W*eb site usage* of the site. The Web site usage data do not distinguish the buyers' visits form the sellers' visits, and is typically measured by "unique visitors" or "page views."

Moreover, different sellers may compete with each other because they list similar (or substitutable) items while some potential buyers may not be interested in bidding for some specific seller's items. Hence, it may not be possible to obtain the exact number of potential bidders faced by a specific seller from the usage data.

In the absence of an appropriate structural model of the market microstructure as well as the exact measurement of the number of potential bidders, this paper will study the significance of the network effect, using the (no) arbitrage condition of the seller's listing behavior between the competing Internet auctions sites, eBay and Yahoo!Auctions. Specifically, we will make some simplifying (reduced-form) assumptions based on the empirical comparison of these competing auctions sites with regard to the auction mechanism, fees and realized (ex post) auction revenues. Then, using the arbitrage condition, we can relate, for given auction mechanisms, the data of Web site usage and listings to a specific seller's expected auction revenue implied by the difference of listing fees, which will support the network effect in Internet auctions as a positive feedback effect between Web site usage and listings.

Due to the dominance of eBay in Internet auctions, however, it is unusual to have the data of the number of listings and Web site usage on auctions sites other than eBay. In this sense, we are fortunate to have unique weekly data of the number of listings and Web site usage on Yahoo! Auctions as well as eBay. Our data cover at most the first 17 weeks of the year 2001, which provides us with a window of opportunity to take a snapshot of the empirical relationship between Web site usage and listings in Internet auctions. However, due to the size of our sample, the statistical inferences in the paper satisfy only small sample properties. On the other hand, the short period of time may be better suited for this reduced-form study, considering the time-varying structural and idiosyncratic changes in the market.

The positive feedback effect between Web site usage and listings at a first glance resembles the liquidity trap in the literature of finance (Economides & Siow, 1988). The liquidity literature usually shows that the expected price in a market is independent of the size of market but the variance of price is lower in a market of high liquidity (with many traders). Traders prefer larger markets because of lower price variance. Hence, liquidity gives rise to a positive externality. The network effect in Internet auctions, however, causes a positive externality because the expected sale price (or auction revenue) increases with the size of a market (the number of potential buyers) and the buyer's net gain from the transaction cost and the expected auction surplus increases

with many traders (the number of listed auction items).

The chapter is organized as follows: The second section discusses empirical observations of eBay and Yahoo! Auctions and then the number of potential bidders faced by a specific seller on an Internet auctions site. The third section utilizes the (no) arbitrage condition of the seller's listing behavior, empirically studying the relationship between sellers' listing behavior and the number of potential bidders. The fourth section discusses our empirical findings in contrast to the theoretical predictions of the traditional auction literature, highlighting unique features of the Internet auctions and inviting more theoretical and empirical studies on the market microstructure of Internet auctions. The Appendix calculates, with additional specifications, the seller's valuation of the number of potential bidders.

INTERNET AUCTIONS, POTENTIAL BIDDERS, AND DATA

Internet Auctions

Internet auctions began in 1995 and have been growing rapidly. As of fall 1999, Internet auctions sites are estimated to have almost $100 million revenue per month, while in May 2001, the estimated total revenue of Internet auctions reached $556 million. Since the beginning of Internet auctions, eBay has maintained a dominant position, although the popular attention and the profitability of eBay induced entries of the two biggest e-commerce firms: Yahoo! in October 1998 and Amazon.com in March 1999. An eBay vice president said in January 2000 that eBay's market share in the Internet auctions market remained approximately 90 percent (Lucking-Reiley, 2000). As of fall 2001, it is still believed to be more than 80 percent.

An Internet auctions site, such as eBay and Yahoo!Auctions, acts as a listing agent, allowing individual sellers to register their items for its Web site and running Web-based automatic auctions on their behalf. Actual exchanges, including payment and shipment, are worked out by the buyer and the seller on their own. The English auctions have been the most dominant format in Internet auctions. However, sellers usually have some control over these Web-based auctions, choosing a set of different parameters for each auction such as the duration days, an opening value, an optional secret reserve price, etc.

A variety of goods are auctioned in Internet auctions, but the largest category by far has been collectibles. Each Internet auctions site has different categories, and there is usually no one top-level category that includes all the types of collectibles. Between September 27 and November 1, 2001, 59 percent of listings on eBay belonged to one of these categories: "antiques & art," "collectibles," "books, movies, music," "coins & stamps," "dolls & doll houses" or "toys, bean bag plush." During the same time period, 54 percent of listings of

Yahoo!Auctions were included in one of the following categories: "antique, art & collectibles," "sports cards & memorabilia," "toys & games & hobbies," or "coins, paper money & stamps."

eBay vs. Yahoo!Auctions

Yahoo!Auctions has kept a distant second place in the Internet auctions market although it has offered a bit more options in auction mechanisms and lower listing fees compared to the leader, eBay. As shown in Table 1, both sites offer similar auction mechanisms (in terms of auction formats and auction parameters), but Yahoo!Auctions offers an additional option, "auto extension," in the closing rule and more flexible duration dates. On eBay, sellers can choose a length of three, five or seven days and a length of 10 days with an extra fee of $0.10 while on Yahoo!Auctions, sellers can choose a length between two and 14 days. However, both sites employ the ascending-bid (English) auction format and offer "proxy bid" in which the Web-based auction automatically raises a bidder's bid, as other bidders increase the bid price, to the

Table 1. Auction mechanism

	eBay	Yahoo!Auctions
Auction format for a single item	English auction	English auction
Proxy-bidding	Optional	Optional
Secret reserve price	Optional	Optional
Duration (days)	3, 5, 7, or 10	2-14
Feedback-and-rating	Available	Available
Buy it now	Optional	Optional
Early close	Optional	Optional
Auto extension	Not Available	Optional

maximum amount set secretly by the bidder in the beginning of the auction. On both sites, bidders can check sellers' ratings (or reputations) before the auction and evaluate sellers after the auction (feedback-and-rating system). Options such as "secret reserve price," "buy it now" and "early close" are available from both sites.

Observation 1: eBay and Yahoo!Auctions offer very similar auction mechanisms, but Yahoo!Auctions has more options in the closing rule.

Despite similar auction mechanisms between eBay and Yahoo!Auctions, these two sites charge *distinctively different* fees to sellers. During the first 17 weeks of the year 2001, eBay charged two types of basic fees to sellers: insertion fees and final value fees. The insertion fees of eBay range from $0.30 to $3.30, depending on the opening values (called also reserve prices or minimum bid levels), while the final value fees are five percent of the final value (called also sale price or closing value) up to $24.99, 2.5 percent from $25.00 up to $1000.00, and 1.25 percent over $1000.00. On the other hand, Yahoo!Auctions charges only insertion fees ranging from $0.20 to $1.50. As indicated in Table 2, eBay charges higher insertion fees for all the ranges of opening values.

Observation 2: eBay charges higher insertion and final value fees.

The basic fees of Internet auctions have not changed frequently. Indeed, Yahoo!Auctions began to charge insertion fees only from the beginning of the year 2001. At the same time, eBay raised its insertion fees a little bit to the levels shown in Table 2. As will be discussed below, these changes of fees had significant impacts on the number of listings on Yahoo!Auctions.

Despite more options in the closing rule and lower listing fees on Yahoo!Auctions, eBay's dominance is evident in terms of both the number of listings and Web site usage. Our data of the number of listings are obtained from the *Downtown Magazine*'s Wednesday Report. *Downtown Magazine* is an unbound magazine available via the Internet (www.dtmagazine.com) and reports its counts of the number of auction listings updated every Wednesday by noon Eastern Time. This weekly data of the number of listings for

Table 2. Listing fees

		eBay	Yahoo!Auctions
Insertion Fees			
Opening Value	$0.01-$9.99	$0.30	$0.20
	$10.00-$24.99	$0.55	$0.35
	$25.00-49.99	$1.10	$0.75
	$50.00-$199.99	$2.20	$1.50
	$200.00 and up	$3.30	$1.50
Final Value Fees			
Closing Value	$0-$25	5%	Free
	$25-$1000	$1.25 + 2.5%	Free
	over $1000	$25.63 + 1.25%	Free

eBay and Yahoo!Auctions were collected from the first week of the year 2001. However, from the second week of April 2001, the Wednesday Report ceased counting the number of weekly listings on Yahoo!Auctions and began to report the number of listings on a monthly basis, and this is the main reason that the number of our observations are very small.

As illustrated in Figure 1, during the first 17 weeks of 2001, the number of listings on eBay remained between 5 million and 5.7 million after an increase in the first week. On the other hand, the initiation of fees on Yahoo!Auctions in the beginning of the year 2001 had a dramatic impact on the listings of Yahoo!Auctions. The number of listings on Yahoo!Auctions declined drastically from more than 2 million to about 250,000 by the seventh week of the year 2001, and then stabilized around 220,000.

In what follows, therefore, our data analysis will focus on the period of the seventh week to the 13th week (the third week of February to the first week of April) after the changes of the fee schedules were fully absorbed in sellers' listing behavior.

The data of weekly Web site usage (measured by "unique visitors" and "page views") of these two auctions sites are obtained from Nielsen/NetRatings for the first 17 weeks of the year 2001 (except in the first week of March for eBay and the first week of January for Yahoo!Auctions). This usage data from Nielsen/NetRatings is unique in the sense that the weekly usage of Yahoo!Auctions is counted separately from the entire site of Yahoo!.

Unlike the number of listings, however, the changes of fees had no substantial effect on Web site usage. As illustrated in Figures 2 and 3, between the seventh week and the 13th week of 2001, eBay had about 6.3 million unique visitors and 763.6 million page views on weekly average while Yahoo!Auctions had about 530,000 unique visitors and 1.7 million page views. It is quite puzzling that the initiation of fees on Yahoo!Auctions incurred the drastic decrease of listings but had no significant impact on Web site usage. One possible explanation is that before the initiation of fees, many sellers on Yahoo!Auctions might have kept listing their items over and over until they were sold and thus the number of the listings were substantially over-counted.

The data of the number of listings and Web site usage shown in Figures 1-3 clearly indicate the following observation

Figure 1. Listings

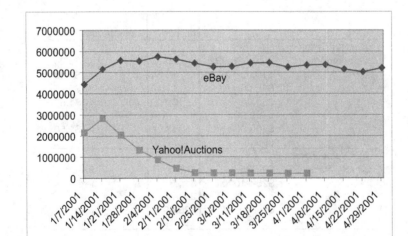

Figure 2. Unique visitors '

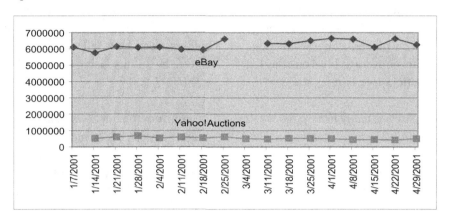

Figure 3. Page Views

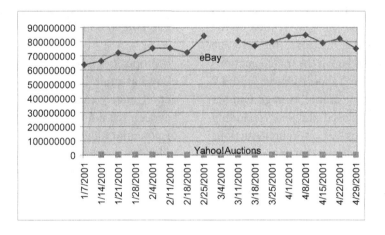

Observation 3: eBay has much larger Web site usage (measured by either unique visitors or page views) and many more listings than Yahoo!Auctions.

Number of Potential Bidders

As discussed in the Introduction, the number of potential bidders faced by a specific seller on an Internet auctions site may not be exactly equal to the numbers of Web site usage of the site. Since different sellers may list similar (or substitut-

able) items in the overlapping time periods, we may infer that Web site usage per listed item is more relevant than the absolute value of Web site usage. However, Web site usage is typically measured by either "unique visitors" or "page views." Hence, it is a question which one is more relevant to the number of potential bidders faced by a seller. To answer this question, we look into our data of unique visitors and page views as well as the number of listings presented in the previous subsection.

It is *striking* to note that during the period in concern (the seventh week to the 13th week of 2001), unique visitors per listing are on average 1.2 on eBay but 2.3 on Yahoo!Auctions while page views per listing are on average 148.4 on eBay but 7.3 on Yahoo!Auctions (see Figures 4 and 5).

Observation 4: eBay has many more page views per listing but smaller unique visitors per listing

Note that "unique visitors" is the (estimated) number of different individuals who visit a Web site while "page views" is the number of unique visitors multiplied by the average unique pages viewed per visitor. As reported in Bajari and Hortaçsu (2001), the average number of (actual) bidders for U.S. mint/proof coin sets was 3.0 on (traded) eBay auctions. In Park (2006) of the Barber Quarter Dollar auctions, the average number of (actual) bidders in the traded auctions turns out to be 4.5 on Yahoo!Auctions and 4.0 on eBay while the conjectured average number of bidders in all the closed auctions (including non-traded auctions) is 0.9 on Yahoo!Auctions and 1.9 on eBay. Considering that unique visitors (including sellers) per listing are on average 1.2 on eBay, we can infer that "unique visitors per listing" may be too small to be the number of potential bidders.

Page views, in addition, reflect the multiple roles of a unique visitor in Internet auctions: A (same) unique visitor may act as a seller, a potential bidder or both, possibly in multiple different auctions. However, different listed items may face competition from different groups of similar (or substitutable) items, and some buyers may not be interested in bidding some items. Hence, the number of potential bidders faced by a specific seller may be item specific. Therefore, the number of potential bidders faced by a seller may be specified as an increasing, item-specific function of Web site usage per listed item.

ASSUMPTION 1: Let U_j denote page views and L_j denote the number of listings on Internet auctions site j. Let N_j^i be the number of potential bidders faced by a seller listing item i on site j and f^i be an increasing real function. Then $N_j^i = f^i(U_j/L_j)$.

From now on, for notational simplicity, we use N_j and f instead of N_j^i and f^i, but it is understood that N_j and f are indexed by the item which a seller is listing. It is difficult to obtain the information of a specific functional form of f, but our analyses that follow do not depend on this specific functional form.

Assumption 1, combined with Observation 4, leads to Proposition 1.

Proposition 1: Under Assumption 1, a seller faces more potential bidders on eBay.

Proposition 1 and Observation 3 indicate that eBay has more listings and more potential bidders. Hence we can infer a *positive correlation* between the number of listings and the number of potential bidders in Internet auctions. In the following section, we proceed to examine whether this positive correlation is caused by the positive feedback effect (i.e., network effect).

SELLERS' LISTING BEHAVIOR AND WEBSITE USAGE

Expected Auction Revenues and Potential Bidders

To study the network effect between the number of listings and the number of potential bidders, we begin by examining whether more sellers list their items on an Internet auctions site if more potential bidders visit the site. In other words, we will examine whether the seller's expected auction revenue increases with more potential bidders in Internet auctions. In principle, a seller's *expected* revenue from listing an item on Internet auctions site j depends on the expected revenue from auctioning the item and the fees charged by site j. Furthermore, the expected auction revenue, say R_j, is affected by the auction mechanism and the number of potential bidders. As discussed above, there are two types of basic fees to sellers: insertion fees, say F_j, and final value fees, say α_j. Then the seller's expected revenue from listing his/her item on Internet auctions site j is:

$$(1-\alpha_j)R_j - F_j. \tag{1}$$

The (no) arbitrage condition implies that the seller's expected revenues from listing the item on any auction Web site must be the same. Then, for any two auctions sites, say e and y, we have:

$$(1-\alpha_e)R_e - (1-\alpha_y)R_y = F_e - F_y. \tag{2}$$

Hence, the number of listings on each site will be determined by this arbitrage condition for a given (expected) number of potential bidders, available auction mechanisms and fees charged by the sites.

As shown in Table 2, eBay charges sellers higher insertion fees for all the ranges of opening values. In addition, only eBay charges the final value fees. Hence, if a potential seller chooses the same (or a higher) range of opening values (for the same item) on eBay, the arbitrage condition in (2) indicates that the seller's expected auction revenue must be greater on eBay. In other words, we expect an *eBay premium* on auction revenues. A seller's choice of an opening value (and thus an insertion fee), however, may be determined endogenously. In the Barber Quarter Dollar auctions on eBay and Yahoo!Auctions closed between November 28, 2001 and December 4, 2001, Park (2006) found that the average opening value of the traded coins was \$26.47 with the average final value of \$41.08 on eBay while the average opening value of the

traded coins was \$6.55 with the average final value of \$14.65 on Yahoo!Auctions. Although we need a broader study of the comparison of auctions on eBay and Yahoo!Auctions for more conclusive arguments, this snapshot indicates that sellers on Yahoo!Auctions set, on average, a lower ratio of opening value to final value. Hence we assume as follows.

Assumption 2: A seller sets no higher opening value on Yahoo!Auctions than on eBay.

As documented in Lucking-Reiley (1999) and Bajari and Hortaçsu (2001), opening value is believed to be the most important determinant of potential bidders' entry into a specific auction. Assumption 2, therefore, seems consistent with Proposition 1 since sellers on Yahoo!Auctions have substantially less potential bidders and thus would set no higher opening values to attract more entries into auctions. The difference in fees shown in Table 2, together with Assumption 2 and the arbitrage condition of (2), leads to the following proposition.

Proposition 2: Under Assumption 2, a seller's expected auction revenue is higher on eBay.

As pointed out in the literature of the auction theory, a seller's expected auction revenue, R_j, on site j, depends on the number of potential bidders, N_j, and auction mechanisms, say m_j, such as available auction formats and a set of parameters which the seller can choose in each auction. That is, $R_j = R(N_j, m_j)$, where R is a real function. If two sites have the same number of potential bidders but one site offers additional options in the auction mechanism than the other, then we can reasonably assume that a seller's expected auction revenue is (*ex ante*) no smaller on the site with additional auction options.

Assumption 3: If two sites have the same number of potential bidders, then a seller's expected auction revenue is no smaller on the site with additional auction options than on the other site.

As discussed in Observation 1, there is no significant difference in the choices of auction formats and auction parameters between eBay and Yahoo!Auctions, but Yahoo!Auctions offers more options in the closing rule. Note that different closing rules may mean different auction formats in practice and different expected auction revenues. For instance, if the end time of an auction is fixed as in eBay, all bidders have incentives to bid only at the last minute. Hence, in this case, the apparent English auctions will be equivalent to the first-price, sealed-bid auctions. On the other hand, in the case of "auto extension", the auction closing time can be automatically extended for five minutes if a bid is placed within the last five minutes of the auction. Hence, "auto extension" can avoid the problem of the fixed end time and restore the English auction mechanism. However, these additional features of Yahoo!Auctions, such as auto extension and more flexible duration days, are optional, and thus a seller may or may not choose them, depending on his/her expected auction revenues resulting from different closing rules. Hence, *ex ante*, *if the sizes of potential bidders are the same*, a seller's *expected* auction revenue on Yahoo!Auctions must be at least as high as that on eBay. However, as indicated in Proposition 2, the seller's expected auction revenue is higher on eBay. Therefore, the implied eBay premium on expected auction revenues can be explained only by more potential bidders on eBay.

Proposition 3: Under Assumptions 1 to 3, a seller's expected auction revenue is increasing in the number of potential bidders in Internet auctions.

Proposition 3 implies that more sellers will list their items on an Internet auctions site as more potential bidders log onto that site. In the Appendix, with additional specifications of the seller's expected auction revenue and the number of potential bidders, we will calculate the seller's valuation of the number of potential bidders.

Web Site Usage of Potential Bidders

Proposition 3 indicates that a seller's expected auction revenue increases with Web site usage per listed item. Hence, if one percent increase in listings induces more than one percent increase of Web site usage, then the expected auction revenue will be raised by increased listings. Therefore, for the completion of the network effect as a positive feedback effect between listings and Web site usage, we have to check whether one percent increase in listings induce more than one percent increase of Web site usage. As discussed in the Introduction, a potential buyer's visit to an Internet auctions site is affected by the number of listed auction items via the buyer's transaction cost and the buyer's expected surplus in the auction. The transaction cost decreases with more listings in an Internet auctions site. However, the buyer's expected trade surplus may increase or decrease with more listings, depending on the market microstructure of the auction mechanism and the number of potential bidder. Hence it is an empirical question whether more potential bidders will visit an Internet auctions site with more listed items.

The comparison of the number of listings and page views on eBay and Yahoo!Auctions provides us with some idea on this quantitative relationship. As discussed above, eBay has more listings and more page views. However, the difference between eBay and Yahoo!Auctions is much bigger in page views than the number of listings. In fact, during the time period in concern, page views per listing are on average 148.4 on eBay but 7.3 on Yahoo!Auctions. Hence, considering that eBay has more listings, these numbers suggest that the elasticity of page views with respect to listings is likely to be greater than one.

To have a more accurate estimate of this elasticity, however, we need to conduct a regression analysis, taking into account that potential bidders can choose to log on to the rival site. Since an appropriate structural model for the market microstructure of the Internet auctions is not yet available (see the next for details) and since it is very difficult to obtain data for potential bidders' actual choices, we use a *reduced-form* analysis of the potential bidders' (aggregate) Web site usage. To quantify the effects of listings on *potential bidders*' Web site usage, say P_j, we employ a logarithm specification as follows:

$$P_j = L_j^{\beta_1} L_{-j}^{\beta_2} e^{c_j}, \tag{3}$$

where L_j is the number of listings, L_{-j} is the number of listings of the rival site and (β_1, β_2, c) is a vector of parameters to estimate. Note that β_1 and β_2 measure the elasticity of Web site usage on an Internet auctions site with respect to its own listings and its rival's listings, respectively. In this reduced-form analysis, we understand that both the market microstructure and the idiosyncrasies of market participants are reflected in the three parameters, (β_1, β_2, c). Hence, a shorter coverage period will be better suited in this reduced-form analysis, which will incur the sample size problem on the other hand.

Since we cannot distinguish the potential bidders' usage from the sellers' usage in our data of page views, we will use page views (or page views minus the number of listings) as a proxy

variable for potential bidders' Web site usage. Then our estimating equation can be derived from (3) as follows:

$$U_j = L_j^{\beta_1} L_{-j}^{\beta_2} e^{c + \eta_j}, \tag{4}$$

where η_j is a measurement error of this proxy variable. Since η_j is not correlated with L_j and L_{-j}, we will apply an OLS estimation procedure to the reduced-form estimating equation of (4).

Table 3 reports these estimation results. First, there is no significant difference in our estimates between the two proxy variables for the potential bidders' Web site usage. Note that our data size is 14 and thus the OLS estimates satisfy only the small sample properties such as the best linear unbiased estimates. However, the logarithm specification fits the data very well ($R^2 = 0.99$). This is mainly because our data cover a short period of time in which there were no significant structural and idiosyncratic changes. As reported in Table 3, the estimates of the elasticity of page views are significant, although the constant, c, is a little bit imprecisely estimated. Our key coefficient, the elasticity of page views with respect to listings (β_1), is estimated to be 1.2. That is, one percent increase of sellers' listings on a site induces 1.2 percent increase of page views.

Hence, the estimation result indicates that an increase in listings will increase the number of potential bidders, eventually raising the seller's

Table 3. Web site usage equation

| Independent Variables | Potential Bidders' Web site Usage | |
| | Pageviews | Pageviews – Listings |
	Estimate (St. Error)	Estimate (St. Error)
constant	11.20 (7.35)	11.25 (8.32)
number of listings	1.20 (0.26)	1.22 (0.30)
number of the rival site's listings	- 0.76 (0.26)	-0.78 (0.3)
R squared value	0.99	0.99
Number of observations	14	14

expected auction revenue in Internet auctions. Since increased expected auction revenues will induce more listings, we can infer a positive feedback effect between the number of listings and Web site usage. The existence of this network effect explains the dominance of eBay even with higher fees in the Internet auctions market.

IMPLICATIONS FROM OUR FINDINGS

Proposition 3 says that the seller's expected auction revenue increases with the number of potential bidders in Internet auctions. This empirical finding, however, seems to contrast to the theoretical prediction in Levin and Smith (1994). Levin and Smith (1994), based on the equilibrium analysis of a symmetric *endogenous* entry with fixed costs, concluded that the expected revenue of any seller who uses his/her optimal mechanism, in either private-value or common-value auctions, *decreases* with the number of potential bidders in a mixed-strategy entry equilibrium when there are too many potential bidders. Hence, if the number of potential bidders is too big, the seller can be better off *ex ante* by restricting the number of potential bidders. Bulow and Klemperer (1996), on the other hand, showed a positive correlation between the seller's expected auction revenue and the number of bidders if the number of bidders is *exogenously* given. In Internet auctions, however, a seller can choose an auction site based on the sizes of potential bidders but cannot restrict the number of potential bidders of a certain site. In addition, the stochastic endogenous entry with fixed costs in Internet auctions is supported by Lucking-Reiley (1999) and Bajari and Hortaçsu (2001). Hence, Internet auctions seem to satisfy the conditions in Levin and Smith (1994), but Proposition 3 contradicts the theoretical prediction of Levin and Smith (1994).

Our intuition for this discrepancy between the theoretical prediction and our empirical finding in Internet auctions is as follows. The theoretical prediction depends on whether there is a sufficient number of potential bidders as well as potential bidders' entry behavior in specific auctions. We first suspect that any Internet auctions site, even eBay, may not have reached the sufficient number of potential bidders (or n^* in Levin & Smith (1994)). As reported in Bajari and Hortaçsu (2001), the average number of bidders for U.S. mint/proof coin sets was only three on (traded) eBay auctions. In Park (2006) of the Barber Quarter Dollar auctions, the average number of bidders in the traded auctions turns out to be 4.5 on Yahoo!Auctions and 4.0 on eBay while the conjectured average number of bidders in all the closed auctions (including non-traded auctions) is 0.9 on Yahoo!Auctions and 1.9 on eBay. In reality, sellers pay more fees for featured auctions and set low opening values (usually with higher secret reserve prices) in order to attract more bidders in Internet auctions. Second, but more importantly, the potential bidders' entry behavior (into a specific auction) in Internet auctions may not be consistent with the underlying assumption of Levin and Smith (1994) in which potential bidders enter a single auction (at a time). Potential bidders on an Internet auctions site may choose to enter specific auction(s) among the (many) auctions listing similar items, and the same seller may list multiple similar items for auctions at the same time. As reported in Bajari and Hortaçsu (2001), there were 100 to 400 U.S. mint/proof set auctions closed on eBay every day between September 28 and October 2, 1998. In addition, the stochastic entry reported in Lucking-Reiley (1999) and Bajari and Hortaçsu (2001) may be generated not by mixed strategies but by things happening in bidders' lives or by different numbers of competing auctions over time. These unique features of the Internet auctions invite more theoretical and empirical studies on the market microstructure of Internet auctions.

CONCLUSION

In this chapter, we empirically examine the network effect in Internet auctions as a positive feedback effect between Web site usage and the number of listings. The (no) arbitrage condition of a seller's listing behavior, combined with our unique data for eBay and Yahoo! Auctions, indicate that a seller's expected auction revenue increases with page views per listing. Our data analysis further indicates that increased listings raise page views per listing. The existence of this network effect explains the dominance of eBay even with higher fees in the Internet auctions market.

The quantitative conclusions in the paper are drawn from the small-sample, reduced-form analyses for only a short period of time. The short period of time may be well suited for our reduced-form study, considering the time-varying structural and idiosyncratic changes in the market. However, due to the size of our sample, the statistical inferences in the paper satisfy only small sample properties. Ideally, we would need to develop a structural model of Internet auctions with data covering a longer period of time.

Our empirical findings also highlight unique features of Internet auctions, especially in the entry behavior of potential bidders in a specific auction, inviting more theoretical and empirical studies on the market microstructure of Internet auctions. Recently, a substantial portion of eBay's business has arisen from the Internet storefront for small retailers, which may not be pure auction transactions. The dominance and high volume of site usage of eBay established by the network effect in the beginning period of the site might have enabled this type of new business, which may add to the complexity of the market microstructure and the possible evolution of Internet auctions.

APPENDIX: SELLER'S EVALUATION OF THE NUMBER OF POTENTIAL BIDDERS

We now proceed to quantify the effects of the number of potential bidders on the seller's expected auction revenue, based on specific functional forms of the seller's expected auction revenue, $R(N_j, m_j)$, and the number of potential bidders, N_j. We will assume a (reduced-form) logarithm specification of a seller's expected auction revenue as follows:

$$R_j = aN_j^b e^{\xi_j}, \qquad (5)$$

where a and b are parameters, and ξ_j represents any idiosyncratic factors which may affect the seller's auction revenues week by week. In equation (5), a reflects the effect of available auction mechanisms on the seller's expected auction revenue, while b measures the elasticity of the seller's expected auction revenue with respect to the number of potential bidders. In principle, a and b are understood to be indexed by the listed item. As discussed in Section 2, Yahoo! Auctions offers additional options to sellers. If these options make a substantial difference in expected auction revenues, the parameter a must differ across the two auctions sites. Later on, we will discuss how the value of b may be affected by this difference in the values of a.

Based on the seller's expected auction revenue function in (5), we will use the arbitrage condition of listing behavior in (2) to calculate b (the elasticity of the seller's expected auction revenue with respect to the number of potential bidders). For the calculation of b, we can first consider an estimation procedure directly from the arbitrage condition of (2). However, the expected auction revenue, R_j, is not observed in this non-linear estimating equation. To calculate R_j, we need a structural econometric model for the Internet auctions which, to our knowledge, is not yet available (see the fourth section).

Hence, to keep our analysis manageable, we will rewrite the arbitrage condition of (2), calculating an eBay premium equivalent to the difference in insertion and final value fees between eBay and Yahoo!Auctions for some representative items. As discussed in second section, the most popular category by far has been the collectibles in Internet auctions. In the U.S. mint/proof coin sets auctions on eBay, as reported in Bajari and Hortaçsu (2001), the average opening value of the traded coins was \$16.28 while the average final value was \$47. The Goldman Sachs study, based on more than 1,000 closed auctions of eBay, estimated the average sale price (final value) to be \$40 in the third quarter of 2001. Hence, in the paper, we will consider as a focal case that a seller lists an expected auction value of \$50 on eBay with an opening value between \$10.00 and \$24.99. We also assume that the seller will choose an opening value no higher than \$25.00 on Yahoo!Auctions. Then, the arbitrage condition in (2) implies that a seller will expect about four percent less revenues from auctioning the same item on Yahoo!Auctions than on eBay. In other words, a seller expects about 4.2 percent $(= 1/0.96 - 1)$ of the eBay premium on auction revenues. Hence, the arbitrage condition in (2) can be rewritten as follows.

$$1 - \overline{\alpha} = R_y / R_e, \qquad (6)$$

where $\alpha_j = 0.04$. If the seller's expected revenue from auctioning his/her item on eBay is \$40 or \$100 with an opening value between \$10.00 and \$25.00, then $\alpha_j = 0.043$ or 0.033, respectively. As another reference case, we will consider that the eBay premium is 10 percent (and thus the corresponding $\alpha_j = 0.091$), which is the eBay premium calculated in the sample of the Barber Quarter Dollar auctions (Park, 2006).

As discussed in the second section, we assume that the number of potential bidders is an increasing function of page views per listing: i.e., $N_j = f(U_j / L_j)$. In what follows, we will use both logarithm and linear specifications, $N_j = c \ln(U_j / L_j)$ and $N_j = c (U_j / L_j)$, where c is a positive constant and understood to be indexed by the listed item. Park (2006) suggests that a logarithm specification is a better fit. Substituting each of these specifications into the seller's expected auction revenue in (5), we can rewrite equation (6) to obtain the following estimating equations for the logarithm and the linear specifications:

$$-\ln(1 - \overline{\alpha}) = b \ln((\ln(U_e / L_e) / \ln(U_y / L_y)) + \varepsilon,$$

$$(7)$$

and

$$-\ln(1 - \overline{\alpha}) = b \{ \ln(U_e / L_e) - \ln(U_y / L_y) \} + \varepsilon,$$

$$(8)$$

where $\varepsilon = \xi_e - \xi_y$. Since ξ_j is not correlated with the numbers of potential bidders, we can apply an OLS estimation procedure for (7) and (8). Recall that, in principle, b depends on the listed item. As discussed above, for a given expected auction revenue of an item on eBay, we can calculate a corresponding eBay premium or α_j. Hence, in our estimating equations of (7) and (8), we will understand that b is indeed indexed by α_j.

Our estimation results are reported in table 4. Before we proceed, we have to concede a couple of limitations in these estimations. First, we have only 7 weekly observations in our estimation. However, the standard errors of our estimates are very small even with this small number of observations. As an alternative (see table 4), we also calculated the values of b (ignoring the error term ε) from the average values of the number of listings and page views, which turned out to be almost the same with our estimates of b (Note that the estimating equations in (7) and (8) have no constant terms). Second, the dependent vari-

Table 4. Seller's valuation of the number of potential bidders

Elasticity with respect to potential bidders	Regression results: estimate (st. error)	Calculations based on mean values
eBay premium = 4.2%		
$N_j = c \ln(U_j/L_j)$	0.044 (0.001)	0.044
$N_j = c (U_j/L_j)$	0.013 (0.0002)	0.014
eBay premium = 3.4%		
$N_j = c \ln(U_j/L_j)$	0.036 (0.001)	0.036
$N_j = c (U_j/L_j)$	0.011 (0.0001)	0.011
eBay premium = 10%		
$N_j = c \ln(U_j/L_j)$	0.102 (0.002)	0.103
$N_j = c (U_j/L_j)$	0.031 (0.0004)	0.032
eBay premium = 15%		
$N_j = c \ln(U_j/L_j)$	0.150 (0.003)	0.152
$N_j = c (U_j/L_j)$	0.046 (0.0006)	0.046
Number of observations	7	

able of the estimating equations (7) and (8) is a constant. In other words, both $\ln(U_e/L_e)/\ln(U_y/L_y)$ and $(U_e/L_e)/(U_y/L_y)$ are expected to fluctuate around a constant, and our data are supportive of this implication. Since our estimating equations are based on the *reduced-form* expected auction revenue function, the short coverage of the time period may help the model to fit the data.

We now discuss our estimation results. There are a couple of interesting patterns in Table 4. First, the elasticity of the seller's expected revenue with respect to the number of potential bidders (b) is increasing in the eBay premium (or decreasing in the corresponding α_j). Due to the fee schedules shown in Table 2, the eBay premium is increasing in the expected auction revenue, and thus we can infer that the elasticity of the seller's expected revenue with respect to the number of potential bidders is higher for a more expensive

item. Consistently, we usually find more expensive items listed on eBay. Second, b is estimated to be higher under the logarithm specification of the number of potential bidders. In our focal case of the eBay premium equal to 4.2 percent, we find that 1.0 percent increase of the number of potential bidders induces 0.04 percent increase of a seller's expected auction revenue under the logarithm specification but 0.01 percent increase under the linear specification. Note that the low elasticity under the linear specification does not necessarily mean that page views per listing induce a smaller increase in the seller's expected auction revenue since we do not have any information of the values of c in Table 4.

Since Yahoo! Auctions offers more options, the parameter a in the seller's expected auction revenue in (5) may be different across these two auctions sites, and thus we will have $(1 - \overline{\alpha})(a_e/a_y)$

instead of $(1-\overline{\alpha})$ in equations (6) to (8), where a_y are a_e the parameters for Yahoo!Auctions and eBay, respectively. If more options in auction parameters, such as more flexible duration days and auto extension, significantly increase the seller's expected auction revenues, we have: $a_y >$ a_e. Hence the eBay premium must be higher than 4.2 percent in our focal case. As pointed out in Table 4, b is increasing in the eBay premium, and thus the above estimate of b in our focal case can be considered a *lower bound* for the true value of b. As discussed in Park (2006), the eBay premium calculated in the sample of the Barber Quarter Dollar auctions is about 10 percent with the average sale price of $41.1 for the traded eBay auctions. Table 4 indicates that if the eBay premium is 10 percent, then one percent increase of the number of potential bidders induces 0.10 percent increase of a seller's expected auction revenue (based on the logarithm specification) or 0.03 percent increase (based on the linear specification).

REFERENCES

Bailey, J. P. (1998). *Electronic commerce: Prices and consumer issues for three products: books, compact discs, and software*. Working paper OECD/GD(98)4. Organization for Economic Co-Operation and Development.

Bajari, P., & Hortaçsu, A.. (2001*). Winner's curse, reserve prices, and endogenous entry: Empirical insights from eBay auctions*. Working paper. Stanford University, Stanford.

Bakes, J. Y. (1991). A strategic analysis of electronic marketplaces. *MIS Quarterly, 15*(3), 295-310.

Bakes, J. Y. (1997). Reducing buyer search costs: Implications for electronic marketplaces. *Management Science, 43*(12), 1676-1692.

Brynjolfsson, E., & Smith, M. (2000). Frictionless commerce? A comparison of Internet and conventional retailers. *Management Science, 46*(4), 563-585.

Bulow, J., & Klemperer, P. (1996). Auctions versus negotiations. *American Economic Review, 86*(1), 180-194.

Chen, P., & Hitt, L. (2002). Measuring switching costs and their determinants in Internet-enabled businesses: A study of the on-line brokerage industry. *Information System Research, 13*(3), 255-276.

Clemons, E. K., Hann, I., & Hitt, L. (2002). Price dispersion and differentiation in online travel: An empirical investigation. *Management Science, 48*(4), 534-549.

Economides, N., & Siow, A. (1988). The division of market is limited by the extent of liquidity. *American Economic Review, 78*(1), 108-121.

Ellison, G., & Ellison, S. F. (2004). *Search, obfuscation, and price elasticities on the Internet*. Working paper. MIT, Cambridge.

Goldfarb, A. (2003). *State dependence at Internet portals*. Working paper. University of Toronto, Ontario.

Harstad, R. M. (1990). Alternative common values auction procedures: Revenue comparisons with free entry. *Journal of Political Economy, 98*(2), 421-429.

Johnson, E. J., Moe, W. W., Fader, P. S., Bellman, S., & Loshe, G. (2003). *On the depth and dynamics of online search behavior*. Working paper. Columbia Business School, New York.

Katz, M., & Shapro, C. (1994). Systems competition and network effects. *Journal of Economic Perspectives, 8*(2), 93-115.

Klemperer, P. (1999). Auction theory: A guide to the literature. *Journal of Economic Surveys, 13*(3), 227-286.

Levin, D., & Smith, J. L. (1994). Equilibrium in auctions with entry. *American Economic Review, 84*(3), 585-599.

Loshe, G., Bellman, S., & Johnson, E. J. (2000). Consumer buying behavior on the Internet: Findings from panel data. *Journal of Interactive Marketing,* 14, 15-29.

Lucking-Reiley, D. (2000). Auctions on the Internet: What's being auctioned, and how? *Journal of Industrial Economics, 48*(3), 227-254.

Lucking-Reiley, D. (1999). *Experimental evidence on the endogenous entry of bidders in Internet auctions.* Working paper, Vanderbilt University.

Matthews, S. A. (1984). Information acquisition in discriminatory auctions. In M. Boyer & R. E. Kihlstrom (Eds.), *Bayesian models in economic theory.* North Holland, New York.

Park, S. (2006). eBay's dominance in Internet auctions. In M. Khosrow-Pour (Ed.), *Encyclopedia of e-commerce, e-government and mobile commerce.* Hershey, PA: Idea Group Reference.

Park, S. (2004). Quantitative analysis of network externalities in competing technologies: the VCR case. *Review of Economics and Statistics, 86*(4), 937-945.

Chapter VI
Mobile Payment Issues and Policy Implications:
The Case of Korea

Youngsun Kwon
Information and Communications University, Republic of Korea

Changi Nam
Information and Communications University, Republic of Korea

ABSTRACT

This chapter introduces three mobile payment plans that have been launched in Korea: mobile banking service, mobile prepaid electronic cash service and mobile phone bill service. Based on the recent experiences of the Korean economy, this chapter discusses the regulatory and monetary policy issues associated with mobile payments. Mobile payments are superior to existing means of payments because of their efficiency and convenience and mobile network operators (MNOs) are on the verge of turning into non-bank financial institutions in their nature. The government needs to facilitate the crossbreed between banks and MNOs to accelerate the development of efficient payment instruments rather than hindering innovation in banking industry.

INTRODUCTION

All business transactions entail at least one method of payment. Traditionally, fiat money has been the most popular method of payment for retail business transactions. But as computer and telecommunication technologies have developed, electronic payment methods, including credit cards, debit cards and electronic payments via online banking, have appeared and are now widely used in most economies. By the latter part of the 1990s, many advanced economies, including Korea, had experienced three important changes: an electronic commerce boom, wider Internet penetration and the spread of mobile communication. As electronic commerce sales expanded, firms and customers needed new electronic payment systems that were more convenient and efficient.

As electronic commerce has grown, Internet banking in Korea also has increased rapidly since its introduction in 1999. In mid-2002, teller service was still the dominant delivery channel of banking services in Korea, with face-to-face transactions accounting for 42.4 percent of total retail banking transactions. By contrast, only 11.7 percent of retail banking transactions was delivered through Internet banking. However, the gap between traditional teller banking and Internet banking has been fast shrinking. Indeed, the number of Internet banking transactions has outgrown teller banking transactions more recently, as shown in Figure 1. The fact that the proportion of transactions done through banking call centers has been relatively stable over time suggests that Internet banking is the main substitute channel for teller service and cash dispensers (CDs)/automated teller machines (ATMs). As a result, the number of Internet banking customers has grown from 1.2 million at the end of June 2000 to 25.4 million at the end of the third quarter 2005. In addition, daily fund

transfers made through Internet banking over the same period have increased about 22 times, from 608 billion Won to 13.5 trillion Won.

However, one limitation is that Internet banking cannot fully satisfy the human desire for mobility, because it cannot provide users with a ubiquitous connection to the communication system. As a result, Internet banking has a critical drawback as a means of payment for retail business transactions because it does not accommodate human beings' mobility. In order to use an Internet banking service, customers often need to use a specific computer, usually their own, which has an authentication file. Although customers can carry their authentication file on a diskette, they have to find a computer hooked up to a network to use the Internet banking service. Therefore, Internet banking cannot satisfy that part of human nature that makes us prefer to move about, rather than staying in one place all the time. By contrast, mobile payments, which we define as the transfer of a currency-denominated value from buyers

Figure 1. Share of Korean banking service channels, 2002-2005 (Source: Bank of Korea [2005])

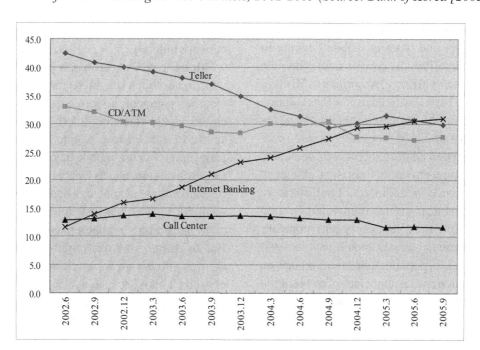

to sellers using mobile devices such as mobile phones and personal digital assistants (PDAs), provide better mobility for customers.

Although mobile banking was introduced in Korea in late 1999, the number of users of mobile devices as a payment tool began to grow significantly after the integrated circuit (IC) chip-embedded mobile phone appeared in the third quarter of 2003. In addition to mobile banking, new mobile payment solutions such as mobile prepaid electronic cash service and mobile phone bill service have been recently provided to customers.

Based on the recent experiences of the Korean economy, this chapter discusses the regulatory and monetary policy issues associated with mobile payments. Mobile payment systems are evolving, so our policy discussions are confined to the current state of the Korean mobile payment systems, which we believe are relatively more advanced than those in other countries. Unfortunately, a rigorous empirical analysis of the effects of mobile payment systems on financial intermediation is almost impossible due to the lack of data. Therefore, this chapter focuses on identifying and discussing the policy issues related to mobile payment systems.

The second section introduces the concept, characteristics and types of mobile banking in Korea and describes the current state of mobile payment systems in Korea. According to Mishkin (1997), three basic forces determine the evolution (or innovation) of payment systems: efficiency (low transaction costs), convenience and security. This section addresses how the superiority of mobile payments stems from their efficiency and convenience. In addition, a brief literature survey on mobile payments is provided. Section 3 discusses the main regulatory and monetary problems caused by the new mobile payment systems in Korea. In particular, Section 3 reports on the competition and resultant lack of cooperation between banks and network operators. Section 4 addresses government reaction to the problems and discusses what the government can do to accelerate the innovation of payment systems. Finally, the fifth section concludes the chapter and suggests future research topics.

MOBILE PAYMENTS: CONCEPT, CHARACTERISTICS, AND TYPES

Concept of Mobile Payments

There are two viewpoints on mobile payments. First, a "process perspective" views mobile payments as just one method of transferring monetary value among people. Kuttner and McAndrews (2001) defined a payment as "a transfer of monetary value from one person to another" (p. 37). Following this, a mobile payment can be defined as a monetary value transferred among economic agents using mobile devices.[1] The alternative "business perspective" views mobile payments as the product of the collaboration between financial institutions, including banks and credit card companies, and mobile network operators (MNOs). In other words, a mobile payment is a new crossbreed service enabled by the collaboration of firms belonging to two different industries—the financial industry and the mobile network industry.

Mobile payments are a new payment method, which can either substitute for or complement existing payment instruments, such as cash, checks, credit cards and Internet banking. They substitute for existing payment instruments if people prefer to use mobile payments for convenience in circumstances where multiple payment instruments are available, whereas they complement existing payment instruments if mobile payments are the only available payment instrument. But no matter what role mobile payments play, their usefulness grows as electronic commerce expands. This is because, as electronic commerce transactions increase—for example, downloading music, avatar and virtual game tools—the need for instantaneous completion of small payment amounts also grows.

Characteristics of Mobile Payments

Mobile payments have unique characteristics that distinguish them from similar electronic payments. First, they provide users with mobility, which Internet payments cannot.[2] If we focus on payments based on bank accounts, the path of money transfer in mobile banking is exactly the same as that of Internet banking. As illustrated in Figure 2, a person with an account in Bank A has access to his/her account using a mobile handset and can transfer some monetary value to a person with an account in Bank B. MNOs provide network connections between mobile handsets and the mobile server located in a bank, which in turn is connected to an Internet banking server. Contrary to Internet banking, users carry a payment instrument, the mobile handset, with which they can complete bank transactions anytime, anywhere. In short, mobile banking is much more convenient to use than Internet banking.

Second, mobile payments provide users with greater ubiquity of service than other electronic payment instruments, such as credit and debit cards, which can be used only at stores that have card readers. By contrast, mobile payments can be used anywhere. As well as being more convenient, online payments, including mobile payments, are usually less expensive payment methods than credit and debit cards, as noted by Kuttner and McAndrews (2001).[3] Third, although cash provides people with high mobility and ubiquity, the major drawbacks are weak security and the inconvenience involved in carrying large amounts. By contrast, even though there is some chance of losing the mobile handset, the chance of losing money using mobile payments is almost zero. In addition, mobile payment instruments substitute for paper currency and coins, because carrying mobile handsets enables users to pay virtually any amount of money for retail transactions. Finally, although checks are close to mobile payments in terms of mobility, they are inferior because many small stores do not accept them and their settlement takes a longer time, whereas

Figure 2. Mobile payment system

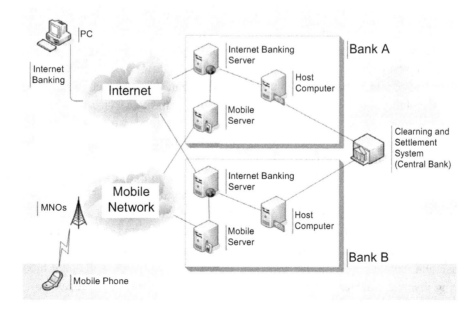

Table 1. Comparison of conventional payment instruments with mobile payments

	Mobility	Ubiquity	Security	Settlement*
Mobile payment	Very High	High	High	Instantaneous
Internet banking	Low	Low	High	Instantaneous
Credit card	High	Medium	High	–
Cash	High	Medium	Low	Instantaneous
Checks	High	Medium	High	1 day

* Settlement indicates how quickly a person can withdraw money that is transferred by another person.

settlement is virtually instantaneous for mobile payments. In addition, mobile payments do not require face-to-face contact. This can be contrasted with checks, which hinder instantaneous or flexible payment.

As summarized in Table 1, mobile payments are the most convenient, secure and efficient payment method available among the competing retail payment instruments. They are more convenient than other conventional payment instruments because people can transfer funds anytime and anywhere as long as the mobile network works effectively. Mobile handsets are also as easy to carry as a credit card or cash. For instance, people cannot transfer funds to those who live in remote areas at midnight with conventional payment instruments, but they can with a mobile payment device. Even cash (not to mention credit cards and checks) is inferior to mobile payments because it is not appropriate for electronic payment. Cash is the lowest payment instrument in terms of security, especially when value is large. In conclusion, it is mobility and ubiquity that make mobile payments unique.

Types and Current Status of Mobile Payments in Korea

In Korea, there are presently three types of mobile payments: mobile banking (usage of which has grown significantly recently), mobile prepaid electronic cash and mobile phone billing. First, mobile banking involves transferring monetary value between the bank accounts of buyers and sellers using mobile handsets. Figure 3 illustrates funds transfer between banking accounts using a mobile banking service. To purchase a product or a service, a payer (a buyer) sends funds to a payee's account by accessing his/her bank account using a mobile device.[4] After confirming that the money is transferred, the payee (seller) sends the product or service to the payer. This type of e-commerce has tended to be limited to retail transactions of less than $100 mainly because there is some risk that the seller may send a defective product or one different from that ordered. Hence, sales have usually been completed directly between the buyer and seller.

Mobile banking service was introduced in Korea at the end of 1999. Initially, adoption of the service was not great, as shown in Table 2. However, with the launch of a new enhanced mobile banking service based on the IC-chip method in the third quarter of 2003, mobile banking service use began to skyrocket.[5] Prior to this, Korea's mobile banking service was based on the Web browser method, which was virtually the same as the Internet banking method. It was clearly inconvenient for users to both surf the Web and type in account information on a tiny display using miniature buttons. Hence, use of the mobile banking service market was not widespread until the MNOs invented new technologies to enhance the convenience and speed of use and reduced the data input process. IC-chip mobile banking reduced the data input process to between five

Figure 3. The mobile payment process based on mobile banking

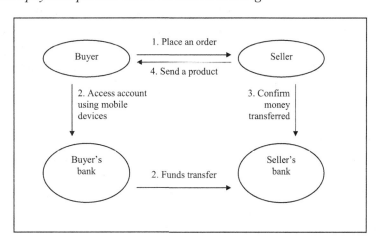

Table 2. Mobile banking use in Korea, 2000-2004 (Note: Transaction numbers are in thousands and the figures in parentheses are the percentage growth rates)

	Dec. 2000	Dec. 2001	Dec. 2002	Dec. 2003	Dec. 2004
Balance checking	200 (−)	692 (246.0)	1,081 (56.2)	2,173 (101.0)	5,013 (130.7)
Funds transfer	2 (−)	18 (800.0)	14 (−22.2)	387 (2,664.3)	1,269 (227.9)
Total	202	710	1,095	2,560	6,281
Ratio*	0.6	0.6	0.6	1.0	1.6

* As a ratio to Internet banking

and six steps, down from the nine to 16 steps required under Web browsers. In addition, the need for mobile banking in Korea increased by 2003, as electronic commerce expanded continuously after 2000. The new technology and the growing need for electronic transactions brought about a dramatic increase in the use of mobile banking from 2003, as shown in Table 2.

The second type of mobile payment is mobile prepaid electronic cash. The mobile prepaid electronic cash service that Korean MNOs currently offer is a digital substitute for bank notes and coins, with which people can transfer funds and pay for small transactions. In order to use the mobile prepaid electronic cash service, a mobile phone user transfers a certain amount of money

from his/her bank account to his/her virtual account opened at an MNO, which is linked to his/her mobile phone number. After storing a certain amount of money in his/her virtual account, users can initiate transactions using mobile devices. Simply by using a mobile phone number, a user can send electronic cash to others, without being required to provide any further information. However, transferring money from a bank account to a virtual account then means users' purchasing electronic cash by paying cash into their bank accounts and MNOs' issuing electronic cash.[6] The service is not popular in Korea because of a fraud that occurred in April 2004.[7]

The third type of mobile payment is a mobile phone bill service. The mobile phone bill service was developed to enable those with mobile handsets to pay for small retail transactions in Internet shopping malls. Online shoppers who chose to pay using the phone bill service are asked to type in their mobile phone number and a certification key when they place an order on the Web. The shoppers type their mobile phone numbers on a Web page and wait a few seconds to receive a certification key sent through a short message service (SMS) by the membership MNOs. The transaction process finishes when online shoppers type in the certification key. They usually receive the commodity after a few days, or, in the case of a digital commodity or online service like virus checking/fixing, receive it immediately. The transaction record is sent to the MNOs, and the price of the service or product is included in the monthly mobile phone bill. After online shoppers pay for the service or product, the MNOs remit the collected funds to the Internet shopping mall. In other words, MNOs simply play the role of rate collectors on behalf of the online shopping malls. SK Telecom, the largest MNO in Korea in terms of its customer base, reported that about seven million users were using the mobile phone bill service in 2003, and that value of transactions completed through the mobile phone bill service amounted to some $US330 million. One merit of using the mobile phone bill service is that online shoppers do not need to provide personal information to shopping malls (Financial Supervisory Service, 2002).

A Brief Literature Survey

Research papers on mobile payments and banking are scant, even though the number of papers on mobile payments and banking are increasing. Major concerns of existing papers on mobile payments have been mobile payment systems, the effects of mobile payments on the banking business and industry, mobile banking consumer behavior, security aspects of mobile payments and financial regulation.

Mobile payments are new services enabled by mobile communications technology, so it is not difficult to find previous literature on mobile payment systems. Examples are Lin, et al. (2006), Kreyer, Pousttchi, and Turowski (2003), Herzberg (2003), Mobile Payment Forum (2002) and Kuttner and McAndrews (2001). These papers summarize and introduce the mobile payment processes and services succinctly.

A group of papers explore the impacts of mobile communications technology on banking business and industry. Kumar and van Hillegersberg (2004) discuss briefly how deregulation, globalization and new communication technology change the shape of traditional financial markets. Warwick (2004) and Orr (2006) describe the evolution of our society toward a cashless society. Mallat, Rossi, and Tuunainen (2004) and Kumar and van Hillegersberg (2004) introduce various mobile banking services. Shin and Lee (2005) introduce an electronic payment platform, MONETA, developed by SK telecom in order to provide mobile payment services.

The papers on mobile banking consumer behavior investigate the determinants of mobile banking usage. Luarn and Lin (2005) draw on an extended technology acceptance model (TAM) to understand mobile banking users' behavior. Wang, Lin, and Luarn (2006) apply the extended TAM model to a set of mobile services. Laukkanen and Lauronen (2005) study the factors affecting consumer value creation in mobile banking services by utilizing a qualitative interview method. Suoranta and Mattila (2004) study the diffusion pattern of mobile banking services in Finland. These papers intend to help financial institutions develop marketing strategies.

Claessens et al. (2002) discusses the security issues of electronic banking systems in terms of engineering perspective. Herzberg (2003) argues that electronic payments with mobile devices are securer than other wired electronic payments, and Mallat, Rossi, and Tuunainen (2004) also point that security is one of characteristics that make people prefer mobile banking to other electronic banking services.

There is not much literature dealing with regulation issues caused by mobile payment service. Penny (2001) discusses the opportunities and threats for UK financial services providers and payments disintermediation issues. Warwick (2004) suggests the adoption of a secure government-operated electronic cash that can replace traditional fiat money. This chapter intends to explore and discuss new policy issues caused by mobile payments in the Korean financial market.

THE MAIN ISSUES CAUSED BY MOBILE PAYMENT SYSTEMS

As discussed, mobile payments are more convenient than other payment instruments, especially in terms of mobility and ubiquity of use, and they are as secure as existing electronic payments, including credit cards and Internet banking. If people choose to use mobile payments when other payment instruments are available, this means that mobile payments are more efficient. In fact, even if people use mobile payments because they are the only available means of payment, again this indicates that mobile payments are more efficient than other forms of payment.[8] However, despite their obvious convenience and efficiency, use of mobile prepaid electronic cash and mobile phone bill services has not spread rapidly in Korea, except for mobile banking. This section attempts to shed some light on the lack of cooperation in the mobile payment industry supply chain, and the regulatory and monetary problems caused by mobile payment systems, all of which have contributed to the lukewarm reception of mobile prepaid electronic cash and mobile phone bill services in Korea.

Lack of Cooperation in the Mobile Payment Industry Supply Chain

Mobile payment services came into existence as a result of the collaboration between banks and MNOs. In the case of mobile banking and mobile prepaid electronic cash, banks are the service providers and MNOs take the role of providing a ubiquitous wireless service delivery channel. As shown in Figure 2, the major role of MNOs is to set up the wireless connection between the mobile server at banks and the mobile handsets. If we focus on this complementary relationship between banks and MNOs, there is no apparent reason for the two parties to compete with each other. However, in the process of launching mobile payment services in the form of mobile banking and mobile prepaid electronic cash in Korea, banks and MNOs have engaged in competitive, rather than cooperative, behavior. Banks view mobile payments as an encroachment by MNOs on the conventional financial market, although they recognize that the devel opment of more efficient and convenient service channels is inevitable. In addition, banks often overstate the possibility that mobile payments can weaken the stability of the payment and settlement system and gradually reduce central bank authority.

This ambivalent attitude of the banks resulted in an inefficient mobile banking service and the near death of prepaid electronic cash. As shown in Table 2, the use of the mobile banking service increased exponentially after the mobile banking service evolved from the Web browser method to the IC-chip method. Therefore, mobile banking in Korea appears to be a success. However, there is still much room for improvement. Currently, one serious problem is that each bank individually issues an IC-chip for mobile banking. Therefore, if users have two accounts at two banks, they have to carry two chips and exchange one with another to access a different account. This is a very inefficient outcome. Technically, MNOs can mount multiple account information on an IC-chip, which would allow users to access multiple accounts one at a time without replacing their chip. However, despite the feasibility of such a solution, it has not been implemented in Korea because banks have the power to issue chips. This awkward mobile banking system was the result of a tug-of-war between banks and MNOs without government intervention.To date, banks in Korea have succeeded in maintaining MNOs as simple network service providers.

Potential Issues Related to the Overall Financial System

There is potential risk involved in the fact that MNOs may undertake some financial institution functions without direct central bank surveillance, which in turn may erode the stability of the financial system. This subsection addresses the financial issues related to mobile prepaid electronic cash and mobile phone bill services that are likely to alter the nature of MNOs.

To understand clearly the impact of the mobile prepaid electronic cash service on the financial system, it is necessary to appreciate in detail how

the service works. In order to use a mobile prepaid electronic cash service, users first need to obtain membership of the service. Upon joining, they have a virtual account to which they can transfer funds from their conventional bank accounts. The virtual account is created in the MNO firm's banking account and identified by the user's phone number. In other words, as illustrated in Figure 4, virtual accounts are individual users' accounts within an MNO's own bank account, with phone numbers as identifiers. Upon transfer from a bank account, the money stored in the virtual account becomes electronic cash that users can, by simply using the phone number, remit to friends or purchase products or services.

The virtual accounts created in an MNO's bank account can be understood as depository accounts leased from the bank because the virtual account is, in fact, identical to a conventional bank account. Transferring money from bank accounts to virtual accounts is comparable to depositing money in virtual accounts. In other words, the electronic cash stored in virtual accounts is not money earned by MNOs from their business, but money deposited by users. The MNOs are then de facto depository institutions without the necessary government license for financial business. How-

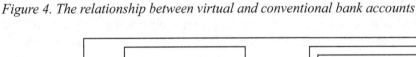

Figure 4. The relationship between virtual and conventional bank accounts

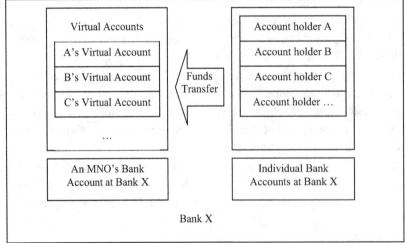

ever, as long as the MNOs do not create credits based on the balance of virtual accounts, and the balance is treated separately in the accounting process, prepaid electronic cash service should not disrupt financial market stability.

After a certain amount of cash is stored in the virtual account, it takes time for account holders to drain their electronic balances. Therefore, on average, at least some balance will remain in the MNOs' bank accounts during the year. A MNO that has a large number of mobile prepaid electronic cash service users will have a large balance upon which it earns financial gains, at least at prevailing market interest rates, without paying interest to depositors (the users). If MNOs make loans using the balance of virtual accounts, they can earn higher financial gains than banks because they are not required to hold some share of balances as noninterest-bearing reserves. Thus, they have an incentive to make loans using the virtual accounts. If they cannot make loans, they can instead use the funds for investment in their original business without cost (interest). Therefore, the mobile prepaid electronic cash service can disturb the long-standing order of the financial market and make it more difficult for a central bank to estimate the amount of money in the economy. Only in the case where MNOs do nothing with the balance—that is, they keep the cash in the virtual accounts intact—will the mobile prepaid electronic cash service not upset the financial market. However, this is implausible without government intervention.

In addition, the mobile phone bill service can potentially work as a disturbing factor in financial markets. If MNOs simply collect rates for products or services that people purchase and then deliver the collected rates to online shopping malls, they function as rate collectors on behalf of the online shopping malls. In this case, the mobile phone bill service does not create any monetary issues. However, MNOs can provide loans to online shopping malls based on transaction records before the rates for products or services are collected and they can

charge fees and interest on these loans. MNOs also have their customers' transaction records so they can evaluate default risk. Therefore, MNOs have sufficient motivation to extend themselves to nonbank financial business.

GOVERNMENT ACTIONS: EVALUATION AND SUGGESTION

To date, the Korean government has taken a hands-off approach to mobile payment services. Mobile payment services are on the verge of burgeoning and the technology for their use is still developing, rather than becoming more stable and standardized. In addition, the size of mobile payment transactions is still very small compared to total financial transactions. It therefore seems appropriate for the government simply to monitor mobile payment market developments, without any regulation.[9]

However, there is much room for the government to facilitate the development of efficient payment instruments by acting as a constructive rule maker in the financial payment market. First, the government needs to monitor and become involved as a market participant in the evolution of the mobile payment system in an attempt to maximize the public interest. This is because new industries, such as online gaming businesses, cannot prosper without an efficient, convenient and secure electronic payment system. An example of inefficiency is the Korean mobile banking service. As shown in Table 2, the demand for the mobile banking service has increased exponentially, but the system is still inefficient because users with multiple accounts at different banks have to change IC-chips. The inefficient mobile banking system is the result of market competition between banks and MNOs. If MNOs had won, a more efficient mobile banking system would have prevailed in Korea, by allowing users access to multiple accounts in different banks with the one chip. With hindsight, the Korean government should have become more actively involved in the standard-setting process for mobile payment systems, to facilitate the evolution of the mobile banking service and the development of the mobile payment market.

Second, the mobile prepaid electronic cash service that utilizes the virtual account system transforms the MNOs into de facto nonbank financial institutions. As the MNOs are not regulated financial institutions, they can compete with banks and other financial intermediaries from a more advantageous position. Therefore, as long as the MNOs act as financial institutions, the government should ensure they compete with conventional financial institutions on a level playing field by imposing the same regulations on MNOs as applied to other financial institutions. The regulations governing MNOs should then include setting a level of non interest-bearing reserves, and imposing rules as to whether the deposit insurance system should apply to the balances in the virtual accounts, protection of customer privacy, and so on.

The government can require MNOs to hold the total balances in virtual accounts as non interest-bearing reserves because MNOs do not pay interest for the funds saved in virtual accounts. The government does then not need to worry about the liquidity and credit risk of the MNOs and extend a deposit insurance system to the balance of virtual accounts. Clearly, however, this inactive policy will result in the inefficient use of financial resources because the balance of virtual accounts will be submerged in accounts unavailable for productive purposes. In addition, such a policy will hinder the advent of new efficient payment media, and in turn, reduce the competition in the banking industry, and deter crossbreeding between banks and MNOs. If the government wants to facilitate crossbreeding between banks and MNOs to accelerate innovation in payment services, it should foster competition in the electronic payment service market by al-

lowing MNOs to provide banking services, and therefore regulate MNOs as banks.

Third, the government should adopt an accounting separation rule for the MNOs because they engage in businesses that belong to different industries. Otherwise, the MNOs can enhance their position in certain markets by cross-subsidizing one business with the profits from another. In addition, a dominant market player in the mobile phone industry can extend its market power over the finance industry by utilizing its customer base in the mobile phone market. This possibility is especially problematic in Korea because it has been a long-standing tradition that industrial capitalists are prohibited from extending their businesses into banking. The MNO providing the mobile prepaid electronic cash service can be considered as either a bank or a nonbank financial institution, depending on how the bank is defined. If the bank is defined as a financial intermediary taking deposits and lending loans, the MNO is not a bank as long as it does not make loans by employing virtual account balances. However, if the ban is defined as a financial institution simply taking deposits, the MNO can be considered a bank.[10] If the government adopts the latter interpretation, the MNO cannot offer the mobile prepaid electronic cash service, which means that the government stifle the evolution of the payment system with outdated restrictive regulation. At the center of the ongoing payment system evolution are computer and telecommunication technologies, with which banks usually are not very familiar. Therefore, the government should allow the MNOs to lead the evolution process of payment systems and abolish or lessen the outdated regulation that separates financial capital and industrial capital. and industrial capital.

Fourth, even though it is too early to state the effects of mobile payments on monetary policy, we can see hat the definition of money and the central bank's monetary control policy are to be redefined in the future. This can be seen from the fact that mobile payments can affect the money creation process outside the central bank's surveillance. For example, MNOs making loans by capitalizing on virtual accounts will eventually undermine the effectiveness of conventional monetary aggregates. While for the time being, the mobile prepaid electronic cash will not have a discernible impact on monetary aggregates and monetary policy because of its small size, the central bank should still monitor the evolution process of electronic cash market and stand ready to remove conventional regulations that block the development of more efficient and convenient payment instruments.

CONCLUSION

Historically, as new technology has developed, new services have appeared in markets. When a new service takes root firmly and successfully prevails in markets, it can develop into a new industry or displace an existing industry through absorption or transformation. In the last decade, computer and telecommunication technologies have created the mobile communication industry and have recently begun to dismantle other Industries, including the banking industry. The MNOs, by providing wireless ubiquitous communication service, can merge and collaborate with conventional firms in existing industries to create better products or services. Some MNOs will definitely attempt to evolve into non bank financial institutions by refurbishing existing services with their superior technology. By nature, innovation threatens the conventional order of market, so incumbent firms and regulatory authorities are likely to be h stile to such change. However, history has repeatedly demonstrated that innovation cannot and should not be annulled by self-protecting incumbents. The central bank needs to facilitate the development of efficient payment instruments by acting constructively,

rather than conservatively, as a rule maker in the financial payment market.

The convergence of the telecommunication and financial sectors creates a dynamic confluence, with many potential research topics being evident. Some future research topics are as follows. First, one can simply trace the evolutionary process of the industry in terms of an historical perspective because mobile payments are an emerging industry. Second, the impact of mobile payments on conventional financial orders are a critical concern for central banks, so research on the effect of mobile payments on monetary systems will be of great importance. Third, the adoption of mobile payments is accelerating because they are more efficient, convenient, and secure than traditional payments. Mobile payments help reduce both customers' and banks' transaction costs, and improve customers' convenience. This is a logical presumption, not confirmed by existing empirical studies. Research on the impact of mobile telecommunication technology on the transaction costs of banking industry would therefore be highly valuable. However, it may not be possible to perform rigorous empirical study in the near future because of the scarcity of relevant data.

ACKNOWLEDGMENTS

This research was financially supported by the MIC (Ministry of Information and Communication), Korea, under the ITRC (Information Technology Research Center) support program of the IITA (Institute of Information Technology Assessment).

REFERENCES

Bank of Korea. (2005). *Press release on the use of Internet banking in Korea.* (Quarterly press releases from 2002-2005).

Bank of Korea. (2004a). Payment and Settlement System of Korea. BOK, Seoul: Bank of Korea.

Bank of Korea. (2004b). *Press release on the use of mobile banking in Korea.* (Payment Information 2004-6).

Bank of Korea. (2004c). *A comprehensive survey on electronic banking.* Seoul: Bank of Korea.

Claessens, J., Dem, V., de Cock, D., Preneel, B., & Vandewalle, J. (2002). On the security of today's online electronic banking systems. *Computers & Security, 21*(3), 253-265.

Financial Supervisory Service. (2002). *Supervisory information on electronic finance.* Seoul: Bank of Korea.

Herzberg, A. (2003). Payments and banking with mobile personal devices. *Communications of the ACM, 46*(5), 53-58.

Kreyer, N., Pousttchi, K., & Turowski, K. (2003). Mobile payment procedures. *e-Service Journal, 2*(3), 7-22.

Kumar, K. & van Hillegersberg, J. (2004). New architectures for financial services. *Communications of the ACM, 47*(5), 27-30.

Kuttner, K. N., & McAndrews, J. J. (2001). Personal on-line payments. Federal Reserve Board of New York Economic Policy Review, 7, 35-50.

Laukkanen, T., & Lauronen, J. (2005). Consumer value creation in mobile banking services. *International Journal of Mobile Communications, 3*(4), 1-11.

Lin, P., Lin, Y. B., Gan, C. H., & Jeng, J. Y. (2006). Credit allocation for UMTS prepaid service. *IEEE Transactions on Vehicular Technology, 55*(1), 306-316.

Luarn, P., & Lin, H. H. (2005). Toward an understanding of the behavioral intention to use mobile banking. *Computers in Human Behavior, 21*(6), 873-891.

Mallat, N., Rossi, M., & Tuunainen, V. K. (2004). Mobile banking services. *Communications of the ACM, 47*(5), 42-46.

Mishkin, F. S. (1997). *The economics of money, banking, and financial markets* (5th ed.). Reading, MA: Addison-Wesley.

Mobile Payment Forum (2002). *Mobile payment forum white paper: enabling secure, interoperable, and user-friendly mobile payments.* Retrieved November 21, 2005, from http://www.mobilepaymentforum.org/pdfs/mpf_whitepaper.pdf

Orr, B. (2006). Cashless society, ahoy! *ABA Banking Journal, 98*(3), 44-45.

Penny, J. (2001). The payments revolution: the growth of person-to-person and 'Generation Y' payments services. *Journal of Financial Services Marketing, 6*(2), 190-201.

Shin, B., & Lee, H. G. (2005). Ubiquitous computing-driven business models: A case of SK Telecom's financial services. *Electronic Markets, 15*(1), 4-12.

Suoranta, M., & Mattila, M. (2004). Mobile banking and consumer behavior: New insights into the diffusion pattern. *Journal of Financial Services Marketing, 8*(4), 354-366.

Wang, Y. S., Lin, H. H., & Luarn, K. N. (2006). Predicting consumer intention to use mobile service. *Information Systems Journal, 16*(2), 157-179.

Warwick, D. R. (2004). *Toward a cashless society. Futurist, 38*(4), 38-42.

ENDNOTES

[1] The Mobile Payment Forum (MPF) defines a mobile payment "as the process of two parties exchanging financial value using a mobile device in return for goods or services" (MPF, 2002, p. 10).

2   Internet payments refer to monetary value transfers by people using the Internet. A good example is Internet banking.

3   In Korea, credit card companies typically charge a fee of 2.25% of the transaction value for credit and debit cards (Bank of Korea (BOK), 2004c).

4   Korea's central bank, BOK, launched an E-Commerce Payment Gateway System in 2000, which is the settlement network for interbank obligations arising from electronic business-to-consumer transactions. This system has been utilized for electronic commerce over the Internet.

5   An IC-chip contains an account number, ID number, and a security program (BOK, 2004b).

6   SK Telecom, a dominant mobile phone service provider in Korea, offers a mobile prepaid electronic cash service called MONETA cash. The maximum amount of money a user can store in his/her virtual account per day is about $US500.

7   In April 2004, 36 million Won (about $US35,000) was fraudulently transferred from bank accounts to virtual accounts and then withdrawn.

8   If people want to purchase a product but do not have the means to pay, they have to spend time finding a store that accepts the payment instrument they have or to obtain a payment instrument circulating in the market. This is quite similar to the situation where a person is traveling in a country without the currency circulated in that country.

9   As at December 2004, some 29.3% of total banking transactions were conducted through Internet banking, as against 1.6% of mobile banking transactions (BOK, 2004a).

10 Kuttner and McAndrews (2001) argue that 'bank' can be defined in two ways (p. 42).

Chapter VII
Innovation Strategies in Digital Convergence:
Nokia and the Digital Home

Raluca Bunduchi
University of Aberdeen Business School, Scotland

Sanda Berar
Nokia, Finland

ABSTRACT

This chapter examines the innovation strategy of one of the major telecom companies—Nokia—in its efforts to develop a sustainable position in the emerging digital home market. The analysis of Nokia's innovation strategy in the digital domain is based on Abernathy and Clark's (1985) classification which differentiates between different types of innovations, depending on their impact on the firm's competitive position. The case study finds that Nokia follows a niche creation strategy, relying on its existing technological competencies in areas such as handset design and open device architecture, while building new market competencies developed either in house, or through collaboration with industry partners. The chapter provides an in depth view into the strategic actions of a large firm which attempts to build a sustainable competitive advantage in an emerging market by taking advantage of the opportunities arising from the convergence of digital home technologies.

INTRODUCTION

The vision of providing technologies and services for home–coined with the label of "home domain" or "digital home"—was born in the mid 1980s out of technological advances in the micro-electronics fields that could make "intelligent" sensors and appliances. The technological innovations to enable seamless interaction among consumer electronics (CE), mobile phones and personal computers (PC) devices have emerged over the past 20 years punctuated by significant breakthroughs in other technologies including digital and multimedia, the Internet, broadband and wireless (TEAHA, 2005).

The concept of "digital home" defines a space where all sorts of home-based electronic devices, ranging from personal computers to TV set-top boxes, video game consoles, stereos and even the refrigerator and the garage door are connected both to one another and to the Internet. The use of the term "*digital* home" rather than "home domain" in recent years reflects also a trend away from analogue towards digital media. The digital home is a home where all sorts of media ranging from music, films and pictures are in digital format. The concept coins both a convergence of the digital content of different media, as well as a convergence in the technologies that enable the connection of various physical devices supporting the delivery of such digital content.

In the last decades, many of the largest companies in the CE, PC, telecom and Internet industries have made strategic decisions to enter the digital home market. CE companies such as Sony and Matsushita are global leaders in digital television, video and music equipment. Computer companies such as Cisco and Intel have special divisions geared towards home entertaining. Microsoft launched Windows Media Central, a version of its Windows operation system that looks more like a TV menu and works via remote control. Telecom companies such as Motorola and Nokia have adopted the digital home vision as one of the cornerstones of their strategy, Motorola with its "seamless mobility" strategy, and Nokia with its home domain "extended mobility" vision.

This chapter examines the innovation strategy of one of the major telecom companies—Nokia—in its efforts to develop a sustainable competitive position in the emerging digital home market.

Competitive advantage arises from a range of sources, including the position of a firm relative to the competitive forces in its industry (Porter, 1980), or its valuable, rare and difficult to imitate resources (Barney, 1991). The accelerating pace of technology developments that nowadays characterises the environment in which firms operate means that increasingly, the pattern moves to favour firms that have the ability mobilise knowledge and technological skills to create novelty in their products and services and to provide timely responsiveness and rapid and flexibly product and service innovation (Kay, 1993; Teece, et al., 1997). Innovation contributes in several ways to the creation of competitive advantage. New products help to capture and retain market share, such as in the case of Sony's Walkman, whilst process innovation explains the dominance of the Japanese manufacturing in the late 20th century across several sectors: cars, motorcycles, shipbuilding and consumer electronics (Tidd, et al., 2005). Consequently, innovation strategies have become a central element of the firm's efforts to build competitive advantage in a fast changing environment.

With the rise of the Internet, the scope for innovation has grown significantly, as the traditional separation between strategies based on offering standard products and services to a large market (high reach) and the ability to offer customised products tailored to a niche audience (high richness) has been "blown to bits." The Internet and accompanying technological innovations are supporting connectivity and common standards that redefine the information channels linking businesses with their customers, suppliers and employees. As a result, the Internet enables the creation of totally new markets and the radical disruption of those which exist in information rich contexts (Evans & Wurster, 1998). In particular, the Internet has been seen as a catalyst for innovations in digital convergence. The technology that has been responsible for platform independence is the IP protocol which enables the transmission of any kind of data through the Internet network, and which has fuelled technology convergence in the late 1990s (Bores, et al., 2003).

The aim of this chapter is to explore Nokia's innovation strategy in an effort to understand the way large companies build their competitive advantage in contexts characterised by rapid technological change, such as the convergence of digital home technologies.

The analysis of Nokia's innovation strategy in the digital home domain is based on Abernathy and Clark's (1985) classification which differentiates between four types of innovations depending on the impact that the technological innovation has on the firm's competencies. The classification that guides the analysis of Nokia's strategy is briefly presented in Section 2. Section 3 provides an overview of the current state of digital home technologies, which sets the stage for the discussion of Nokia's approach to the convergence of digital home technologies in the following section. The final section summarises the main lessons from Nokia's case and discusses future areas of concern.

TYPES OF INNOVATION STRATEGIES

Starting with Schumpeter (1928), technology innovation is seen in social research as an evolutionary process: Technology evolves through periods of incremental or normal changes along a defined technological path, punctuated by technological breakthroughs when new technological paradigms emerge (Abernathy & Clark, 1985; Dosi, 1982; Nelson & Winter, 1977; Tushmand & Anderson, 1986). In environments characterised by rapid technological change, where these technological breakthroughs succeed at fast pace, the competi-

tive advantage of firms rests of their ability to build and acquire a range of capabilities or competencies (Prahalad & Hamel, 1990; Teece, et al., 1997). These competencies range from material resources to human skills and relevant knowledge and can be classified into competencies related to technology and production and competencies related to market and customer. The former include the resources, skills and knowledge linked to competition through their effect on the physical characteristics of the product, such as the design and embodiment of technology, the production system of the firm, the labour, managerial and technical skills and the firm's knowledge and experience base. The latter include the relationship with the customers, the range of customer applications, the channels of distribution and service, customer knowledge and the modes of customer communication (Abernathy & Clark, 1985).

The innovation strategies pursued by firms can be classified depending on the effect that a particular technological innovation–such as the convergence in digital content and automation technologies to create the digital home—has on the firm's competencies (Abernathy & Clark, 1985). The four types of innovation strategies are presented in Table 1.

Architectural innovation disrupts and renders established technical and market competencies obsolete, practically laying down a new architecture of the industry which defines the new "rules of the game" within which competition occurs. For example, the development of the Internet repre-

Table 1. Types of innovation strategy

Type of innovation	Impact on firm's competencies	Examples
Architectural innovation	Disrupts technology & market competencies	Internet & Amazon / e-bay
Niche innovation	Builds upon existing technology competencies Disrupts market competencies	Personal computer & Apple
Regular innovation	Builds upon existing technology & market competencies	Chemicals & DuPont; office supply & Bic pen
Revolutionary innovation	Disrupts technology competencies Builds upon existing market competencies	RFID & supermarkets

sents an architectural innovation for a number of industries, such as book publishing and antique auctions. Firms such as Amazon and e-bay have created new ways of serving and relating with customers, have built new channels of distribution and have altered the way in which firms communicate with their customers, practically redefining the market competencies required to compete in the bookselling and auction industry. In order to survive, incumbents such as Borders had to acquire not only new technological competencies, such as adopting Internet technologies to reach customers, but also new market competencies, for example in terms of online distribution.

Niche innovation opens up a new market opportunity through the use of existing technologies. This type of innovation characterises firms which improve, refine or change a stable and well-defined technology in order to support a new marketing trust. The scope of these improvements is to build on the firm's established technological competencies and apply them to satisfy newly emerging needs. For example, the first personal computer developed by Apple was based on a regression of current computer manufacturing technologies, rather than an improvement or innovation. However, by reducing the power and hence the cost of computers —i.e., using existing technologies—Apple opened up an entirely new market—the individual users, which required incumbents such as IBM to develop new channels of distribution and service for a new category of customers. Incumbents were required to develop new market competencies in order to compete on a product based on what was originally seen as an inferior technology built on existing and limited technological competencies.

Regular innovation builds on established technical and production competences that are applied to existing markets and customers. Innovation here consists in incremental changes in the process technology in order to raise productivity and increase process capacity. One of the best known studies of regular innovation is

Hollander's (1965) study of Dupont rayon plants which finds that cumulative gains in efficiency are often much greater over time than those coming from occasional radical changes. Another example of regular innovation is Bic ballpoint pen which was originally developed in 1957, but still remains a very strong product with annual sales over 14 millions due to gradual improvements in the original product.

Finally, *revolutionary innovation* disrupts technical and production competencies, but targets an established market. Here the firm's strategy focuses on linking emerging technological innovation with existing market needs. The adoption of radio frequency identification (RFID) technologies to replace barcodes in supply chain management is an example of revolutionary innovation. Retailers such as Tesco and Wal Mart and their suppliers have to invest in new types of technologies associated with radio frequency (e.g., encryption and reading applications), which are applied to an existing market—item tracking and tracing along the supply chain. The users are the same—retailers and their suppliers—and they build their competitive position in the RFID market based upon their existing market and customer competencies. However, the technological competencies required to deploy RFID systems are entirely different from those required by the incumbent technology—the barcode—which relies on optical rather than radio frequency technologies.

The four types of innovation require firms to engage in different types of competence building strategies in order to compete effectively under the different innovation regimes. Architectural innovation requires firms to use new technological breakthroughs to create new markets based on new needs and values, while firms operating under conditions of niche innovation create new markets using existing technologies. Successful regular innovators compete through constantly building efficiency improvements, while the revolutionary innovator applies a new technology to satisfy existing customers needs.

BACKGROUND: THE DIGITAL HOME

Since the late 1990s, many of the largest CE, PC and telecom companies have joined in the digital home vision (*The Economist*, 2005) attracted by the expectations for rapid growth in the digital home in both Europe and U.S. markets (ABI research, 2003; Elliott, et al., 2005). Two sets of triggers explain the current growth of the digital home market. First, convergence is fuelled by the proliferation of digital media and IP networking among existing customers, including increases in the sales of digital devices (music players, cameras, camcorders, DVD players, video game consoles and multimedia mobile phones), widespread broadband adoption (DSL and cable) and spiralling home network adoption (wired and wireless, ad-hoc and infrastructure configuration). Second, over the past years, advances in digital technologies laid out the foundation for the building of the interactive, digital homes. Such advances include interactive/digital TV sets in the CE industry, multimedia phones in mobile telephony and PC tuner and Microsoft Media Technologies in PC devices and software sectors.

The "digital home" is populated by a range of products which can be broadly classified into three categories: the PC products, including products such as standalone computing and printers; CE products, including traditional CE such as TVs, DVD and CD players, as well as broadcast products including set-top boxes; and mobile products, such as multimedia phones, PDAs and laptop computers. Additionally, domestic appliances could also be added as a fourth category (i.e., intelligent refrigerators that re-order groceries). However, at the moment, the players within the digital home focus on the sharing of digital content (i.e., the entertaining aspect of the digital

home), rather than on the home automation side (*The Economist*, 2004, 2005). Therefore, the focus here will be on the first three types of devices that support the entertaining function in the digital home domain.

The digital home market is characterised by strong competition between the industry players concerning which device plays the central role in the digital home. The current model for the digital home involves the connection of specialised devices as "spokes" around the house, which would all be connected to one central "hub." PC companies, such as Intel and Microsoft, see the PC as the natural choice; CE companies, such as Sony, see video consoles or the digital TV as playing the role of the Hub; cable operators are lobbying for their set-top boxes, while telecom companies, such as Nokia and Motorola, are promoting the mobile phone.

Currently, the market is characterised by a number of challenges. First, in their hope to recreate the dominance that Microsoft achieved in the PC era through setting Windows as the de facto industry standard, the different digital home products vendors are reluctant to make their technologies interoperable. As a result, the existing home networks are currently built based on multiple products from multiple vendors, which are complex and difficult to manage. This creates confusion in the market, with customers wondering which of the different products offer better performance/price and which will be compatible with the future standard.

Second, existing open industry standards are often too flexible, which means that products built by different vendors all too often fail to interoperate well. In addition, certain technologies are covered by multiple standards creating confusion amongst producers and customers alike, regarding which one to adopt. In contrast, other technological areas are not covered by any definite standard. This leads to limited interoperability, which increases customer scepticism. And finally, the protocols and technologies, especially the higher levels of the multimedia interconnectivity stack, are proprietary. Whereas current end-to-end solutions based on proprietary vertical implementations speed up the time to market, they fail to create an established new category of products in the market (DLNA, 2004).

Consequently, the current state of digital home technologies is characterised by limited interaction between the various devices, with current technologies being far too complex to use and often failing to properly work together, and with the major PC, CE and telecom companies competing to play the central role in the digital home. This paper focuses on the strategy of Nokia which, as a later mover into the digital home domain, attempted to build a defendable competitive position in a market already dominated by PC and CE companies.

NOKIA: COMPETITIVE STRATEGY AND TECHNOLOGICAL INNOVATION

Nokia is the world's largest producer of mobile phones, and one of the leaders in the mobile network infrastructure market. In an environment characterised by high uncertainty and rapid technological advances, Nokia's strategy is based on a combination of technological innovation and focus on core competencies (Leinbach & Brunn, 2002; Sadowski, et al., 2003). For example, the success of Nokia in the GSM market can be explained based on the company's efforts to develop technological competencies in digital signal processing, electronics manufacturing, software platforms and architectures. These technological investments are complemented by Nokia's marketing efforts to develop a strong position in niche markets within the telecom market (Leinbach & Brunn, 2002).

The development and exploitation of leading edge technologies has been one of the key characteristics of Nokia's strategy over the past years

(Leinbach & Brunn, 2002), for example its early involvement in GSM has been one of the crucial factors explaining its success in the emerging European telecom market in the mid 1990s. The development of technology competencies that enabled Nokia to build a strong competitive position in the GSM market had often relied on an industry-wide collective innovation effort. Through building up innovation networks, Nokia has not only learned from collaborating with other industry players, but has also been able to focus on its core competencies (e.g., in the GSM case) while purchasing the reminder from specialist suppliers. Such innovation networks were built around the GSM technology. They enabled Nokia to spread the costs of developing the new technology, reduced the product-development times and fostered reciprocal innovation (Keil, et al., 1997).

The transition towards the third generation of mobile telecommunications as well as the potential convergence of future mobile technologies with other trajectories in telecommunications meant that Nokia has had to develop new competencies to build a sustainable position in the third generation mobile market. As in the case of the second generation, Nokia has pursued a strategy of collaboration with the other industry players to support new technological developments, for example, in areas such as Wireless Application Protocol (WAP forum was established in 1997), EPOC systems (Symbian joint venture was created in 1998) and Bluetooth applications (Bluetooth industry group was founded in 1998) (Sadowski, et al., 2003).

Nokia pursues similar innovation strategies focused on building and/or acquiring new competencies in the digital home market. The digital home strategy is anchored in Nokia's "extended mobility" vision. Coined by the slogan "Life Goes Mobile," the vision for extending mobility is one of the three cornerstones of Nokia's current competitive strategy, together with driving consumer multimedia and expanding mobile voice. The vision is to provide users with access to digital content and services anytime, anyplace and is fuelled by the convergence of digital technologies. Nokia's "extended mobility" vision covers the home domain (including products such as multimedia sharing), the mobile domain (for example multimedia messages over the phone), the Internet and media domain (represented by products such as Internet browsing and digital content download) and the enterprise domain (where Nokia offers corporate e-mail access services through mobile phones).

Two aspects of Nokia's strategic approach to the convergence of digital home technologies are discussed here: (1) what does the digital home represent for Nokia and how does it fit with Nokia's overall strategy?, and (2) the way Nokia develops, uses and/or acquires technology and market competencies to address the market for the digital home.

New Market Opportunities

The major players in the home domain market are CE manufacturers (e.g., Sony, Philips & Samsung) and PC companies (Microsoft & Intel). The market emerged as a result of CE manufacturers' efforts to standardise the interaction between the different CE devices 20 years ago. The first step toward connecting different devices was the development of a range of regional standards for home automation in the mid 1980s. In 1984, the Consumer Electronic Bus (CEBus) specifications were developed by the Electronic Industries Association in the U.S., and were later ratified as an ANSI standard. In Europe, a collaboration between the European CE companies and the government on home automation started in 1984 and led to the development of the European Home System network specifications in 1995. Similar standards for controlling the CE devices within the home were developed in Japan since 1981 under the name of the Home Bus System.

PC companies entered the home domain market a decade ago with a number of software products for content management, access and storing. For example, the first two versions of Microsoft's Windows XP Media Centre Editions were niche products, targeting computer enthusiasts who wanted to record TV shows on their computer drive. The Media Centre product was destined for high end machines and was sold only on about one million PCs. The price was accordingly excessive for the usual buyer, higher even than the price for the Windows XP professional edition. In contrast, the 2005 version targets the mainstream PC buyer, with a significantly lower price than the previous versions. As for CE manufacturers, most of the TVs sold today are digitally enabled, and are at least partially interoperable with other home products (e.g., DVDs, stereos, and PCs). Consequently, what originally was a niche market for CE and PC manufacturers became a mass market during the last years, with CE and PC companies targeting "home domain" products as their mainstream market. In contrast, mobile phone companies have only recently addressed the market created through the convergence of digital home technologies in an effort to (1) increase their current market (i.e., supporting communication within the extended home), and to (2) support growth outside traditional markets (i.e., managing home infotainment).

First, the mobile phone has already become the primary communication device within families, allowing extension of family relationships outside the boundaries of the physical home. This allows the mobile phone to play new roles in meeting specific communication needs within the "extended home."

Second, the digital convergence of content and home infotainment defines a new potential area of application for mobile phones: the mobile phone assisted home infotainment. The mobile phone can be used to enable mobility, authentication, billing and personality in the home domain. It can also support the management and access of personal and commercial content. For example, digital content such as videos and music can be received and/or stored in a mobile device and then sent over short range technology to the TV or a gateway device. The mobile phone can be used to select the display device and to control the content presentation functionalities. These functionalities mean that the mobile phone can support the entertaining function within the digital home domain, alongside the PC and CE. For example, Motorola formed a new "connected home" division in 2003 to sell wireless cable modem gateways, digital set-top boxes and other digital home products such as home networking components and phones to consumers. Nokia is also developing handsets that enable the sharing of files for home entertaining between mobiles, PCs and CE.

Consequently, the convergence of digital home technologies not only allows mobile phone companies to grow within their existing markets, but it also opens up a new market for providing entertaining functionalities within the digital home. Mobile manufacturers are seizing the opportunity provided by the convergence of digital home technologies by deploying and acquiring new competencies in the digital home domain that enable them to build a sustainable competitive position in the new market.

Technical and Market Competencies

Nokia has a number of core competencies in the digital home area, both in the technological and production area and in the marketing and customer relationship areas.

1. Nokia applies a range of its existing generic **technological competencies** to support its presence into the home domain (see Table 2).

Over the years, emerging media concepts like Visual Radio, mobile TV, mobile blogging and music, gaming and video downloads were gradually incorporated into Nokia's devices. Since 2004, six new *smartphones* were delivered. Nokia 7610 imaging smartphone, Nokia's first megapixel imaging device, started sales in May 2004 and quickly became the best selling megapixel GSM imaging smartphone globally. Nokia 6630, the latest 3G WCDMA smartphone, was offered by more than 30 operators worldwide, including in Japan. Sales of Nokia's first EDGE-enabled Series 60 smartphone, Nokia 6620, started in the Americas in July 2004. In 2005, Nokia introduced its Nseries range (N70, N90 and N91) of hi-end multimedia devices which feature 3G technologies, Symbian Series 60 software, 2MP and digital cameras, Bluetooth and stereo output. The handsets enabled

Table 2. Nokia's technical competencies

Technical competencies	Support for the digital home domain
Handsets	The development of handsets to support digital home technologies
Open device architecture	The development of open device architecture for the digital home
Industry wide standards	Participation in digital home standardisation consortium (DLNA)
Series 60 platform	Platform for the digital home enabled handsets
Connectivity solutions	Solutions for connectivity amongst different digital home devices
IP networks	IPv6 standard which is at the core of the architecture for digital home technologies
Core networks	Model to support service delivery for digital home customers

sharing of a range of digital content (pictures, sounds and video) to support the digital home. A number of competencies contribute to these developments, including open device architecture, open, industry-wide standards, mobile platforms and local connectivity solutions.

Nokia's device architecture is characterised by harmonized interfaces across products, modularity in hardware to add performance and layering in software to add functionality. The device architectures vary depending on the domain and the use situations that a particular device is designed for (mobile domain, Internet and media domain, enterprise domain and home domain). Therefore, architecture evolution has to ensure interoperability between systems and devices within and across all domains. This is achieved through the support of *open architecture and open source paradigm* in all domains. The open source strategy is in line with Nokia's overall technological strategy; examples include Series 60 platform, licensed to seven top mobile phone manufacturers, Symbian OS, owned and licensed by major vendors and JavaTM, used by four million application developers worldwide. The open source strategy enables Nokia to reap the benefits of collective innovation, as risks, costs and information are shared between the users involved in the development of technology.

Nokia has constantly supported *industry wide standards*, rather than proprietary solutions. Examples include participation in consortia that developed standards for communication systems (GSM, WCDMA, CDMA and IP), local connectivity (Wireless LAN, Bluetooth, IrDA, USB and Near Field Communication), computing platforms (Mobile Industry Processor Interfaces alliance) and applications (Open Mobile Alliance).

Nokia *Series 60 platform* is currently the leading the smartphone platform in the world. It is licensed by some of the foremost mobile phone manufacturers in the world including LG Electronics, Nokia, Panasonic, Samsung, Sendo and Siemens. The licensing agreement supports a large Series 60 device base, and a diverse product portfolio which spread the risks while reaping the benefits of scale.

Nokia posses a range of technical competencies concerning *connectivity solutions* which were either developed in-house through the development of proprietary Pop-Port™ connectivity, or acquired from collaborators through participation in industrywide alliances, including Bluetooth, IrDA, WCDMA, Digital Video Broadcasting for Handheld (DVB-H), USB and WLAN connectivity functions and the Near Field Communication.

Nokia was an active participant in the development of *IPv6* specifications—one of the core technologies enabling digital home convergence—through the IPv6 working group in the IETF (Internet Engineering Task Force). The expertise in IPv6 has been leveraged for the development of key products, as Nokia deploys both IPv6 routing and security appliances.

The change in the range of services provided by mobile devices beyond the simple calling functionality required a similar change in the *core network*. Network technologies are seen in Nokia as a tool to support and enhance the evolution of the handsets (terminals) toward the "more than a phone" concept. The Intelligent Edge is a new service and business machine that enhances present packet core networks. Intelligent Edge gives operators new tools for maintaining greater control over services and revenues, providing new possibilities for positioning themselves in the value chain, beyond the basic access charging as in today's fixed networks. Service awareness enables precise differentiation of the traffic carried as well as engaging content owners in revenue sharing with an unprecedented flexibility. Nokia Intelligent Edge also drives new applications. For example, the IP Multimedia Subsystem specified by 3GPP/3GPP2 enables direct terminal-to-terminal IP connections. New person-to-person applications allow mobile devices to share media such as video streaming or instant direct-call voice service, and support interaction services such as the exchange of game data.

2. **Market competencies in digital home enhancement:** There are two ways in which Nokia labours to acquire market competencies in this area: alone and through intra- and inter-industry collaborations. Table 3 presents the market competencies developed by Nokia in the digital home domain.

Nokia has developed **in-house** a number of services and products for the home domain over the years, such as the Digital Set-Top-Box (STB) products. These products interoperate with mobile devices in order to share content. Such an experience allowed Nokia to test its products and evaluate its technical and market competencies in the home domain area against the real customer demand, and to assess the customers' appetite for these new products and technologies. At the same time, the experience served as a learning process, enabling Nokia to develop further its technologies and adapt its competencies in this area. However, the home domain is dominated by PC and CE manufacturers (i.e., Microsoft, which dominates the market for home products software with the new OS-Window XP Media Centre Edition released October 2004, and Sony and Philips, which entered the market with products such as interactive TVs). Therefore, in order to extend the functionality of mobile devices, and enter the home domain market, emphasis was placed on ac-

quiring competencies through collaboration with the leading experts in this market. Collaboration and alliances with a range of players in the home domain area enables Nokia not only to add to its own technical competencies, but also to capture customers and market knowledge.

Nokia *works together with operators and content providers* to provide premium content and services through multiple service delivery channels to both mobile users and users at home, hence acquiring new competencies in marketing and distribution of products and services to the home market. For example, until recently mobile services were mostly SMS-based ring tone, logo download. The emergence of new technologies and terminals now make it possible to provide technologies such as MMS (for images, video and sound clips), Java (for downloadable applications) and XHTML/CSS (for colour browsing) that greatly enrich users' experience beyond SMS and voice. Whereas person-to-person services (like voice and person-to-person MMS) are well understood by the industry, the business models for content-to-person services are still evolving, with many of the latter services introducing third parties into the value-chain. Nokia is closely collaborating with operators and content providers to develop the ways in which content-to-person services such as mobile browsing, streaming and downloading can be best marketed and delivered to customers. Such collaboration benefits Nokia, which gains insight into the operators' understanding of the end customer, whereas the

Table 3. Nokia's market competencies

Source	Market competencies
In-house	Development of digital set-top-box products to identify customers' requirements & reaction to digital home products
Intra industry collaboration with operators and content providers	Acquiring competencies in marketing and distribution of products and services to the home market
Inter industry collaborations within UPnP, DLNA consortia	Gain market and customer knowledge from CE and PC manufacturers

operators can benefit from Nokia's insight into the technologies.

Early involvement in Digital Living Network Alliance (DLNA) also enables Nokia to gain access to the other DLNA members' strong market and customer knowledge in the home domain area (CE and PC manufacturers). DLNA is a consortium of firms representing the CE, PC and mobile industries which focuses on defining a standard architecture that would enable interoperability between all the devices involved in the digital home. For example, whereas for Nokia the digital home domain is an emerging market, CE manufacturers have years of experience in developing and marketing digital, smart CE devices for the home.

DISCUSSIONS AND CONCLUSION

Current innovation in the digital home occurs as incumbent firms build upon their existing technological competencies to address new opportunities either within their existing market (for CE manufacturers) or outside their traditional market (for the telecom industry). Nokia pursues a niche creation innovation strategy in order to address the convergence of digital home technologies by using its existing technological competencies (e.g., digital home enabled handsets and connectivity solutions) to target new and emerging markets (mobile services to support the entertaining functionalities of the digital home domain). The Nokia case study has revealed the strategic actions taken by a large telecom firm to support the process of competencies building in the context of an emerging innovation. Nokia builds upon its technological knowledge and competencies in the digital home domain area, and acquires customer and market capabilities through participation in industrywide alliances to develop a strong competitive position in the emerging digital home market. For example, the early involvement in the shaping of digital home

technologies in the DLNA has enabled Nokia to consider incorporating digital home applications in the (new generation) platform which would considerably reduce the time to market for the new mobile products once home domain products are available.

There are also significant risks and uncertainties associated with such concentrated competence building efforts. For example, digital technologies are still under development. Their embeddedness in the platform might lead to a loss in robustness reflecting a trade-off between platform flexibility and first mover advantage on one hand and platform robustness on the other hand. Additionally, whereas currently the analysts predict increasing demand for home domain products and services, forecasts have been wrong in the past. As Tidd, et al. (2005) pointed out, information about future customers needs is rarely available and accurate, which renders traditional forecasting methods inappropriate to forecast the demand for future technological innovations.

Moreover, depending on the future shape of the digital home domain—whether PC/CE-centric or mobile-centric—Nokia''s position in the market will change. The nature and shape of the standard for the overall domain architecture (whether DLNA or other) will also affect Nokia's ability to deploy its existing technical competencies in the market. In the end, some of Nokia's competencies might prove to be of limited applicability, while others will be developed to match new requirements in the digital domain market as they emerge. This study therefore provides a snapshot view of Nokia's competencies developing efforts to address the current state of the emerging market for digital home, some of which might have been missed by a retrospective analysis when the digital home market has stabilised.

Finally, it is likely that in the near future Nokia will have to involve the end users into its competencies building efforts. Innovation research suggests that end users play a significant role in shaping the innovation process (Fleck,

1987; Ornetzeder & Rohracher, 2006) and often represent an important source of innovative ideas (Luthje, 2004). The current Nokia efforts focus on acquiring second-hand knowledge about end users behaviour and requirements from collaborations with operators and content providers and with CE and PC manufacturers. However, such knowledge has to be matched with direct data regarding the digital home end users behaviour and requirements gathered through the involvement of the users in the innovation process—what Fleck (1987) calls innofusion—if Nokia is to develop market and customer competencies that enable it to build a foothold in the digital home market.

REFERENCES

ABI research. (2003). *The US digital home enterprise: Connected home automation.* Accessed on August, 2005, from http://www.abiresearch.com/reports/HAS.html

Abernathy, W.J., & Clark, K.B. (1985). Innovation: Mapping the winds of creative destruction. *Research Policy, 14*(1), 3-22.

Barney, J. (1991). Firm resources and sustained competitive advantage. *Journal of Management, 17*(1), 99-120.

Bores, C., Saurina, C., & Torres, R. (2003). Technological convergence: A strategic perspective. *Technovation, 23*(1), 1-13.

Dosi, G. (1982). Technological paradigms and technological trajectories. *Research Policy, 11*(3), 147-162.

Fleck, J. (1987). *Innofusion or diffusation? The nature of technological development in robotics.* (Working Paper No. 4). Edinburgh: Edinburgh University PICT.

Hollander, S. (1965). *The Sources of increased efficiency: A study of Dupont rayon plants.* Cambridge, Massachusets: MIT Press.

The Economist. (2004). The digital home: Life in the vault. *The Economist,* July 1, 2004. Accessed on October, 2005, from http://www.economist.com

The Economist. (2005). *The digital home: Science fiction?* Special Report, September 1, 2005. Accessed September 1, 2005, from http://www.economist.com

Elliott, N., Fogg, I., & Mulligan, M. (2005). *European digital home forecast, 2005 to 2010.* 21st of September, 2005, Jupiterresearch Report.

Evans, P., & Wurster, T. (2000). *Blown to bits: How the new economics of information transforms strategy.* Cambridge, Massachusets: Harvard Business School Press.

Kay, J. (1993). *Foundations of corporate success: How business strategies add value.* Oxford: Oxford University Press.

Keil, T., Autio, E., & Robertson, P. (1997). Embeddedness, power, control and innovation in the telecommunications sector. *Technology Analysis & Strategic Management, 9*(3), 299-316.

Leinbach, T.R., & Brunn, S.D. (2002). National innovation systems, firm strategy, and enabling mobile communication: The case of Nokia. *Tijdschrift voor Economische en Sociale Geografie, 93*(5), 489-508.

Luthje, C. (2004). Characteristics of innovating users in a consumer goods field: An empirical study of sport-related product consumers. *Technovation, 24*(9), 683-695

Nelson, R.R., & Winter, S.G. (1977). In search of useful theory of innovation. *Research Policy, 6*(1), 37-76.

Ornetzeder, M., & Rohracher, H. (2006). User led innovations and participation processes: Lessons from sustainable energy technologies. *Energy Policy, 34*(2), 138-150.

Porter, M.E. (1980). *Competitive strategy.* New York: The Free Press.

Prahalad, C.K., & Hamel, G. (1990). The core competence of the corporation. *Harvard Business Review, 68*(3), 79-91.

Sadowski, B.M., Dittrich, K., & Duysters, G.M. (2003). Collaborative strategies in the event of technological discontinuities: The case of Nokia in the mobile telecomunication industry. *Small Business Economics, 21*(2), 173-186.

Schumpeter, J. (1928). The instability of capitalism. *The Economic Journal, 38*(151), 361-386.

TEAHA (2005). *The worldwide markets for the connected home: Status and trends.* TEAHA Market Background Document, TEAHA Project IST-2004-507-029, Deliverable D7.1.2.

Teece, D.J., Pisano, G., & Shuen, A. (1997). Dynamic capabilities and strategic management. *Strategic Management Journal, 18*(7), 509-533.

Tidd, J., Besant, J., & Pavitt, K. (2005). *Managing innovation: Integrating technological, market and organizational change* (3rd ed.). Chichester: John Wiley & Sons.

Tushman, M.L., & Anderson, P. (1986). Technological discontinuities and organizational environments. *Administrative Science Quarterly, 31*(3), 439-465.

Chapter VIII
Open Systems in Digital Convergence[1]

Ken Krechmer
University of Colorado, USA

ABSTRACT

The greater the degree of digital convergence, the higher the potential for monopoly behavior. Open systems minimize the possibility of monopoly behavior. But what are open systems? This paper explores the different meanings and criteria suggested by the term open systems and the many ways openness is viewed. It specifically discusses open systems, open architectures, Open Source, open interfaces and open standards to better understand each. Identifying and agreeing upon what constitutes openness is an important step to avoid any disadvantages of digital convergence.

INTRODUCTION

Digital convergence potentially offers many desirable attributes: easier use, lower cost, ubiquity, greater interactivity, more lifelike video and more realistic audio. The many different communications channels we use today (telephone, Internet, cellular, broadcast TV, cable, satellite and wireless) may one day converge into a single interface for all communications. However, converging all the communications of a home or office onto a single communications pathway might also decrease overall flexibility and reliability. Such a loss of flexibility and reliability could occur in a market dominated by a single supplier, where there are no alternative communications pathways.

Initially, the passage of information necessary for a free society only required freedom of the press. Later, broadcasting opened new pathways for society to receive information. Then came telephony (wired and much later wireless) communications. Next the Internet emerged, providing society's first interactive information pathway. Now, digital convergence offers the possibility to bring together these independent pathways that keep society connected into a single stream, more interactive, more dynamic and more ubiquitous than any information pathway of the past. For digital convergence to be acceptable to society, these important pathways that inform, entertain and interact with us must remain open. Digital convergence only increases the importance of open systems to a free society.

As with the evolutionary hierarchy of life, the more successful communications systems are those which are the more flexible and adaptable. *Open* is usually used to describe ICT (Information and Communications Technology) systems or aspects of such systems that are perceived by the observer to be more flexible or adaptable. Of course, any understanding of *flexible* and *adaptable* is strongly skewed depending on the vantage point of the viewer. Original equipment manufacturers, software developers, end users, public standardization development organizations (SDOs) or private ones (consortia), judicial systems, national and local governments and international organizations all have their own views of what criteria constitute "openness as applied to ICT systems."

The terms "open architecture," "Open Source," "open interfaces" and "open standards" are frequently used to describe open systems. There are many cases in the literature where different criteria are related to these terms. The purpose of this Chapter is to identify the criteria commonly used to describe openness, and to describe the criteria most closely related to each of the above terms for openness. Perhaps when everyone agrees on the meaning of open systems, it will be possible to achieve them, and strengthen digital convergence.

SOME DEFINITIONS

Open System embodies the terms "open architecture," "Open Source," "open interfaces" and "open standards" to support an open systems environment (Grey, 1991; Hugo, 1991). Originally the IEEE standard POSIX 1003.0 defined open

systems. Currently, the International Organization for Standardization/International Electrotechnical Commission (ISO/IEC) standard TR 14252 defines an open system environment as "the comprehensive set of interfaces, services and supporting formats, plus user aspects, for interoperability or for portability of applications, data or people, as specified by information technology standards and profiles" (Critchley and Batty, 1993). A 1994 report sponsored by the US National Science Foundation described an open data network as being open "to users, to service providers, to network providers and to change" (NRENAISSANCE Committee, 1994). To maintain interoperability and portability, an open system needs to be responsive to change.

Open Architecture. The definition of an architecture used in ANSI/IEEE Std 1471-2000 is: "the fundamental organization of a system, embodied in its components, their relationships to each other and the environment, and the principles governing its design and evolution." Based on this definition of architecture, two current definitions of an open architecture emerge:

- Open architecture is a type of computer architecture that allows users to upgrade their hardware in all of the computer components (for example the IBM PC has an open architecture). This is the opposite of a closed architecture, where the hardware manufacturer chooses the components, and they are not generally upgradeable, for example the AMIGA-500 home computer had a closed architecture (Wikipedia, 2001-2005, http://en.wikipedia.org/wiki/Open_architecture).

- An architecture whose specifications are public. This includes officially approved standards as well as privately designed architectures whose specifications are made public by the designers (Webopedia, 2001-2005, http://webopedia.com/TERM/O/open_architecture.html).

These two definitions are interrelated: The open architecture (modular system) suggested in the first requires the public specifications mentioned in the second. But it is possible to have public specifications and yet a closed system, at least from the users view, if the user finds only a single vendor of the system and its components. An open architecture also supports Open Source software, object oriented software or open standards for hardware and software interfaces. So these two definitions of open architecture do not address all the aspects of openness.

All the aspects of open architecture represent sufficiently complex openness requirements that most modular system architectures currently are proprietary. That is, expansion or openness requires purchasing from the original vendors. This is acceptable to many users if the original vendors maintain their architecture for reasonable periods and offer acceptable migration strategies to new architectures.

Open Source describes a process of software development that makes use of multiple independent software developers. Due to copyright laws, this process requires specific arrangements of licensing that provide the legal framework to allow multiple independent software developers to change and extend the software while maintaining the software available to all (Rosen, 2005). Open Source does not require that software available to all is free.

Software development follows two major directions: proprietary and Open Source. Commercial software developers, the proponents of proprietary programs, state that they adapt their programs to changing user needs based on economic incentive. The more users who are willing to pay for a specific change, the more responsive the software developer will be. Open source software developers may work for payment or work altruistically.[2] Free Open Source programs rely on the somewhat altruistic interest of programmers to continuously modify the program. Users then rely on the flow of changes to include the changes they

desire. Many users find it more effective to pay for the changes they wish. With specific software programs (e.g., GNU Ada), free Open Source has been an efficient way to offer the program while commercial viability is achieved by charging for maintenance and integration needs (http://www.gnu.org/philosophy/categories.html).

Often Open Source systems make use of *open standards* for operating systems, interfaces or software development tools, but the purpose of Open Source is to support continuous software improvement (Raymond, 2002) while the purpose of open standards is to support common agreements that enable an interchange available to all. The Open Source Initiative uses the Open Source Definition (http://opensource.org/docs/definition_plain.php) to determine whether or not a software license can be considered Open Source. The definition was based on the Debian Free Software Guidelines, written and adapted primarily by Bruce Perens.

Under the Open Source Definition, licenses must meet ten conditions in order to be considered Open Source:

1. **Free Redistribution:** The software can be freely given away or sold.
2. **Source Code:** The source code must either be included or freely obtainable.
3. **Derived Works:** Redistribution of modifications must be allowed.
4. **Integrity of the Author's Source Code:** Licenses may require that modifications are redistributed only as patches.
5. **No Discrimination Against Persons or Groups:** No one can be locked out.
6. **No Discrimination Against Fields of Endeavor:** Commercial users cannot be excluded.
7. **Distribution of License:** The rights attached to the program must apply to all whom the program is redistributed without the need for execution of an additional license by those parties.

8. **License Must Not Be Specific to a Product:** The program cannot be licensed only as part of a larger distribution.
9. **License Must Not Restrict Other Software:** The license cannot insist that any other software it is distributed with must also be Open Source.
10. **License Must Be Technology-Neutral:** No click-wrap licenses or other medium-specific ways of accepting the license must be required (Wikipedia, 2001-2005, http://en.wikipedia.org/wiki/Open_Source_Definition).

Open Standards. J. West (2004) defines 'open' for a standard as meaning rights to the standard are made available to economic actors other than the sponsor." This definition offers a succinct economic view of open standards. But economic rights cannot not be maintained without supporting political rights such as balance, consensus and due process. In order for the economic rights associated with compatibility standards to be available, some technical process (mutually agreed changes) and technical functionality (revision level negotiation) are also required. In order for specific economic rights associated with Intellectual Property (IP) to be available, specific licensing procedures must be defined.

B. Perens (no date) offers a software engineering perspective of open standards. He presents six criteria and related practices. The criteria proposed are: (1) availability, (2) maximization end-user choice, (3) no royalty, (4) no discrimination, (5) extension or subset and (6) no predatory practices. These six criteria are discussed further below.

Standards are a multi-disciplinary field. The criteria of open standards should address each of the related disciplines—economics, law, engineering, social and political sciences. From the legal perspective, each of the criteria that make up an open standard may be a legal right of a specific group. As J. West (2004) notes, each of these criteria has an economic cost and a benefit to specific stakeholders. From an engineering perspective, the criteria that create equal opportunity for manufacturers and developers directly impact communications equipment design. From a social science perspective, the dynamics of different stakeholders impact the requirements that make up open standards. From a political science perspective, the political criteria are basic to any fair political process, including standardization.

Many see Open Source and open standards as complementary (Siegel & Soley, 2005). Standards are codified common agreements that enable information transfer, directly in the case of ICT standards, and indirectly in the case of all other standards. Open Source describes a process of ongoing software development that often changes. Systems that combine Open Source and Open Standards suggest that the software programs evolve continuously while some interfaces remain fixed for spans of time to maintain compatibility.

The term "open standards" has also been associated with zero intellectual property costs (Rosen, 2005, chapter on Open Standards) by proponents of free Open Source software.

Other definitions: The term "Standards Setting Organization" (SSO) refers to any and all organizations that set, or attempt to set, what are perceived as standards. The term *SDO* refers to any SSO recognized directly or indirectly by a government. Consortium is the term used for any SSO that is not recognized directly or indirectly by a government.

The terms open interfaces and open standards are closely related. An interface is the description of the relationship between two (or more) compatible entities that are capable of communicating or interworking. Most commonly, an open interface would be specified using open standards.

THREE VIEWS OF OPENNESS

The definitions given above address what these terms mean but do not indicate who views the definition. Different views of the meaning of openness affect the meaning of openness considerably. This section identifies the different criteria of openness as they relate to one or more of the interested parties–the stakeholders. Openness impacts system concepts and system development (design, development, meeting regulatory requirements and any required standardization). Openness also impacts system implementation and system use (by users).

Stakeholders may be grouped into three categories–external, implementers and users. To identify all the requirements of openness, it is necessary to understand what these three categories of stakeholders would consider the broadest reasonable criteria of openness. Each group of stakeholders is driven by specific desires:

- The external view of openness is driven from the government policy, legal and economic theory perspectives. From this view, openness is a public good that should be monitored and protected, independent of commercial concerns.
- The implementation of openness is driven by production and distribution cost efficiencies.
- For the user, the use of standards and software that are deemed open is driven by an efficiency improvement associated with using a standardized product or system.

While there is some overlap among these desires, e.g., open meetings are more likely to create multiple procurement sources, each stakeholder group has a distinct motivation. Thus it is necessary to consider each stakeholder category independently.

The External View of Openness

The external view (e.g., a governmental view) of open systems, open architecture or Open Source is different from the implementer's or the user's view as it tends to focus on policy issues rather than product issues. However, the external criteria that define an open system may have significant impact on the implementer or user. An unfair political process or asymmetrical economic exchange in the creation of the systems or their interfaces may indicate some restraint of commerce. Many of the legal requirements surrounding the external dimensions are based on the need to protect the end users. In economic terms, the seller has a natural advantage by knowing more about their product than the buyer/user. The solution to this asymmetric advantage is for the user to examine multiple sources of a similar product and thereby learn enough about the product to make a fair choice. But multiple sources may be reduced when possible implementers are excluded by proprietary specifications, unfair political processes, excessive IP costs or trade barriers. Regulations that restrict the system, its uses or components may impact trade. Reduced markets may also increase user costs where trade restrictions appear. Implementers, not surprisingly, often have self-serving feelings about trade restrictions, favoring those trade restrictions that favor them, and not favoring the trade restriction that do not.

It is easiest to identify the view of SDOs about open standards. Many SDOs' Web sites state what open or openness of standardization means to them:

The Institute of Electrical and Electronic Engineers (IEEE): "For over a century, the IEEE-SA has offered an established standards development program that features balance, openness, due process, and consensus" (http://standards. ieee.org/sa/sa-view.html).

The European Telecommunications Standardization Institute (ETSI): "The European model for telecom standardization allows for the creation of open standards" (http://www.etsi.org/%40lis/background.htm).

The American National Standards Institute (ANSI) National Standards Strategy for the United States (2002): "The process to create these voluntary standards is guided by the Institute's cardinal principles of consensus, due process and openness ..." (http://www.ansi.org/standards_activities/overview/overview.aspx?menuid=3).

It is interesting to contrast these views with a view from the European Commission, which as a government represents the policy view (Interchange of Data Between Administrations, 2004). The following are the minimal characteristics that a specification and its attendant documents must have in order to be considered an open standard:

- The standard is adopted and will be maintained by a not-for-profit organization, and its ongoing development occurs on the basis of an open decision-making procedure available to all interested parties (consensus or majority decision, etc.).
- The standard has been published and the standard specification document is available either freely or at a nominal charge. It must be permissible to all to copy, distribute and use without fee or at a nominal fee.
- The intellectual property—i.e., patents possibly present–of (parts of) the standard are made irrevocably available on a royalty-free basis.
- There are no constraints on the re-use of the standard.

Most SSOs follow rules to ensure what they consider an open standards creation process by requiring open meetings, consensus and due pro-

cess. Most SSOs do not suggest "the standard is made irrevocably available on a royalty-free basis" (the highest level of open IPR). Krechmer (2006) provides a more detailed view of the openness of different standards development organizations.

The Implementer's View of Openness

The implementer, considered from an economic viewpoint, is within the production function of an organization that creates the open system or its components. Consider commercial developers of software, manufacturers of hardware or communications service providers as examples of implementers of open ICT systems. They want the ability to compete on an equal basis with their competitors. This concept has often been termed a *level playing field*. An implementer would describe a system as open when it is without cost to them, it serves the market they wish, does not necessarily obsolete their prior implementations, does not preclude further innovation and does not favor a competitor. These five requirements ensure a level playing field.

As an example of the broad usage of the term open, Microsoft often refers to their implementation of Word as open, meaning that they make their implementations of Word widely available to users and the applications programming interface (API) of Word available to non-competitors (Gates, 1998). Certainly Microsoft does not plan to make the software of Microsoft Word open in a manner similar to Open Source. Commercial companies desire to have some controllable advantage over their competition. This reasonable commercial desire of an implementer to maintain a commercial advantage can become the basis for legal conflict when competitors feel that the playing field is tilted unfairly.

The purpose of the criteria open meeting, due process and consensus is to make possible a level playing field when defining an open system. But these criteria do not address two of the implementers' legitimate requirements: serves the market they wish and does not favor a competitor. Many recognized SSOs are national or regional while many implementers' markets are international. Most recognized SSOs allow intellectual property to be included in their standards. This is not in the interests of the implementers who do not have similar intellectual property to trade.

Consortia have, in many cases, done a better job of addressing the needs of standards implementers. Many consortia offer international standardization and allow IP rights negotiation within their process (which recognized SSOs do not). Because consortia address more of the implementers' requirements, there has been an increase in standardization by consortia.

The User's View of Openness

The user is an office or factory of an organization that uses implementations of the open standard or Open Source software. A communications service provider may be both a user of hardware and software supplied by implementers as well as an implementer of communications services supplied to its users. The simple goal from the users' perspective is to achieve the maximum possible return on their investment. While many aspects of the users' return on investment are not related to openness (e.g., the implementation quality), four aspects are:

- The implementation operates and meets local legal requirements in all locations needed.
- New implementations desired by the user are compatible, as desired, with previously purchased implementations.
- Multiple interworking implementations from different sources are available.
- The implementation is supported over the user-desired service life.

It is worth noting that users, with the exception of communications service providers, do not often participate in ICT standardization (Naemura, 1995). Perhaps that is because many of these requirements specific to users are not even considered in most SSOs.

Understanding the Requirements of Open Systems

Table 1 identifies eighteen individual criteria that relate to open systems. Open Systems, Open Standards and Open Interfaces potentially include all 18 criteria. Open Architecture and Open Source appear to relate to a subset of the 18 criteria. The columns indicating the criteria suggested for Open Architecture and Open Source are the author's opinion based on the definitions given above.

The political criteria provide a more detailed view of what constitutes a fair political process used to create an Open System. The economic and legal criteria offer more of a governmental view of what constitutes an open system. The implementer and user criteria are directly related to the interests of those groups (Cargill, 1997). It is interesting to see that the criteria suggested by Open Architecture and Open Source are more related to the users' and implementers' interests and less related to the process of developing the system.

Different viewpoints see the criteria of openness differently. From each viewpoint, specific criteria of openness emerge. The importance of specific criteria will even rise and fall based on the tenor of the times. Table 1 identifies five possible viewpoints and 18 related criteria. Of course the names of these 18 criteria are arbitrary and it is possible to imagine combining different groups into one category, so there is no importance to the number 18. It appears that the legal viewpoint of openness may be expanded into far more criteria than shown. What is important is that these criteria, by whatever name, are the criteria that reasonably may be identified as part of the criteria that make up Open Systems.

Table 1. The criteria of openness for open systems and open standards

	Criteria of openness:	Open architecture	Open Source
1.	**Political: A fair process**		
1.1	Open meeting		x
1.2	Consensus		
1.3	Due process		
2.	**Economic: Open trade**		
2.1	No trade restrictions		
2.2	Symmetric exchanges		
3.	**Legal: Fair IP costs and controls**		
3.1	Commercial licensing		
3.2	Licensing only to non competitors		
3.3	Non discriminatory licensing		x
3.4	Pass through licensing		x
3.5	Reverse engineering allowed		x
3.6	No IPR costs		x
4.	**Implementer: Fair competition**		
4.1	A level playing field for all competitors	x	x
4.2	Mutually agreed changes	x	x
4.3	Available documents	x	x
5.	**User: Improve investment**		
5.1	Multiple procurement sources	x	
5.2	Implementation assessment		
5.3	Aftermarket additions	x	x
5.4	Support over the service life		x

The first three viewpoints (political, economic and legal) are external viewpoints distinct from the implementer and user of an Open System who are more focused on the related product or service. These three viewpoints relate most directly to the creation, design or development of an Open System. The last two viewpoints (implementer and user) are most relevant to the implementer (e.g., software developer or original equipment manufacturer) and the user of an Open System. There is some overlap of the effect of these viewpoints (e.g., a fair political process is more likely to result in multiple procurement sources).

There is considerable current interest from the legal and governmental spheres in Open Systems focusing on viewpoints 2 (economic) and 3 (legal). However, implementers and users are far more interested in viewpoints 4 and 5. Table 1 identifies the strong implementer and user interest in the terms "Open architecture" and "Open Source," which more closely address their viewpoints.

UNDERSTANDING THE REQUIREMENTS OF OPENNESS

Table 1 shows that the criteria of the major stakeholder groups are sometimes similar and sometimes divergent. Users have little interest in how a standardization process is conducted. The concept that open meetings, consensus and due process support the development of multiple sources of implementation of a completed standard is recognized but rarely supported by users. Users are focused on being able to purchase compatible equipment from multiple sources. History does suggest that open meetings, consensus and due process facilitate the creation of multiple sources. In the case of the legal viewpoint, even though all the stakeholders have an interest, their interests are quite different. SSOs appear satisfied to support reasonable and non-discriminatory (RAND) IPR policies. Commercial implementers require a means to identify and control their IPR cost, which RAND does not offer. This pushes implementers to form consortia. Users are often unwilling to pay high prices caused by multiple IPR claims irrespective of which SSO (public or consortia) produced the standard. So, users may be put off by the impact of RAND policies.

The first three criteria in Table 1 (1.1, 1.2 & 1.3) are oriented to the stakeholders focused on open systems creation. The first four criteria (1.1, 1.2, 1.3 & 2.1) are also at the heart of the World Trade Organization (WTO) Agreement on Technical Barriers to Trade, Code of Good Practice (http://www.wto.org/english/tratop_e/ tbt_e/tbtagr_e.htm#Annex%203). The ANSI open standards concept requires the first three criteria for all ANSI accredited standards organizations (American National Standards Institute, 1998). The fourth criteria, no trade restrictions, is supported by ANSI but not required. Criteria 3.3, non-discriminatory licensing, has been formally added to the U.S. standards development process by ANSI and many SSOs.

Currently the widest interest regarding open standards focuses on Fair Trade and Fair IPR. Fair Trade addresses standards as barriers to trade or enablers of trade. Fair IPR impacts the profitability of all communications equipment companies today. The additional seven criteria listed under 4 and 5 represent open standards requirements which are emerging, but are not yet supported by most SSOs. Table 1 identifies that these seven criteria are more oriented to the implementation and use of standards.

The following provides descriptions of the five viewpoints and discusses the 18 criteria identified as they relate to open standards and Open Source. Once these concepts are fully described, the definitions of open interface, open architecture and open systems may be refined by identifying which of the concepts apply.

POLITICAL CONSIDERATIONS

The political process associated with developing open standards appears quite different from the political process associated with developing Open Source software. Standards are developed in an SSO while Open Source is developed in an ad hoc group led by one or a few project leaders. However, most standards development projects have just a few key contributors–similar to most Open Source software development projects, and consensus is usually sought among the participants of each. So underneath the different organizational veneers, the political operation is not as different, on average, as it first appears. The unencumbered licensing approach usually desired for Open Source software is very different from the reasonable and non-discriminatory (RAND) licensing often used by SDOs or the commercial licensing often used by consortia. Open source discussions are less fractured by specific economic goals. However, standardization meetings often have more formal rules to minimize polarization. Since open standards and Open Source are the concepts underlying open architecture and open systems, the political process that determines the generation of Open Source and open standards directly relates to how open the systems and architectures are.

Open Meeting

Open Meeting—All may participate in the standards or software development process. Currently openness of meetings is deemed to be met under many SSO requirements if all current stakeholders may participate in the standards creation process. But, as technology has become more complex, user participation in standards creation has declined significantly (Foray, 1995). When the largest number of stakeholders (users) no longer participate, such a definition of open meetings is no longer functional.

In Open Source software development, the users of specific software tools or processes are often the developers of the same Open Source software. This occurs because only those with some interest are likely to become developers.

"All stakeholders can participate," is a mantra of many recognized SSOs. But this mantra does not address all the barriers to open meetings. Recent social science research has identified 27 barriers to open standards meetings and grouped these into five categories: the stakeholders themselves, the rules of recognized standardization, the way the process is carried out, the role of the technical officers of the committee and the culture of the committees (de Vries, Feilzer, & Verheul, 2004).

A major barrier to standardization and software development participation is economic. Some recognized SSOs (e.g., International Telecommunications Union [ITU]) and many consortia (e.g., World Wide Web Consortium [W3C]) require membership before attendance. Paying to become a standardization committee member is a significant economic barrier when a potential standardization participant is not sure they are interested in attending a single meeting. Participation expenses, unless quite low, are part of the real barriers to standardization participation for students, many users and even start-up companies in the field. Currently only a few SSOs, such as the Internet Engineering Task Force (IETF), the standardization organization for the Internet and the IEEE offer low cost per meeting participation.

The costs to become an Open Source software developer are quite low (a subscription to SourceForge is $39.00 per year). Of course making the time necessary to actively participate in Open Source software development or standards

development is a very significant cost. While some pursue such development from their own resources, the development costs are often borne by the participant's employer.

Consensus

Consensus—All interests are discussed and agreement found, no domination. Different SSOs define consensus differently. Ideally, consensus requires that no single stakeholder group constitutes a majority of the membership of an SSO. This concept is less practical for Open Source development as the Open Source software developers may have a similar background. Consensus may be identified by vote of the standardization committee or may mean without active or informed opposition, what the IETF describes as "rough consensus." Surprisingly, the IETF, which many find to be an example of a more open SSO, does not support full consensus as the IETF Area Directors have a dictatorial level of control over the standardization decisions in their area (IETF, 1998).

In Open Source software development, the project leaders often have a similar dictatorial level of control.

Due Process

Due Process—Balloting and an appeals process may be used to find resolution. Different SSOs describe due process differently. In general it requires that prompt consideration be given to the written views and objections of any participants. A readily available appeals mechanism for the impartial handling of procedural complaints regarding any action or inaction is part of the due process requirement. As explained above, the three requirements: Open Meetings, Consensus and Due Process, are considered fundamental by recognized SSOs to the openness of their standardization process.

Due process is less likely to available in an Open Source development project. It is also less available in the IETF standardization process although the IETF is evolving its standardization system.

ECONOMIC CONSIDERATIONS

From an economic viewpoint, open systems, open architecture, open standards and Open Source are all means to support open trade. Open trade occurs when there are no trade restrictions and each transaction is symmetric (the buyer and seller are equally well informed). Open trade is more concerned with open standards than Open Source software. Open source software impacts on open trade can occur where licensing restrictions or government security concerns, usually over encryption capabilities in the software, impede open trade.

Trade Restrictions

No trade restrictions requires the same standard for the same capability, worldwide. This criteria is supported by the WTO to prevent technical barriers to trade. The International Federation of Standards Users (IFAN) also supports uniform international standards (IFAN, 2000). However, politically this can be a very contentious area. There are national standards for food processing that are based on religious beliefs (e.g., halal and kosher). There are standards for the environment, health, medical care and social welfare that cause an imbalance in cost between countries that implement them (often richer) and countries that don't (often poorer). To avoid these contentious issues, most recognized SSOs currently support, but do not require, coordination of their standards work with worldwide standards. This allows, but does not favor, divergent regional or national standards.

In the richer countries, the decline of publicly funded research and aggressive commercialism has made it more difficult to achieve a single standard for a single function worldwide. The five different incompatible wireless technologies of the 3G cellular standards (W-CDMA, cdma2000, UWC-136, TD-CDMA & FD-TDMA) are an example of these effects. Initially these five 3G versions will operate in different geographic areas but eventually users will demand worldwide compatible cell phone operation. It appears likely that standardization organizations will continue to create incompatible standards for similar capabilities. This may be viewed as an indication of the failings of recognized standardization (Cargill &Bolin, 2004), or as an indication of the need to increase aspects of the support of a level playing field (see 4.1, below).

The political criteria of open standards have been addressed and in large measure resolved in most SSOs. The requirement for open trade is supported by the three recognized worldwide SSOs: ISO, IEC and ITU, but many nations cling to the view that giving up their national standardization prerogatives would be giving up an aspect of their nation's sovereignty. Consortia standardization, which is unimpeded by such political issues, usually creates worldwide standards.

Symmetric Exchanges

Economic transactions tend to favor the seller, who has greater knowledge of the product or service for sale. To ensure a more symmetric exchange, the buyer relies on standards that define aspects of the product or service as well as an ability to purchase from multiple competing sources (see Multiple Procurement Sources, below). In this way open standards are quite important to enabling more symmetric exchanges.

Open Source supporters suggest that software developed and maintained by multiple individual software developers will be better understood and more available to users, but this criteria is currently neither controlled nor experimentally shown.

LEGAL CONSIDERATIONS

Open Source software and open standards require specific licensing mechanisms to ensure that implementers and users of the software and standards are not unreasonably constrained by others' IPR.

Most recognized SSOs and many consortia consider that holders of Intellectual Property Rights (IPR) must make available their IPR for implementation on Reasonable And Non-Discriminatory (RAND) terms. IPR associated with implementations (hardware or software) has generally proved to be useful to motivate innovation. IPR on interfaces, which define a relationship between two or more implementations, is of greater concern. Five major variations of IPR and IP control on interfaces are generally considered:

1. Commercial licensing may be the most prevalent legal way to use IPR. It is also the least open. In this case the holder of IPR and the implementer of the IPR agree privately on commercial terms and conditions for the implementer to use the holder's IPR.

Band (1995) described four additional levels of increasing openness relating to IPR associated with interfaces:

2. Microsoft believes that interface specifications should be proprietary, but will permit openness by licensing the specifications to firms developing attaching (but not competing) products.
3. The Computer Systems Policy Project (CSPP) also believes that interface specifications can be proprietary, but will permit openness by licensing the specifications on RAND terms for the development of products on either side of the interface.
4. The American Committee for Interoperable Systems (ACIS) believes that software

interface specifications are not protectable under copyright, and that therefore reverse engineering (including disassembly) to discern those specifications does not infringe the author's copyright.

5. Sun Microsystems believes that critical National Information Infrastructure (NII) software and hardware interface specifications should receive neither copyright nor patent protection. This variation precludes commercial advantage. Using the concepts discussed under Level Playing Field below, some commercial advantage could be maintained (Band, 1995).

The range of possible refinements in this contentious area is probably limitless. Some refinements include:

An additional variation of licensing that can impact all five variations above is pass-through licensing, which allows a licensee, who is an implementer, to pass through to other implementers the licensing terms negotiated without additional actions.

The CSPP variation (3, the manner of operation of most SDOs currently) might be more acceptable to implementers if an IPR arbitration function existed when IPR is identified during the creation/modification of a standard (Shapiro, 2001).

Sun Microsystems variation (5) might be more acceptable to implementers if claims on basic interfaces were precluded but IPR on proprietary extensions was allowed. This could be technically feasible using the concepts identified in the "Level Playing Field" section.

SUMMARY OF THE EXTERNAL CRITERIA

The current practice of many SDOs, to require RAND licensing, appears to increase the number of consortia as it does not allow implementers to determine the impact of standards-based IPR on their costs. The semiconductor industry, where manufacturing cost drops rapidly with volume, exacerbates IPR problems for implementers. In the case of semiconductors, IPR costs may be based on fixed unit charges. Such charges can be the largest single cost component of a semiconductor. Semiconductor implementers must control their IPR costs. It seems only fair that any implementer has a right to determine the exact cost of IPR to them before they accept its inclusion in a new standard. This issue has led many implementers to join consortia as consortia often require joint licensing of related IPR. This practice defines the cost of the IPR to the implementer. While commercial licensing may seem the least open process, it may not be more costly than the RAND approach to specific implementers.

For emerging countries, RAND policies also appear to be causing an undesirable situation. China is rapidly developing into the major supplier of communications systems and equipment but Chinese companies do not have a portfolio of IPR that can be used to trade with commercial organizations in more developed countries who have IPR in communications standards. This may cause the Chinese to consider developing non-standard technologies for existing communication systems so that they do not have to pay for previous IPR standardization decisions that they did not participate in (Updegrove, 2005).

The Web site Cover Pages (2005) maintains a section on open standards and collects many different descriptions of open standards. The view of open standards from the SSOs quoted on this site follows the political and legal criteria identified here. The view of other organizations is more divergent and includes criteria discussed below.

IMPLEMENTER CONSIDERATIONS

The implementer of the products or services that are based on standards and the developer of software products or services that utilize Open Source software are affected by a number of criteria that impact the openness of the standards or Open Source.

Level Playing Field

Manufacturers or service providers must compete in order to offer multiple sources of their products and services. As was noted above, without competition the seller becomes more dominate as asymmetrical transactions become more likely. Standards represent a means to help balance the buyers' and sellers' information, but when everything about a transaction is standardized there is no longer any grounds for product competition (only price competition). In similarity standards, a balance is achieved by standardizing some aspects of a product or service but not others. Interface (compatibility) standards, in order to support a level playing field, should offer means to support proprietary advantage as well as compatibility.

Interfaces that are open, not hidden or controlled and support migration, can also support proprietary advantage. Such interfaces which exhibit both proprietary and public advantages, termed Open Interfaces, are an emerging technical concept applicable to interface standards used between programmable systems. Programmable systems with changeable memory make possible multi-mode interfaces that can be changed to support backward and forward compatibility. The idea that Open Interfaces should embody both public and private advantage is relatively new. But interest is increasing due to the considerable success of open interfaces in facsimile (T.30), telephone modems (V.8 and V.32 auto baud procedures) and Digital Subscriber Line transceivers (G.994.1 handshaking).

One way of achieving open interfaces is to implement a fairly new technique called an *etiquette* (Krechmer, 2000). Etiquettes are mechanisms to negotiate protocols. While a protocol terminates an X.200 (OSI) layer, an etiquette, which may negotiate multiple OSI layer protocols, does not terminate (replace) any protocol layer function. An etiquette is used only for negotiating which protocol, options or features to employ. The purpose of etiquettes is connectivity and expandability. Proper etiquettes provide:

- Connectivity, negotiating between two or more devices in different spatial locations to determine compatible protocols.
- Means to allow both proprietary and public enhancements to the interface that do not impact backward or forward compatibility.
- Adaptability, so that one communications system can become compatible with a different communications system.
- Easier system troubleshooting by identifying specific incompatibilities.

As long as the etiquette is common between the equipment at both ends, it is possible to receive the code identifying each protocol supported by the equipment at a remote site. Checking this code against a database of such codes on the Web or in a manual, the user can determine what change is necessary in their system or the remote system to enable compatibility.

One of the earliest etiquettes is ITU Recommendation T.30, which is used in all Group 3 facsimile machines. Part of its function includes mechanisms to interoperate with previous Group 2 facsimile machines while allowing new features (public as well as proprietary) to be added to the system without the possibility of losing backward

compatibility. Another etiquette is the ITU standard V.8, which is used to select among the V.34 and higher modem modulations. More recently, ITU G.994.1 provides a similar function in Digital Subscriber Line (DSL) equipment.

As an example of the usefulness of Open Interfaces, consider Microsoft APIs. Assume that a standard based upon the Microsoft Windows API is created. Then any vendor could create an operating system (OS) to work with Microsoft's applications or create applications to work with Microsoft's OS. If any vendor (including Microsoft) identified a new function such as a music delivery service or IPTV that was not supported across the basic API, that vendor could then offer the new function, as an identified proprietary feature across the API, to users that purchase that vendor's OS and appropriate applications. Since an Open Interface supports proprietary extensions (Krechmer, 2000), each vendor controls the way the new function is accessed across the API, but does not change the basic compatibility of the API. In this manner a vendor is able to maintain control and add value, based on the desirability of the new function.

Some aspects of the issue of open interfaces were explored in technical detail in 1995 (Clark, 1995). Since then, seven technical aspects of open interfaces have been identified (Krechmer, 2000).

Mutually Agreed Changes

To maintain openness, all changes to existing standards need to be presented and agreed to in a forum supporting the political criteria identified above. Controlling changes is a powerful tool to control interfaces when system updates are distributed over the Internet and stored in computer memory. Even with the most liberal of IPR policies identified (see Legal Considerations, above), Microsoft would still be able to control its Windows Application Programming Interfaces (APIs) by distributing updates (changes) to users that updated both sides of the API interface. But without a similar distribution at the same time, competing vendors' products on one side of the same API could be rendered incompatible by such a Microsoft online update.

The only way that interfaces can remain open is when all changes are presented, evaluated and approved in a committee that supports the political criteria identified above. Considering today's environment of computers connected over the Internet, identifying and requiring mutually agreed upon changes is vital to the concept of open standards. Surprisingly, this is not widely understood. The original U.S. judicial order to break-up the Microsoft PC-OS and application software monopoly did not address this key issue (United States District Court). On March 24, 2004, the European Commission (EC) announced its decision to require Microsoft to provide their browser (Explorer) independently of the Windows operating system and make the related Windows APIs available to others (European Union, 2004). This decision did not address the necessity for mutually agreed change. The EC announced on June 6, 2005 receipt of new proposals from Microsoft addressing Microsoft's support of interoperability (European Union, 2005). Unfortunately these proposals still do not directly address mutually agreed change.

Mutually agreed change is also a significant issue for the Open Source software development community, as the concept of Open Source allows independent change based on any programmer's desire. While this maximizes the freedom the programmer has to develop new applications, it is also responsible for the splintering of some Open Source software systems into multiple similar but not fully compatible software systems (e.g., UNIX).

Available documents

Committee documents, completed standards and software documentation should be readily avail-

able. This criterion allows any stakeholder to be able to see any documents that relate to an open standard or Open Source program. The openness of a standardization meeting or software development project to outsiders is closely related to the availability of the documents from the meeting. All technical documentation falls into two classes: work-in-progress documents (e.g., individual technical proposals and meeting reports), and completed documents (e.g., standards, source code and test procedures). Different stakeholders need to access these different classes of documents. Standards implementers and software developers need access to work-in-progress documents to understand specific technical decisions, as well as access to completed standards or source code. Implementation testers (users and their surrogates) also need access to completed documents.

The Internet Society (ISOC) supports a non-government recognized standards-making organization, the IETF, which has pioneered new standards development and distribution procedures based on the Internet. While the IETF does not meet the criteria for Consensus and Due Process, the IETF is perhaps the most transparent standardization organization. Using the Internet, the IETF makes available on the web both its standards, termed RFCs, and the drafts of such standards at no charge. Using the facilities of the Internet, IETF committee discussion and individual technical proposals related to the development of standards can be monitored by anyone and responses offered. This transparent development of IETF standards has been successful enough that some other SSOs are doing something similar. In July 1998, ETSI announced that their technical committee, TIPHON (Telecommunications and Internet Protocol Harmonization Over Networks), would make available at no charge all committee documents and standards drafts.

SourceForge also uses the Internet to provide software developers a forum to access Open Source development projects. Currently, the Open Source concept does not define the level of software documentation required: how well the source code is commented, how changes are documented and how the specific software developers are identified. Some Open Source development projects provide excellent documentation and others do not.

Ultimately, as technology use expands, everyone becomes a stakeholder in technology and the technical documents that describe it. Using the Internet, access to documents and discussion may be opened to all. In this way, informed choices may be made about being involved in a specific committee or project, and potential new participants could evaluate their desires to participate.

USER CONSIDERATIONS

The end users' view of openness is critical to the success of any product or service that claims openness. However, this perspective has been overlooked by many (e.g., governments) who are more concerned with how openness impacts the political and economic processes. Companies that are strongly focused on serving their markets address the users' view. However, such companies may be seen as not open because they may not support open political and economic processes.

Multiple Procurement Sources

From the users' perspective, the most significant aspect of openness is the availability of multiple sources for products and services the user desires. The importance of this from the user's perception of openness cannot be overstated. If a product or service is only available from a single supplier, the product or service is obviously proprietary. This is true irrespective of the political process or economic criteria. From the users' view, proprietary products or services are acceptable if the cost is acceptable for the function performed. But many users recognize that their desire for aftermarket additions (see below) and support over the life

of the product (see below) may be compromised when products or services are only available from a single source.

Implementation Assessment

A user requires the means to determine if a product or service will be suitable. Implementation assessment identifies the importance to users of reliable implementations. A user may trust an implementation based on previous performance, its brand or simply familiarity with the requirements. When such trust is not reliable, compliance, conformance and/or certification mechanisms for implementation testing, user evaluation and identification may be necessary. This more exact form of implementation assessment is termed conformity assessment. Implementation assessment is supported by ANEC (no date), a European organization that focuses on consumer issues associated with standardization. ISO/IEC 17000 defines conformity assessment as the "demonstration that specific requirements relating to a product, process, system, person or body are fulfilled" (ISO/IEC 17000). Conformity assessment procedures, such as testing, inspection and certification, offer assurance that products fulfill the requirements specified in the appropriate regulations or standards.

Implementation assessment covers all possible parameters that may need to be identified as conforming for accurate, safe and/or proper use. Such parameters could include physical access (e.g., access by people with disabilities), safety (e.g., CE or UL mark, the European and U.S. indications that equipment is designed safely) and correct weights and measures (e.g., certification of scales and gasoline pumps). Achieving implementation assessment may be as simple as identifying a known brand or requiring testing by implementers, regulators, users or their testing agencies as well as displaying known and controlled identification marks (e.g., UL and CE) to indicate conformity to certain requirements.

Implementation assessment may represent requirements on the standardization process or software development process as well as requirements on implementations that use the standard to identify and assure compliance and, if necessary, conformance. For a manufacturer of a scale to measure weight, a self certification process traceable to national standards may be required. For a communications equipment or communications software manufacturer, an interoperability event may be needed (often termed a plug-fest) to test that different implementations interoperate. For the user, a simpler mark of conformity is often desirable. As an example, in the European Union (EU), the CE marking is the manufacturer's indication that the product meets the essential (mostly safety) requirements of all relevant EU Directives. This specific marking indicating compliance reduces the user's safety concerns. Many consortia support plug-fests and compliance testing as part of their members' desire to promote associated products. Open Source software is just beginning to develop implementation assessment procedures, e.g., Linux is a more user trusted UNIX version.

Aftermarket Additions

One way the end users maximize their capital investment in products and services is to acquire extensions of such products or services that increase the service life or functionality. For the user, one advantage of products and services that dominate in their respective markets is that such products or services often attract aftermarket additions. Smaller suppliers often complain about users being unwilling to purchase from any but the dominant supplier. But users often turn to the dominant supplier because of the expected availability of aftermarket additions. Some suppliers (e.g., Microsoft) provide proprietary interfaces and yet support large aftermarkets. Sometimes an interface seen as open attracts aftermarket suppliers. But open standards and Open Source cannot guarantee aftermarket additions. Successful Open Source software may attract continued software development, but Open Source software itself is no guarantee of aftermarket additions.

Support Over the Service Life

Products and the related software should be supported until user interest ceases rather than when implementer interest declines. Ongoing support of hardware, software and services and associated standards is of specific interest to end users as it may increase the life of their capital investment in equipment or software. The user's desire for implementer independent ongoing support is noted

Table 2. The phases of support during a standard's lifetime

Phase	Activity	Description	Major Interest Group
0.	Create standard	The initial task of SSOs	Creators
1.	Fixes (changes)	Rectify problems identified in initial implementations	Implementers
2.	Maintenance (changes)	Add new features and keep the standard up-to-date with related standards work	Users
3.	Availability (no changes)	Continue to publish, without continuing maintenance	Users
4.	Rescission	Removal of the published standard from distribution	Users

by Perens (1999) as one of the desirable aspects of Open Source software. While this is true, the Open Source community does not provide a mechanism to ensure users that Open Source software will be maintained. The support of an existing standard, which directly impacts any products that utilize the standard, consists of four distinct phases after the standard is created (Table 2).

It is difficult to interest users in the first phase of standards development (creation) shown in Table 2 (Naemura, 1995). Even the second phase, fixes, may be of more interest to the developers and implementers than the users. The next three phases, however, are where users have an interest in maintaining their investment. Currently, few SSOs actively address maintaining their standards based on user desires. Possibly greater user involvement in the ongoing support of standards would be practical by taking advantage of the Internet to distribute standards and allowing users to track potential changes in specific standards. Increasing the users' involvement with the maintenance phases of the standardization process may also represent new economic opportunities for SSOs. The ITU-T Telecommunications Standardization Bureau Director's Ad Hoc IPR Group report, released in May 2005, includes "Ongoing support–maintained and supported over a long period of time" as one element of its Open Standards definition (http://www.itu.int/ITU-T/othergroups/ipr-adhoc/openstandards.html).

CONCLUSION

By looking at a full list of criteria that define open, it is clear that the terms "open systems," "open architecture," "open standards," "open interfaces" and "Open Source" have been misapplied in the past. This accounts for much of the confusion that they engender. What a government deems to be open has little relation to what a user deems to be open. Commercial implementers are often caught between these two forces. In the author's opinion, no SSO or Open Source project meets all of the criteria described. In fact, different SSOs and Open Source projects differ significantly in which criteria they do support.

Digital convergence offers many desirable opportunities, but it also may increase the opportunity for monopoly behavior on the part of information pathway suppliers. The increased compatibility required for digital convergence reduces the types of information pathways, creating the possibility of single vendor systems. Open systems can increase the number of information pathways by allowing competition. But achieving open systems is not straight forward and has not been well defined previously.

The 18 criteria developed here are a broad view of the meaning of openness. Are fewer criteria sufficient? That question can only be answered when each stakeholder understands the consequences of what they may be giving up. Users are advised to be alert to the pros and cons associated with digital convergence.

REFERENCES

American National Standards Institute (1998). *Procedures for the development and coordination of American national standards.* Washington, DC: American National Standards Institute.

ANEC, the European consumer voice in standardization. Retrieved from http://www.anec.org/

Band, J. (1995). Competing definitions of "openness" on the NII. In B. Kahin & J. Abbate (Eds.), *Standards policy for information infrastructure.* Cambridge, MA: The MIT Press.

Cargill, C. (1997). *Open systems standardization.* Upper Saddle River, NJ: Prentice Hall.

Cargill, C., & Bolin, S. (2004). *Standardization: A failing paradigm.* Paper presented at the Standards and Public Policy Conference, Federal Reserve Bank of Chicago, May 13-14, 2004.

Clark, D. C. (1995). *Interoperation, open interfaces and protocol architecture.* Retrieved from http://www.csd.uch.gr/~hy490-05/lectures/Clark_interoperation.htm

Cover Pages (2005). *Technology reports: Open standards.* Retrieved October 6, 2005 from, http://xml.coverpages.org/openStandards.html

Critchley, T. A., & Batty, K. C. (1993). *Open systems: The reality.* Hertfordshire, UK: Prentice Hall.

de Vries, H., Feilzer, A., & Verheul, H. (2004). Removing barriers for participation in formal standardization. In F. Bousquet, Y. Buntzly, H. Coenen, & K. Jakobs (Eds.), *EURAS proceedings 2004*, 171-176. Aachen, Germany: Aachener Beiträge zur Informatik, Band 36, Wissenschaftsverlag Mainz in Aachen.

European Union (2004). *EU commission concludes Microsoft investigation, imposes conduct remedies and a fine.* Delegation of the European Commission to the USA. Retrieved March 24, 2004 from http://www.eurunion.org/news/press/2004/20040045.htm

European Union (2005). *Delegation of the European commission to the USA.* Retrieved from http://europa.eu.int/rapid/pressReleasesAction.do?reference=IP/05/3&format=HTML&aged=0&language=EN&guiLanguage=en

Foray, D. (1995). Coalitions and committees: How users get involved in information technology (IT) standardization. In R. Hawkins, R. Mansell, & J. Skea (Eds.), *Standards, innovation and competitiveness.* Hants, England: Edward Elgar Publishing Limited.

Grey, P. (1991). *Open systems: A business strategy for the 1990s.* Blacklick, OH: McGraw-Hill.

Hugo, I. (1991). *Practical open systems: A guide for managers.* Manchester, Oxford: NCC/Blackwell.

IETF Working Group Guidelines and Procedures. RFC 2418, September, 1998. Retrieved from http://www.ietf.org/rfc/rfc2418.txt

IFAN strategies and policies for 2000-2005. Retrieved from http://www.ifan-online.org/

Interchange of Data Between Administrations (IDA; 2004). *European Interoperability Framework section 1.3 "Underlying principles," derived from the eEurope Action Plan 2005 as well as the Decisions of the European Parliament.* November, 2004. Retrieved from http://xml.coverpages.org/IDA-EIF-Final10.pdf

ISO/IEC 17000: 2004. *Conformity assessment–Vocabulary and general principles.* Geneva: International Organization for Standardization (ISO).

Krechmer, K. (1998). The orinciples of open standards. *Standards Engineering, 50*(6).

Krechmer, K. (2000). The fundamental nature of standards: Technical perspective. *IEEE Communications Magazine, 38*(6), page 70.

Krechmer, K. (2006). Open standards requirements. *Journal of Information Technology Standards Research (JITSR), 4*(1).

Naemura, K. (1995). User involvement in the life cycles of information technology and telecommunications standards. In R. Hawkins, R. Mansell, & J. Skea (Eds.), *Standards, innovation and competitiveness.* Hants, UK: Edward Elgar Publishing Limited.

NRENAISSANCE Committee (1994). Computer and Telecommunications Board, National Research Council. *Realizing the Information Future.* Washington, DC: National Academy Press.

Perens, B. (1999). The open source definition. In C. DiBona, S. Ockman, & M. Stone (Eds.), *OpenSources voices from the open source revolution,* 171-189. Sebastopol, CA: O'Reilly & Associates.

Perens, B. (no date). *Open Standards Principles and Practice*. Summarized at http://xml.coverpages.org/openStandards.html

Raymond, E. S. (2000). *Homesteading the noosphere, section 2*. Retrieved August 25, 2000 from, http://www.csaszar.org/index.php/csaszar/interesting/the_open_source_reader

Rosen, L. (2005). *Open source licensing*. Upper Saddle River, NJ: Prentice Hall.

Shapiro, S. (2001). Setting compatibility standards: cooperation or collusion. In R. C. Dreyfuss, D. L. Zimmerman, & H. First (Eds.), *Expanding the boundaries of intellectual property*. Oxford, UK: Oxford University Press.

Siegel, J., & Soley, R. M. (2005). Open source and open standards–Working together for effective software development and distribution. In S. Bolin (Ed.), *The standards edge: Open season*, p. 131-141. Ann Arbor, MI: Sheridan Books.

United States District Court for the District of Columbia. Civil Action No. 98-1232 (TPJ).

Updegrove, A. (2004). Best practices and sandard setting (How the "pros" do it). In S. Bolin (Ed.), *The standards edge, dynamic tension*. Ann Arbor, MI: Bolin Communications.

Updegrove, G. (2005). China, the United States and standards. *Consortium Standards Bulletin, IV*(4). Retrieved from http://www.consortiuminfo.org/bulletins/apr05.php#editorsnote

West, J. (2004). What are open standards? Implications for adoption, competition and policy, paper presented at the *Standards and Public Policy Conference*. Federal Reserve Bank of Chicago, May 13-14, 2004.

Webopedia (2001-2005). *Webopedia, An online dictionary and search engine for computer and Internet technology definitions*. Available at http://webopedia.com

Wikipedia (2001-2005). Wikipedia, the Free Encyclopedia. Available at http://en.wikipedia.org

ENDNOTES

[1] This chapter is an expansion of an earlier paper submitted to the Journal of Information Technology Standards Research (JITSR Vol. 4 No. 1). In turn the JITSR paper is a significant revision of a paper published in the Proceedings of the 38th Annual Hawaii International Conference on System Sciences (HICSS), January, 2005. In turn, the HICSS paper is a major revision of Krechmer (1998).

[2] See http://www.slackbook.org/html/introduction-opensource.html for a Linux view.

[3] SourceForge is the world's largest development and download repository of Open Source code and applications. http://sourceforge.net/

Section III
Root and Content Governance

Chapter IX
Issues in Internet Governance

Oliver Q. C. Zhong
University of Michigan – Ann Arbor, USA

Kenneth S. Flamm
University of Texas at Austin, USA

Anindya Chaudhuri
National Center for Educational Accountability, USA

ABSTRACT

"Internet Governance," not to be confused with "e-government," refers to the complex interaction of hardware (root-servers), software and public and private entities through which content is made available over the World Wide Web. The largely libertarian origins of Internet management, which helped it spread in a decentralized fashion, are under increasing pressure from various interest groups. The outcome of this tussle, and the future structure of Internet governance, will have significant geopolitical repercussions, especially in the context of the continuing tendency of digital convergence.

DEFINING INTERNET GOVERNANCE

The phrase "Internet governance" is frequently confused with "e-government," the transference of many governmental transactions into cyberspace. It is also misconstrued as the bylaws of the Internet Corporation of Assigned Names and Numbers (ICANN), the central authority of the Internet's naming space, or as the Requests for Comments (RFCs), the important technical documents underpinning the Internet's architecture or even as regulatory procedures like domain name registration. Still more confusing, many read "governance" in the more dynamic and forceful sense of "governing."

However libertarian the Internet used to be in its early stages of growth, the balance of control today keeps tilting towards regulators and big commercial players at the expense of end users.

The founders of ICANN attempted to distance themselves from the image of "the ruler" by employing terms such as "technical management" in reference to their activities (Mueller, 2002, p.7). If not deliberately misleading, the characterization was at least unintentionally opaque. Sound management of the technical infrastructure is pivotal for the Internet's functionality, but the spectrum of management activities extends far beyond the technical band. What matters more, invariably, is how content on the Internet are governed. Content-side governance, due to the rich variety of types of content and their corresponding jurisdictions, necessarily involves not uniform but discrete mechanisms that determine, most importantly, property rights.

Thus, a good definition of "Internet Governance" must represent this technology-content duality, as well as the variety and the complexity embedded. Some official progress has recently been made in that regard. The Working Group on Internet Governance (WGIG) has, in its June 2005 report, furnished its definition (WGIG, 2005a, P.4), which ICANN in a response agreed as "appropriate" (ICANN, 2005):

Internet governance is the development and application by governments, the private sector and civil society, in their respective roles, of shared principles, norms, rules, decision-making procedures, and programs that shape the evolution and use of the Internet.

The mere fact of this working definition being accepted by major stakeholders is cause for celebration. For a more forward looking definition, however, this chapter proposes that Internet governance be a two-tier construct of "Root Governance" and "Content Governance." By using the term throughout this chapter, we are referring to:

a.   laws, policies and technical standards that shape the architecture of the Internet and;

b.   institutional mechanisms by which real-world interest groups compete for content rights in the virtual world by working through established real-world rules or competing to legislate new ones for the unchartered waters of the Internet, at international, national and regional levels.

We now turn to examine the state-of-being of root governance and content governance respectively. We first identify the "root" of the Internet through a technical examination of the naming space, followed by a brief look at its history and a survey of its current issues. Subsequently, we provide an overview of important aspects of content governance, with a narrow focus on recent developments in intellectual property rights (IPR) on the Internet.

Root Governance and the Naming System

To understand how the Internet is governed, it is necessary to first understand the technical foundations on which the governance rests. In this section, we first go through some very basics of technical rationales underlying the Internet. Then, we explain IP addresses and domain names and discuss how the interaction between the two naming systems constitutes the "root" of the Internet.

The IP Address System

In a sense, misconception about the nature of the Internet can be attributed to its own popularity. The very name "Internet" is so entrenched in everyday vocabulary that it is very often considered a substantial "thing," and the presence of "www" so ubiquitous, that the Internet is often confused with the World Wide Web. In fact, the Internet, unlike telegram or telephone, is not a new, tangible communication network that stands on its own; the Web is only one part of it. It is really a global

Table 1. Classes of IP address (Source: Networking Next)

Class	Leftmost bits	Start address	Finish address
A	0xxx	0.0.0.0	127.255.255.255
B	10xx	128.0.0.0	191.255.255.255
C	110x	192.0.0.0	223.255.255.255
D	1110	224.0.0.0	239.255.255.255
E	1111	240.0.0.0	255.255.255.255

network of existing heterogeneous devices connected via a variety of channels, each of which has already existed for some original purpose: telephone lines, TV cable, fiber optics, radio waves and even electric cable. On this network, many useful applications other than WWW are available, such as ftp, mail, chat and newsgroup.

Every application, however different, involves the same core technical process: principled data transfer from one computer to another. Mass information flow is made possible because every networked computer is installed with TCP/IP—software suites which work as a common language known by all computers. It uses a hierarchically layered interface where each layer performs different functions and talks only to the same layer on the other computer. In a nutshell, information is cut into small pieces called "packets." Each packet is labeled with its destination address and is routed to the destination computer by TCP/IP on the host computer. Packets for one piece of information don't necessarily go through the same path, but upon arrival, they are received by the corresponding layers on the local computer and reassembled into one piece seamlessly.

Analogous to a traditional mailing system, delivery can be accurate only if destination addresses actually exist and do not have duplicates. In the Internet space, every computer is assigned a unique, IP address. The IP address system currently in use, named IPv4 ("Version 4"), takes the form of a binary string of 32 digits, or bits, thus theoretically being able to accommodate about 4.3 billion different addresses. For the sake of human comprehension, each octet (byte) of eight bits is

converted to the decimal system and a dot is used as a separator in between. This is the IP address as we know it. Each octet can theoretically range from 0 to 255, with some restrictions. IP addresses can go further on to be divided into five classes, Class A to Class E: those start with "0" belong to Class A; those start with "10" belong to Class B, and so on. The classification has technical implications and the difference is seen in the assignment process. Class D and E are virtually not used due to technical reasons. Class A and B are mostly reserved by large organizations. The only class open to the general public is Class C.

Given the geometric expansion of the Internet, the exhaustion of the address pool under the current IPv4 regime is no longer a remote possibility. In response, IPv6 ("version 6"), using 128 bits instead of 32, is being developed by the Internet Engineering Task Force (IETF). In the new system, the address resource will be practically inexhaustible, at least speaking in current terms.

The Domain Name System

Even under the present IPv4 regime, remembering the four octets of a single address, not to mention the 32 bits of 0s and 1s, is difficult. A specific IP address does not provide any obvious clue as to its actual contents. Moreover, changes in a network can result in a change in the IP addresses of affiliated devices. For instance, if a company changes its ISP, all the hosts for its Web site must be renumbered. From a user's perspective, this can be overwhelming.

The Domain Name System (DNS) was developed to tackle precisely these issues. It is a naming system consisting of hierarchically organized character strings separated by dots, like www.yahoo.com. The hierarchy, in contrast to that of the IP address system, goes from far right to far left. For example, ".com" is the most common top-level domain name (TLD), ".yahoo" is a popular second-level domain (SLD) and "www" is a third-level domain.

Like the IP address system, domain names are unique: No two computers share the same domain name. Unlike the IP address system, the DNS space is virtually inexhaustible. Under the current structure, there can be as many as 127 levels of hierarchy and on each level, the string can be up to 63 characters in length, where 37 different ASCII characters are eligible for use. This amounts to an astronomical number of theoretically available domain names. Further plans to introduce non-ASCII character domain names are under consideration as well.

In contrast to the theoretical abundance, however, actual domain name supply suffers from what economists refer to as the "artificial scarcity." All together, only 261 TLDs are in use. SLDs are controlled by a registration process which, closely related to the control of the "root" of the Internet, has become a multimillion-dollar business.

The Root

A two-way translation process, the resolution and the inverse resolution, intermediates between the IP address and the DNS systems. In the early days of the Internet when the total number of addresses was very limited, the correspondence between numerical and verbal addresses was maintained in a file called "host.txt" at the Network Information Center (NIC). Every computer on the network did the resolution locally according to a downloaded copy of host.txt. This flat scheme was soon overwhelmed by the unforeseen growth of the network. A more sophisticated system was thus developed, but with a similar philosophy.

To guarantee "universal resolvability," i.e., the idea that on a networked computer anywhere, resolving one domain name should always result in the same IP address, there needs to be an accurate, reliable and up-to-date database which also must be always available to every networked computer. Like the DNS, this key database system is structured hierarchically. A "registry" for a TLD, that is, an organization managing the registration of domain names under a top-level domain like .com keeps all the important resolving information within the domain it manages. All computers within the domain rely on the registry's database. At a higher (practically the highest) level, 13 "root servers" around the world, coordinated by ICANN, contain the very same, most accurate and up-to-date DNS information (the "root zone files"). They back each other up and keep the registry name servers updated. Thus, if the Internet has a root, it "actually refers to two distinct things: the root zone files and the root name servers" (Mueller, 2002, p.47).

The root is the core of Internet stability. If it's disrupted from providing correct revolving information properly, the DNS system will eventually collapse, bringing down the whole Internet. However, because of mass caching and transfer of information between name servers at all levels, there is no critical reliance on any particular node. For instance, when seven root servers were paralyzed and two others failed intermittently during one of worst "denial of service" (DoS) attacks on the root, Internet traffic was not significantly disrupted. However, Internet security experts said one more server failure would have resulted in damage to Web browsing and e-mail functions. To put it another way, the Internet has some flexibility to take outages, but without a healthy root, that flexibility would not be adequate protection.

ICANN and Root Governance

No one particularly cared about the ownership of what would later become the Internet when it was first developed in the 1970s as ARPANET, an experiment within the U.S. military with the help of several U.S. educational institutions and governmental departments. Without the slightest anticipation of its future commercial possibilities, the control of the network was not much of an issue. When the profitability of the Internet began to be apparent in the early 1990s, Network Solutions Inc. (NSI), a private government contractor later purchased by VeriSign Inc., and Internet Assigned Numbers Authority (IANA), a

technical community, were in *de facto* control of the domain name and IP address systems, after a series of contractual transactions.

On January 30, 1998, the U.S. National Telecommunications and Information Administration (NTIA) under the Department of Commerce (DoC) published the *Green Paper*, which asserted the U.S. government's authority over the root and an intention to relinquish the authority in a way that "involved Internet stakeholders internationally" (NTIA, 1998a). Proponents welcomed it for bringing direction to what had been a chaotic process. Opponents like the Government of Australia, on the other hand, saw it as a nationalistic intervention in a self-regulating international community

Figure 1. ICANN organizational chart before 2002 (Source: ICANN)

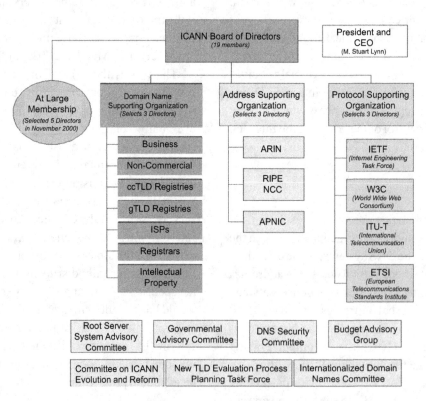

at best, and a coup d'état by the U.S. to secure its jurisdiction over the global Internet, at worst.

Under mounting pressure from warring parties, the Clinton administration released a plan in the legally nonbinding *White Paper* on June 5, 1998, to privatize the Internet before the contract with the NSI was to expire on September 30 that year (NTIA, 1998b). The White Paper did not pass any specific verdict on the future of Internet governance. Instead, it defined an international non-profit authority to be developed by the private sector based on consensus. However, the International Forum on the White Paper (IFWP), a series of four conferences where an assortment of Internet activists met to try to build a new consensus-based Internet regime as envisioned in the *White Paper*, failed to be the Constitutional Convention of the Internet. Powerful governmental contractors, the IANA and the NSI could not compromise with each other and with smaller players. In a move to break the stalemate, the DoC proposed an organization called the "Internet Corporation for Assigned Names and Numbers," or the ICANN, as the authority envisioned in the *White Paper*. On November 25, 1998, the DoC entered into a Memorandum of Understanding (MoU) with ICANN.

The MoU entrusted ICANN with the following functions: (a) Set policy for and direct allocation of IP number blocks to regional Internet number registries; (b) Oversee operation of the authoritative Internet root server system; c) Oversee policy for determining the circumstances under which new TLDs are added to the root system and; d) Coordinate the assignment of other Internet technical parameters as needed to maintain universal connectivity on the Internet.

ICANN's 19-member board rested on three Supporting Organizations (SOs): the Address SO (ASO), the Protocol SO (PSO), and the Domain Name SO (DNSO). They were the three nerve centers where specific policies were formulated and day-to-day work performed. Apart from the SOs, there were an At-Large Membership Com-

mittee, a Governmental Advisory Committee (GAC) and various other ad hoc committees performing different functions.

In September 1999, the NSI entered into a series of trilateral agreements with the DoC and ICANN, agreeing to sign a registry contract and a registrar accreditation contract with ICANN and provide some funding for the new regime. This move marked the significant completion of ICANN's efforts to integrate the domain name registration market and, in some sense, the real start of its global authority. The second highest priority for ICANN was about intellectual property protection. ICANN successfully established a Uniform Dispute Resolution Policy (UDRP) by defining it in its contract with every registrar. In addition, as mentioned earlier, ICANN released more gTLDs as an answer to market demand.

After three years of running, ICANN faced a shortage of resources. Stuart Lynn, then president, painted a bleak picture in his *Letter to the Internet Community* on February 24, 2002:

… But despite this progress, all the original expectations of ICANN have not been realized. ICANN is still not fully organized, and it is certainly not yet capable of shouldering the entire responsibility of global DNS management and coordination. ICANN has also not shown that it can be effective, nimble, and quick to react to problems. ICANN is overburdened with process, and at the same time underfunded and understaffed. For these and other more fundamental reasons, ICANN in its current form has not become the effective steward of the global Internet's naming and address allocation systems as conceived by its founders. Perhaps even more importantly, the passage of time has not increased the confidence that it can meet its original expectations and hopes. (Lynn, 2002)

Bad management cannot have been the major blame. ICANN's employees, many of them volunteers, had been working diligently with the resources available to them. ICANN's original mission—"to create an effective private sector policy development process capable of administrative and policy management of the Internet's naming and address allocation systems"—as Dr. Lynn put it, was "incredibly ambitious." Unfortunately, this ambitious agenda were not substantiated by reality. The NSI regarded the new organization as "more of a debating society than as an effective operational body" (Lynn, 2002). Many other stakeholders were playing a much less active role than they should have been. The real beneficiaries of the Internet—the major industry users, ISPs and backbone providers—were not keen to join the club just to pay. The RIRs, not wishing to see their established regional power eroded, couldn't be more lukewarm. The 243 ccTLDs made no commitment at all. The GAC largely failed in its mission to get support from many national governments. All these deficiencies resulted in nothing but very limited legitimacy, executing power and, most critically, disposable resources.

To make things worse, a significant portion of that already meager resource pool was used for non-essential purposes. An ideal of direct, global representation was entrenched in some of the Internet's top decision makers and was obsessively pursued in a hopelessly unrealistic way, namely, the At-Large membership elections, which were highly counterproductive in practice and seriously questionable in rationale. As Lynn rightly put it, "[it] is simply unrealistic to expect ICANN—thinly-staffed, underfunded, technical-oriented ICANN—to be able to achieve what no other global institution has: a global electorate expressing its will through stable representative institutions" (Lynn, 2002).

After Lynn's reform proposal, ICANN set up the Committee on Evolution and Reform (ERC) which started a reform process marked by the publication of a blueprint in June, a final implementation report in October and the organization's new Bylaws in December. When the reform process concluded in early 2003, it became clear that it had not gone quite the way Lynn had suggested. The June blueprint was already very different from the Lynn proposal. The final version of new Bylaws, accepted in December, hardly resembled the initial plan. Aimed at bringing about dramatic changes, the Lynn proposal had heavily focused

Table 2. Comparison of board composition proposals at different stages (Source: ICANN)

Document	Composition & Selection	Terms
Lynn Proposal	"5+5+5+2 Trustees" 5 (one from each ICANN geographic region) + 5 (nominated by open process) + 5 (CEO, Chairs of Address and Numbering Policy Council, Generic TLD Names Policy Council, Geographic TLD Names Policy Council and Technical Advisory Committee) + 2 (Designee of the Internet Architecture Board and Chair of Governmental Advisory Committee, as nonvoting liaisons)	Staggered three-year terms; maximum service two terms
Blueprint	"8+6+1+5 Directors" 8 (selected by the Nominating Committee) + 6 (two from each of the three Supporting Organizations) + 1 (the President) + 5 (selected by the Technical Advisory Committee, the IAB/IETF, the DNS Root Server System Advisory Committee, the Security Advisory Committee and the Government Advisory Committee, as nonvoting liaisons)	Staggered three-year terms; maximum service three terms
Final new By-Law	"8+6+1+6" One more nonvoting liaison added from a newly-created At Large Advisory Committee, the rest unchanged from the Blueprint	One-year term for liaisons subject to reappointment

on restricting At-Large Membership, bringing in more national government involvement and diluting the power of the largest players. But conservatism apparently took over and the reform ultimately became much more reserved.

Two of the three former ICANN Supporting Organizations were reshuffled in the reform. ICANN now rested on an Addressing Supporting Organization, a Country-Code Names Supporting Organization (ccNSO) and a Generic Names Supporting Organization (GNSO). This change in structure signaled a move toward providing more international and content-oriented services. Another positive move was a more effective integration of the GAC with the other constituent bodies of ICANN. National governments and country code registries were now in a better position to participate.

However, the problem of At-Large elections has sustained, and even worsened to some degree. The pursuit of representativeness of the "entire community," never clearly defined, is still the driving philosophy under ICANN. The Nominating Committee, ultimately selected by an At-Large election process, is playing an extremely powerful role in personnel decisions. This only helps strengthen, not dilute, the dominance of existing powerful players and prevent more interest groups from joining the international effort of Internet root governance.

U.S. vs. UN? The Future of Root Governance

The unmistakable trend of the ICANN reform has been a shift of control over the root away from its initial holders–the U.S. governmental, military, educational entities and their private contractors. Today, ICANN's 21 directors come from all over the world, and many national governments are actively engaged in the process.

It should be emphasized that the perception of a U.S. grudgingly ceding its monopoly of the Internet which it had held for its narrow national benefit is quite wrong. Even before ICANN became more international, the U.S. government had exerted very little micromanagement over its operations. In addition, it had always expressed a desire to exit the central role at an appropriate juncture despite the fact that its control was based on perfectly legitimate proprietary ownership. Quite a few national governments ignore this simple fact. They argue for an immediate transfer of control on the grounds that information technology has become essential for every country, but that the benefits are at present skewed towards the richer nations (WSIS, 2003).

The movement for taking over the Internet from the U.S. has achieved some institutional success, best seen in the launch of the aforementioned World Summit on the Information Society (WSIS), authorized by the UN General Assembly Resolution 56/183 in December 2001. The WSIS is clearly a parallel operation specifically designed to bring the Internet root under the control of the UN, or more directly, the International Telecommunications Union (ITU). The first-phase meeting in Geneva in 2003 produced a Declaration of Principles and commissioned a Working Group on Internet Governance to be operative till the scheduled second-phase in Tunis in November 2005.

The final report of the WGIG, presented on July 18, 2005, proposed a number of alternative structures or "Models" to the existing one under ICANN (WGIG, 2005b). For example, "Model 1" contemplated a "Global Internet Council" of representatives of national governments to take over the responsibilities of Internet governance from the U.S. Department of Commerce and ICANN. The GIC was to be "anchored in the United Nations" (WGIG, 2005b, p.12). A good deal of emphasis was placed on "regional and national coordination" under the aegis of a steering committee (WGIG, 2005b, p.15).

ICANN, understandably, is not enthused with the idea. It with all due decorum sent its At Large Advisory Committee Chairman, Vittoria Bertola, to attend the summit, making an implicit statement that it considered the conference no more than a liaison opportunity. In responding to the WGIG report which laid out strong recommendations over matters currently within ICANN's turf, ICANN did not hide its displeasure by effectively stating that while "the WGIG report [had] provided an important contribution to the WSIS discussions," ICANN had carried out reforms on its own agenda and, regarding the multi-stakeholder model the WSIS only had on paper, ICANN had been testing it in practice and it proved not to be easy (ICANN, 2005).

There are at least two justifications for this reluctance, not only on the part of ICANN and the U.S. government but that of many other national governments and individual observers as well. First, the system in place is working well and there does not seem to be any strong case for switching to an international bureaucracy. In fact, many, if not most, of the WSIS's declared principles are lofty slogans, hardly demonstrating any immediate relevance to what is required for root governance. The tempo of the diplomatic world seems an ill fit for what is required of some of the key objectives of root governance—flexibility combined with stability, for example. Particularly disturbing is the apparent attempt to bundle root governance with the agenda of the Millennium Declaration, a remarkably ambitious but not commensurately efficient development plan adopted under Secretary-General Kofi Annan.

Second, many fear the ideals of the Internet community will almost certainly be lost in an international talking society where many countries are performing under par in areas such as free speech. Indeed, the U.S. government probably will not forget Libya's democratically-elected chairmanship of the UN Human Rights Commission in 2003. It, together with many other Western countries, probably would not like to see, for instance, Saudi Arabia chair the "Internet Commission" either.

The U.S. does not have an obligation to give up the root, and exterior pressure is not yet strong enough to persuade it to do so. What is left to disgruntled developing regional powerhouses, as some have observed, is always the option to propagate an alternate Internet— a separate system of root files and root servers. For example, this is what China now appears to be flirting with, by recently announcing three Chinese-language TLDs. This is due cause for concern because, as the Chinese Internet authority has exclusive control over the DNS information for these TLDs, there is the *potential* of complete independence from the root administered by ICANN. However, a closer inspection reveals that the domain names under these Chinese TLDs are SLD shortcuts under the ICANN-governed ".cn" domain, for the ease of use by Chinese speakers. The potential of gaining independence remains real but hypothetical.

That the reality is less threatening than it first appeared to be was not immediately obvious even to veteran technology policy insiders. The perceived threat in fact illustrates the strength of the existing system, in which interconnection relies on the two pillars of Net Neutrality and Universal Resolvability. In the absence of national government interference, the current system has ensured smooth delivery of IP packets, wherever the points of origin or destination. These principles have become so entrenched that any large-scale alternative would necessarily create chaos and confusion. Hence, the strength of the status quo can be assumed despite the fact that a determined government not worried about consequences could upset the cart. In essence, had an alternative and better Internet been viable financially and technologically, it would have existed already.

CONTENT GOVERNANCE

Content governance is a highly complex matter. The complexity comes from two dimensions. First, the subject matter can have a very wide range. The most prominent ones and the most commercially important, discussed below, are intellectual property rights (IPR) issues. Second, these subject matters are governed by multiple real-world jurisdictions of law, regulation and governmental policies, which often creates difficult legal problems. For example, some online content may be illegal under U.S. copyright law but remain lawful under the law of The Netherlands, thus giving rise to the legal problem known as "IP arbitrage."

In this section, we limit our scope to IPR issues only because of its relative importance. A substantial portion of intellectual property has migrated from the physical world to the Internet, which has become one of the most influential channels of information flow on the earth and is still growing with fantastic speed. The Internet offers unprecedented opportunities for intellectual property-related industries to develop, whereas its peculiarity gives rise to many new, often difficult, problems in terms of intellectual property protection. This Section is an overview of the latest developments in the protection of online copyright, trademark (especially domain names) and patents.

Copyright and Related Rights

There is a strong consensus among national governments worldwide to protect copyright, in order "to promote the progress of science and useful arts ... by securing for limited times for authors and inventors the exclusive right to their respective writings and discoveries." Empirical data show that the copyright industry has not only promoted human intellectual innovation, but also become an increasingly important force driving the economy, especially in countries where copyright protection is strict and effective. For example, in the U.S., the core copyright industries in 2001 contributed an estimated 5.24% to gross domestic product (GDP) or $535.1 billion. They grew at an average annual rate of 7.01% over the previous 24 years (1977-2001), while that of the rest of the economy moved along at 3%. The total copyright industries employ eight million workers, or 5.9% of the total workforce, more than many of the traditional leading industries, such as aircraft manufacturing, steel, textiles and pharmaceuticals, do (Siwek, 2002).

The fast growth of copyright industries in recent years, in particular, owes much to the development of Internet-related technology, which facilitates creation through easier and closer global cooperation. However, the Internet also offers unprecedented convenience for copyright infringement, first because of the quality, availability of materials, unrestricted volume, speediness and cheapness of copying on the Internet; second because of its global nature that seriously complicates the compatibility between different jurisdictions to even agree on the scope of rights before any protection is enforced at all. A deeper conflict may reside in the opposing philosophies behind the two. Copyright, according to the Berne Convention, the most important international agreement in copyright, protects right holders' "exclusive right of reproduction in any manner or form." The Internet, however, is essentially a global network for exchanges of information stored on originally separate, individual computers, with "copying" the very prerequisite for such exchanges to happen in the first place.

To address the difficult problems of copyright protection in the new medium of the Internet and other digital technologies, great efforts have been made in an attempt to apply traditional legal principles appropriately, or create new ones where necessary. More importantly, significant progress has been made both internationally and nationally in terms of building common legal platforms where national or regional jurisdictions are able to engage in dialogues and resolve territoriality-sensitive disputes.

Two treaties were adopted in 1996 by consensus at the World Intellectual Property Organization (WIPO): the WIPO Copyright Treaty (the "WCT") and the WIPO Performances and Phonograms Treaty (the "WPPT") (commonly referred to as the "Internet Treaties"). The WIPO Internet Treaties are updates to the old international treaties in effect, namely, the Berne Convention and the Rome Convention, incorporating previously excluded provisions of the World Trade Organization (WTO)'s TRIPS Agreement into the WIPO legal framework.

In the U.S., Congress in 1998 passed two legislations that had significant impact on U.S. copyright law: the Sonny Bono Copyright Term Extension Act (the "CTEA"), extending the length of copyright protection by 20 years; and the Digital Millennium Copyright Act (the "DMCA"). Critics of the CTEA challenged its constitutionality under the Copyright Clause and the First Amendment, which was later upheld by the Supreme Court on January 15, 2003 in a 7-2 verdict in *Eldred v. Ashcroft*.

The DMCA created a much larger controversy because it stretched U.S. copyright law in an important way. The WIPO Internet Treaties require that member states provide two types of basic legal protection concerning the enforcement and management of copyright and related rights: "anti-circumvention" and "rights management information" protection. The former inhibits circumvention of technologies that authors use against piracy. The latter protects electronic data identifiers attached to copyrighted works from being deliberately removed or altered. However, the treaties only provide principles, leaving much discretion to national legislatures to stipulate details. The DMCA, in implementing the WIPO treaties, fully exercised that discretion in pushing the balance between rights protection and innovation and free speech toward the former.

As mentioned above, the emergence of the Internet as a mass storage medium adds to the complexity of determining the scope of rights that the law should protect. A common understanding, confirmed in the WIPO Internet Treaties, is that uploading into a computer's hard drive is an act of reproduction which has traditionally been exclusive to copyright holders. There is still no consensus, however, on whether making local copies of data into a computer's RAM, which is an integral part of Internet browsing, is of the same nature. Whatever the result of the debate, the Internet has significantly changed the way that both right holders and users deal with copyrighted work. Increasingly, public access to such materials is governed more by contract as opposed to by possession. Content providers are using more technological measures to prevent unauthorized copying as opposed to seeking legal remedies after such copying has been completed. Therefore, they expect a major shift of the role of copyright law from passively protecting the rights only to actively securing contractual enforcement and protecting the technological safeguards they implement. The DMCA, precisely reflecting this preemptive rationale, provides the desired shift.

The impact of DMCA on the U.S. copyright law can be best seen in a series of high-profile cases related to Peer-to-peer (P2P) systems, which, represented first by Napster then by the likes of KaZaA and Grokster, allows swapping of audio and video files on the Internet between users without a central server. Proponents contend that such swapping is analogous to borrowing and lending books and should be legal. Opponents not only found such swapping absolute copyright violations, but also sought to hold the provider of the software technology contributory liable.

P2P activities had had two potential "safe harbor" theories under earlier copyright law. For the unauthorized use of copyrighted materials itself, there was the "fair use" doctrine, a principle widely adopted by national laws aiming at keeping the balance between providing incentives for creations and innovations and securing reasonable public access to them. Similarly, international treaties have established a "Three-Step Test" to determine the permissibility of "fair use" exceptions in new circumstances on the Internet: they must be permitted in "certain special cases" that "do not conflict with a normal exploitation" of the work and "do not unreasonably prejudice the owner's legitimate interests." Regarding the underlying technology, the Supreme Court in its landmark 1984 ruling in *Sony v. Universal Studios*, 464 U.S. 417 (1984), decided that technologies (Sony's Betamax VCR, in that case) with significant non-infringement uses (SNIUs) could not be held contributory liable for copyright infringement by third-party users.

Both safe harbors were being tested and, in a sense, destabilized by recent cases. A decisive court ruling from *A&M Records, Inc. v. Napster*, 114 F. Supp. 2d 896 (N.D. Cal. 2000), decided that "repeated and exploitative copying of copyrighted works, even if the copies are not offered for sale, may constitute commercial use" and thus was not a "fair use" under U.S. copyright law. That ruling soon led to Napster's shutdown. In Napster's wake, later P2P systems employed more sophisticated technologies and more crafty legal circumvention, thus giving the courts a tougher task to determine the liability of P2P technology providers. In the widely-watched case of *MGM v. Grokster*, 125 S. Ct. 2764 (2005), the Supreme Court unanimously decided that Grokster was contributorily liable for infringement. The copyright industry's sense of victory would soon be reinforced with an international flavor when a federal court in Australia similarly ruled against KaZaA.

The ground realities are less skewed than seems apparent. The *Grokster* court practically left the *Sony* safeguard untouched, deciding instead on conventional common law rules. That gives the verdict limited precedential power for future cases. Piracy is still a widespread phenomenon. According to estimates of the International Federation of the Phonographic Industry (IFPI), there were three million users and 500 million files available for copying on P2P services worldwide in May 2002 (IFPI, 2002). Content industries are expected to continue putting pressure on ISPs and implementing more aggressive technological protection. On the part of Congress and courts, five years under

DMCA has created a deep division between the content and technology industries, and the struggle shows no sign of abating.

Finally, there is the often overlooked area of the protection of databases. Huge investment is needed to compile a sophisticated database, and its commercial value is often much higher than that of the unorganized sum of individual data it contains. However, because less "creativity" is involved in the compilation process, copyright protection for databases has been weak. The Berne Convention does not rule out the protection of databases, though it fails to provide support in clear language. Such support was first explicitly included in the TRIPS Agreement in 1994 and then recognized in the WCT in 1996. However, internationally agreed upon protection is still thin, and does not extend to non-original databases.

The European Union took the lead in regional legislation on offering database protection. The Directive of March 11, 1996 on the legal protection of databases requires member states to provide *sui generis* protection for databases. No similar legislation has been adopted in the U.S., due to constitutionality concerns and different legal doctrines. In the landmark case of *Feist Publications v. Rural Telephone Service Co.* in 1991, the U.S. Supreme Court decided that the sole basis of protection under U.S. copyright law was creative originality, which databases did not have as much as traditional copyrightable materials did. New proposals on copyright protection on databases are being developed in WIPO, the U.S. Congress, and other national legislatures.

Trademark and Other Rights in Distinctive Signs

A trademark is a distinctive sign identifying a specific person or enterprise as the producer or provider of certain goods or services. A trademark owner enjoys the exclusive right to use or authorize others to use (usually at a price) the identifier, and that right is often of indefinite duration.

Trademarks have been important to businesses to distinguish themselves from competitors. Like copyright, trademark rights have significantly migrated to the Internet, where they have become even more important, because online consumers, for instance, tend to have loyalty to a certain brand name. Today, most successful private and public entities, even those in traditional industries that don't involve online transactions, take "Internet presence" a must, often by running Web sites using domain names identical to their established trademarks in the physical world, such as Cocacola.com and GE.com. For many IT companies (once known as dotcoms), domain names are themselves famous trademarks, such as *Amazon.com* and *Yahoo.com*.

There have been some common understandings toward trademark protection in the new media, "that the protection of trademarks should extend to the Internet" and "that such protection should neither be less nor more extensive than outside the Internet." However, the global nature of the Internet proves particularly problematic here, as "trademark rights are territorially limited and important characteristics of trademark rights result from their territoriality."

International Treaties

In an attempt to reconcile this contradiction and establish international standards to protect online trademarks, WIPO established the Standing Committee on the Law of Trademarks, Industrial Designs and Geographical Indication (SCT) in July 1998. Based on SCT's studies, WIPO adopted the Joint Recommendation Concerning the Protection of Marks, and Other Industrial Property Rights in Signs, on the Internet in September 2001 and the Joint Recommendation Concerning Provisions on the Protection of Well-Known Marks earlier in September 1999 (commonly referred to as the "Joint Recommendations"). Although without the force of treaties, the Joint Recommendations have been used by member states as guidelines

for coordinated trademark protection concerning several important issues described below.

Important Trademark Issues on the Internet

Jurisdiction and applicable law. The first problem with a trademark dispute on the Internet is often to determine the jurisdiction and the applicable law. Parties in different jurisdictions competing for an identical or similar trademark usually seek the help of local courts to win injunctions in their favor to block the other side from using the sign online. Most of the time, they get what they want. This is why jurisdiction harmonization is critical. The Joint Recommendations do not answer this hard question, leaving it to international private law. They do stipulate, however, that not every single use of a sign on the Internet should be deemed a use taking place in a certain member state, even though it can be shown on a computer screen somewhere in that state. Only the use that has a "commercial effect" in that state should be. Detailed but non-exhaustive factors to determine "commercial effect" have been listed by the Joint Recommendations.

Infringement, acceptable unauthorized use and co-existence of rights. The territoriality of the trademark determines that an infringement claim can be justified only if the alleged abuse is deemed to have occurred in a jurisdiction where the claimant enjoys protection of the disputed trademark. There is no international obligation to protect foreign trademarks. To keep in line with this territoriality principle, simply putting a sign online should not be deemed an infringement in potentially every territory on the earth, because that would give a nationally established trademark automatic international protection. A more restrictive approach has been adopted, requiring a "tangible effect" in a jurisdiction where the sign is protected. However, like the copyright law, exceptions also exist in the trademark law for the "fair use" of a protected trademark, when it is used fairly and in good faith in a purely descriptive or informative manner. Other "fair use" scenarios include non-commercial use, comments quotes and so on.

A similar but different scenario is the use of an identical or confusingly similar sign in different jurisdictions by different and unrelated users. To achieve a "fair balance of interest" between right contenders without complicating too many business transactions on the Internet, the Joint Recommendations set up a two-step, "notice and avoidance of conflict" procedure. First, sign users in good faith are exempt from liability up to the point when they are notified by a foreign claimant about a conflicting right. Second, having received the notification, they have to take reasonable measures to avoid or end the conflict.

Extraterritorial effect of injunctions. Again, due to the territoriality of trademarks, an Internet-wide injunction is usually not an appropriate answer to infringement because its effect would extend far beyond the territory where the conflict of interest occurs. A "proportionate" remedy would be an injunction limited to preventing or removing the "commercial effect" the infringement exerts on the said territory.

Forms of trademark infringement online. Trademark infringement on the Internet takes on multifaceted, new and changing forms, including but not limited to abusive use of meta tags, unauthorized sale of key words, pop-up advertisements, deep linking and framing. However, the greatest controversies have involved domain names and other Internet identifiers.

The practice of registering famous names as domain names in bad faith, also known as cybersquatting, was particularly exuberant during the .com boom of late 1990s when a eye-catching domain name promised unlimited value. As a result, many domain names were registered by people having no or only peripheral connections to people or companies the names pointed to, and many disputes and lawsuits ensued. As mentioned earlier, after a period of temporary disorder, all such disputes were covered under the Uniform Dispute Resolution Policy (UDRP), a standardized dispute resolution scheme set up by ICANN.

Patents

A patent is a temporary monopoly granted for an invention, that is, a new product or process to do something new or do something in a new way. For a limited period of time, usually 20 years, the patent owner enjoys exclusive rights to the commercial exploitation of the invention. After expiration, the invention enters the public domain. The purpose of the whole system of patent protection is to encourage innovation by offering inventors both recognition and material reward for their creativity.

The patent system, unlike copyrights and trademarks, affects the Internet in a rather indirect way. Currently based on the Paris Convention, the TRIPS Agreement and regional and national legislations, patent protection is critical for the Internet as it maintains the order and legal relevance of the underlying Internet technical infrastructure. The Internet is still growing fast. Possibilities are wide open for new applications that can be performed online to be developed. Essentially, e-commerce is infiltrating into more traditional industries and more geographical areas. All these developments result in an urgent need for more and better computer hardware and software. Sound patent protection serves as both an incentive to the need for innovation and guarantee of the need for stability of existing technologies in use.

However, also because the background is so new and changing so fast, many legal controversies, like the patentability of "business methods" online, are yet to reach resolution. The United States Patent and Trademark Office (USPTO) is working closely with the Japan Patent Office

(JPO) and the European Patent Office (EPO) on this issue.

The peculiarities of the Internet in turn seriously complicate patent-related legal issues with respect to "prior art." It's much more difficult to probe the authenticity, veracity and integrity of a single piece of online prior art as it's much easier to forge online. Also, due to the instantaneity and universality of the Internet, it's equally difficult to determine the timing and location of the disclosure of prior art.

WIPO established a Standing Committee on the Law of Patents (SCP) to work on harmonizing patent laws around the world, with a particular emphasis on the definition of prior art. As an initial success, the Patent Law Treaty (PLT) was adopted in June 2000, starting to provide some general rules internationally. More substantive harmonization work is still underway.

CONCLUSION

Establishing a workable definition of Internet Governance, based on the duality of "Root Governance" and "Content Governance," is a difficult proposition. Erecting a conceptual framework and fleshing it out with current developments in theory and practice is made difficult by the peculiarly contentious nature of the subject. Governing the Internet can have long term strategic values to national governments over and above obvious commercial gains. This has caused a great deal of acrimony and tension over a technology whose origins, ironically, were marked by openness and cooperation.

At its core, the transfer of data packets on the Internet remains a set of simple processes. The technology was originally designed to be unselective with regard to content; were it not so, it is doubtful whether it could have expanded the way it has since its inception, much less been able to support the huge number of applications it now does. The engineer's emphasis on simplicity

rather than the bureaucrat's obsession with order and control lay at the heart of the Internet's architecture, and that basic structure has proved to be both scalable and adaptable beyond anything its creators could have possibly imagined.

This happy state of affairs could not have lasted forever. Interestingly, a move away from the status quo may be driven by fundamental changes in the architecture of the Net itself. One of the main strengths of the present system is also one of its greatest weaknesses, namely its inability to differentiate between the contents of data packets. Useless, disruptive or even malicious packets are channeled through with the same speed as useful ones. In addition, the variety of networked devices has already gone well beyond computers or even hand-held devices. To tackle these and other technological issues, research is currently underway to better channel the flow of information. In essence, the next generation architecture may be much more controlled than the present unrestricted model. But a move away from self-governing simplicity to managed complexity inevitably raises the question of who would be in charge of the management.

However, the biggest question regarding Internet Governance is probably not going to be technological, but continue to be political. Traditionally, the U.S. has taken a remarkably hands-off approach regarding the Internet, which is hardly imaginable from any European or Asian country. On the other hand, the rest of the world has a perfectly reasonable case in raising a concern about the current governance structure. Even at the hardware level, a disproportionate number of the root servers are physically located on U.S. soil; most, if not all, are administered by the U.S. or its allies, and none of the rising powers such as China and India have even a single one under ther control.

If the continuation of the present system is doubtful, the case for the oft-suggested alternative model, namely an international bureaucracy under the UN, is even more dubious. The recent

WSIS summit in Tunis forcefully drove home the inadequacy and incoherence of any collective geo-political governing framework. The net outcome of the much hyped summit was two documents which were more wish-lists than any concrete technological or managerial plans. The heavy pre-summit rhetoric of wresting control of the Internet did not translate into any change from the current, U.S.-supervised structure of root governance.

This was hardly surprising. As pointed out in this chapter, although the expansion of the Internet has shifted the root governance from the immediate control of a small cadre of U.S.-based technologists to a much wider set of real-world interests and national governments, there is as yet no realistic pressure on the U.S. government to relinquish its residual rights. In fact, due to the peculiar requisites of root governance – fast response, highly complex technical demands, commitment to freedom and openness—there is a strong argument for the U.S. to continue its role as the guardian of the Internet.

REFERENCES

Almquist, P. (2002). *Type of service in the Internet protocol suite*, RFC 1349. Retrieved March 19, 2006 from, ftp://ftp.rfc-editor.org/in-notes/rfc1349.txt

CIPR (2002). *Integrating intellectual property rights and development policy.* Commission on Intellectual Property Rights. Retrieved March 21, 2006 from, http://www.iprcommission.org/papers/pdfs/final_report/CIPRfullfinal.pdf-Falstrom, P., Hoffman, P., & Costello, A. (2003). *Internationalizing domain names in applications (IDNA)*, RFC 3490. Retrieved March 19, 2006 from, ftp://ftp.rfc-editor.org/in-notes/rfc3490.txtICANN (2005). Internet corporation for assigned names and numbers. *Comments on the report of the working group on Internet governance*, p. 4.

Retrieved October 1, 2005 from, http://www.icann.org/announcements/ICANN-WGIG-report-comments-15aug05.pdf

IFPI (2002). *IFPI music piracy report: June 2002.* International Federation of Phonographic Industry.Retrieved March 21, 2006 from, http://www.fimi.it/documenti/piracy%20report%202002.pdf

Lynn, Stuart (2002). *ICANN—The case for reform.* President's Report, February 24. Retrieved March 21, 2006 from, http://www.icann.org/general/lynn-reform-proposal-24feb02.htm. Mueller, Milton L. (2002). *Ruling the root: Internet governance and the taming of cyberspace.* Cambridge, MA: The MIT press.

NTIA (1998a). *A proposal to improve technical management of Internet names and addresses.* National Telecommunications and Information Administration, US Department of Commerce. Discussion Draft 1/30/98. Retrieved March 19, 2006 from, http://www.ntia.doc.gov/ntiahome/domainname/dnsdrft.htm

NTIA (1998b). *Management of Internet names and addresses.* National Telecommunications and Information Administration, US Department of Commerce. Retrieved March 19, 2006 from, http://www.ntia.doc.gov/ntiahome/domainname/6_5_98dns.htm

Postel, Jon. (1981). *Internet protocol*, RFC 791. Retrieved March 19, 2006 from, ftp://ftp.rfc-editor.org/in-notes/rfc791.txt

Samuelson, Pamela. (2004). Intellectual property arbitrage: How foreign rules can affect domestic protections. *University of Chicago Law Review.* Vol. 71, No.1, pp.223-239. Retrieved March 21, 2006 from, http://www.law.berkeley.edu/faculty/profiles/facultyPubsPDF.php?facID=346&pubID=128.

Siwek, Stephen E. (2002). *Copyright industries in the U.S. economy: The 2002 report.* Economists

Incorporated. Prepared for International Intellectual Property Alliance. Retrieved March 21, 2006 from, http://www.iipa.com/pdf/2002_SIWEK_FULL.pdf

WGIG (2005a). Working group on Internet governance. *Report of the working group on Internet governance*, p.4. Retrieved October 1, 2005 from, http://www.wgig.org/docs/WGIGREPORT.pdf.

WGIG (2005b). Working group on Internet governance. *Report from the working group on Internet governance*, Document WSIS-II/PC-3/DOC/5-E. Retrieved March 10, 2006 from, http://www.itu.int/wsis/docs2/pc3/off5.pdf

WSIS (2003). *Declaration of principles*. World summit on the information society. Document WSIS-03/GENEVA/DOC/4-E, pp. 1-2. Retrieved October 1, 2005 from,http://www.itu.int/dms_pub/itu-s/md/03/wsis/doc/S03-WSIS-DOC-0004!!PDF-E.pdf

Chapter X
European Regulatory Challenges for Developing Digital Content Services in Modern Electronic Communications Platforms

Ioannis P. Chochliouros
Hellenic Telecommunications Organization S.A. (OTE), Greece and
University of Peloponnese, Greece

Stergios P. Chochliouros
Independent Consultant, Researcher, Expert in European Policies, Greece

Anastasia S. Spiliopoulou
Hellenic Telecommunications Organization S.A. (OTE), Greece

Tilemachos D. Doukoglou
Hellenic Telecommunications Organization S.A. (OTE), Greece

ABSTRACT

The European Union (EU) has recently applied a more proactive and consistent regulatory approach in the wider electronic (mainly Internet-based) communications areas, also including a variety of modern broadcasting activities, aiming to promote their strategic and commercial importance. New requirements imposed by the converged information society technologies are currently demanding high-performance access and high-quality facilities (or services) for the benefits of all market actors involved (both for operators-providers and consumers). More specifically, the continuous expansion of the Internet creates considerable potential for growth, in terms of market and business activities. The latter, however, indicate that different and adequate forms of "content" should be legally available for use, treatment, storage and distribution in various technological platforms, operated from the private and the public sectors. The proposed chapter deals with the major European regulatory challenges for the development and the effective provision either of audio-visual or of other forms of digital content services, in parallel with other important issues (intellectual property rights and copyright, digital rights management, privacy issues, consumers' interests, e-commerce, etc.). Content is a crucial factor in the digital economy, and plays a key role both economically and socially.

INTRODUCTION: ACCESS ISSUES TO MODERN INFRASTRUCTURES AND AVAILABILITY OF CONTENT

Quite apart from the multiple effects generated by convergence in its role as an "enabler" of the Information Society (European Commission, 1997), there is likely to be a direct and positive impact on technical development, market growth and social cohesion. Expansion of the market and the continuous demand for "innovative" forms of content and related services generate new needs for people (including all potential "actors"). In particular, as content providers and network or service operators "re-orient" themselves in the new market reality, they combine their use of standardised and already deployed digital platforms (such as the Internet) with software skills to develop customized applications aimed both at business (corporate) clients and residential customers.

The major task is to take full advantage of technological convergence by integrating the diverse components of telecommunications, media and IT sectors to produce innovative services. In addition to technical and economic aspects, social, cultural and political aspects are also of great importance for further evolution and development. More specifically, knowledge and innovation through the dispersion of "converged" content-oriented facilities should be expected to act the proper "engines" to promote growth and development, especially towards building a fully inclusive information society, based on the widespread use of Information and Communication Technologies (ICT) in public services, enterprises and households. In fact, ICT are a powerful driver of the modern digital economy: A quarter of the European Union's (EU) gross domestic product (GDP) growth and 40% of productivity growth are due to ICT. Differences in economic performances between industrialised countries are largely explained by the level of ICT investment, research and use, and by the competitiveness of information society and media industries (European Commission, 2003b). Consequently, ICT services, skills, media and content are, without doubt, a growing part of the economy and society.

The matter of access in modern platforms-networks-infrastructures is mainly an issue for commercial negotiation/agreement between market "players," dependent on the overall safeguards provided by the general EU competition rules. However, there is currently a "sort of asymmetry" in that access rules apply only for certain categories of networks (e.g., the interconnection and "open network provision" (ONP) rules which traditionally apply to telecommunications networks), but not to infrastructures used for broadcasting activities. (Correspondingly, a frame exists for conditional access systems for digital television, but not for all sorts of digital services.) As for access issues correlated to content, ordinary commercial principles apply, tempered only by related competition rules. One exception to this option is the "management" of certain "premium" content in the EU Member States, such as national sporting events where the revision to the "Television without Frontiers" ("TVWF") Directive has considered the mutual recognition across the European Community of events reserved by Member States for free-to-air television broadcasting (Council of the European Union, 1989).

If market and technology trends continue to expand, there is likely to be a "shift" in the market value chain, such that content production, packaging and relevant service provision rise in value (though not necessarily as distinct business activities), whilst delivering services over a network may, as reflected in some merger activity, become a comparatively low-value activity. This trend can be accompanied by attempts on the part of today's network operators to extend their activities into higher value business areas (such as the satellite).

Recently, many ICT developments have gained pace to arrive at the threshold of massive growth in information society and media, made possible by widespread fast communications, connecting a multiplicity of systems, platforms and devices as well (Chochliouros & Spiliopoulou-Chochliourou, 2003b). Traditional content (such as films, video and music) is now available in many digital formats, and new services that are "born digital," such as interactive software, are both emerging and covering, gradually, sectors of the market. Thus, the digital convergence of information society and media services, networks and devices is finally becoming an everyday reality: ICT will become smarter, smaller, safer, faster, always connected and easier to use, with content moving to three-dimensional multimedia formats.

CONDITIONAL ACCESS SYSTEMS AND ACCESS TO CONTENT: TRENDS AND OPPORTUNITIES

Conditional access (CA) systems are the technical means by which content and service providers can recoup their investment either through subscriptions or charges for individual consumption. CA

formulates an interesting example as it shows the distinction between interoperability and access (Chochliouros & Spiliopoulou-Chochliourou, 2003c). The Television Standards Directive builds a regulatory framework for conditional access to digital television services, based on a proper requirement for legal persons operating corresponding systems to offer broadcasters technical services on a fair, reasonable and non-discriminatory basis (European Parliament and Council of the European Union, 1995).

As a general guiding principle, "practices" applied between network operators, content providers and right owners are a matter for commercial agreement. If exclusively is granted, this may be an issue for competition rules. Exclusive arrangements between content providers and content carriers may limit consumer choice by excluding access to content provided by competitors, especially until there is effective competition in the provision of "delivery channels" to the user (Neale, Green & Landovskis, 2001). Broadcasters wanting to offer pay services over a particular platform need to negotiate access to the relevant facilities on fair and transparent terms, in the context of fully liberalised market. Possession of rights to key-content, such as major sporting events, may give market players particular commercial power.

Although the content industry is profoundly scale-dependent, it generally makes use of these specific economies of scale by cautious management of distribution windows (e.g., cinema, video rental, video sell-through, pay-per-view, pay television and free-to-air television). Exclusivity of distribution is often a feature that secures this process for the content owners. Expansion in the means of delivery brought on by improvements in technology may shift any existing bottleneck and/or limitations from delivery to content; this however may lead to a shortage of adequate content in the medium term. Premium content is already a key-factor for success in both digital and analogue television markets. Continued shortages could inhibit new market entry, and with it, competition and innovation.

THE ROLE OF PUBLIC SERVICE BROADCASTING AND DISTRIBUTION OF CONTENT

The public service mission entrusted to public service broadcasters is recognised as one of cultural importance and the organizations with responsibilities in this regard are entitled to appropriate funding, subject to compatibility with the rules of the Treaty establishing the European Community (the "Treaty"). Market development may however enable many more sources of audiovisual information to be accessed by viewers (Norcontel Ltd., 1997). Public Authorities will need to monitor, on a continuing basis, the extent to which desired policy objectives are being achieved by normal market activity, including the impact of other media, and whether, *as a consequence*, regulatory obligations placed on broadcasters may be lightened. Traditional public broadcasters will need to reappraise their role in the wider information society environment (Ofcom, 2004).

On the one hand, their market share is likely to diminish, as users face an increasing choice in a market already near to saturation in terms of the individual potential for consumption of audio-visual services within a 24-hour day (UK's Consumers' Association, 2001). Moreover, escalating prices for premium content could subject them to budgetary pressures that might outstrip the capabilities of existing funding mechanisms. The issue will be whether these broadcasters can continue to have access to attractive content in the face of fierce competition for the acquisition of program rights within the constraints of their financial support mechanisms. Many are preparing to exploit their reputation and their customers' "brand loyalty" to compete with new pay-television broadcasters. On the other hand, technological development offers public broadcasters a range

of new possibilites, in terms of activities and potential avenues to viewers and listeners (Reimers, 2000). This option can enhance their current role and provide valuable new sources of revenue alongside current funding. The new European regulatory framework should allow broadcasters to take advantage of these new opportunities (Chochliouros & Spiliopoulou-Chochliourou, 2003c). It should also permit them to benefit from economies of scale and scope where these also bring benefits for the consumer. However, if state funds intended to support a public broadcaster in fulfilling its public service mission were used to leverage and cross-subsidize these new activities (or even the use of new technological platforms such as the Internet), then such practices would be subject to the Treaty rules on competition and on the freedom to provide services.

GENERAL POLICY MEASURES FOR CONTENT REGULATION IN THE EUROPEAN UNION

CHALLENGES AND OPPORTUNITIES

The EU has both identified and promoted challenges and opportunities of the digital era, which all demonstrated the necessity for changes and reformation to make the audiovisual sector practically competitive at international level by means of complementary European, national and local policies.

Within the context of the Convergence Green Paper (European Commission, 1997), it has been recognised that the function of the European regulation was the confirmation of the progressing need to fulfil a series of public interest objectives (such as the protection of minors and human dignity, cultural and linguistic diversity and pluralism) whilst promoting investment, especially for modern audiovisual services and enhanced electronic communications applications. The above initiative has practically investigated the potential regulatory "interfaces" between the traditionally existing transmission policies and the wider content regulation. The transmission aspect has led to the *"1999 Review"* of the Telecommunications Regulatory Package (European Commission, 1999), which was the initiative for the promotion of the new 2002 Electronic Communications Regulatory Framework (European Parliament and Council of the European Union, 2002c).

The European Commission has forwarded several basic principles and guidelines for the EU's audiovisual policy in the digital age (European Commission, 2002b). In particular, it has identified the major significance of European content and, as a consequence, the need to uphold and promote appropriate support measures, while bearing in mind the need to promote complementarity and synergy between national and Community measures as well as the need to safeguard cultural diversity; at the same time, suitable initiatives have been strengthened to identify measures to enhance the competitiveness of the European content industry in the digital age while, *among others*, promoting synergy between the relevant Community instruments (Directorate General Information Society of the European Commission, 2002). A core issue focuses upon the fact that more practical policies are needed to respond to the fundamental changes, especially in technology. Therefore, digital convergence requires policy convergence and a willingness to adapt regulatory frameworks where needed, so that they should be consistent with the emerging digital economy at global levels.

The Double-natured Character of the EU Audiovisual Sector

In the EU, the audiovisual sector is characterised from the cultural viewpoint by diversity, and from the economic viewpoint by the fragmentation of the internal market. That is, the audiovisual sector

essentially has a cultural dimension (DigiCULT Project, 2002) and constitutes not only an expression of creativity, particularly of identities, and a fundamental means of promoting democracy, but also an economic activity of growing importance. It becomes evident that the relevant content aspects are strongly related both to competition policy and the industrial activity. The contribution of broadcasting activities to the promotion of the wider information society sector is quite significant (European Commission, 2002b). It also plays an active role in the development of modern electronic communications services, which afford all citizens easier access to innovative applications and relevant facilities.

The Common EU Principles

The fundamental activity of EU in Information Society sector is aimed to ensure that *"Europe continues to play a leading role in shaping and participating in the global knowledge and information based economy"*. To this aim, the European policies have very early identified (European Commission, 2001a) distinct measures and suitably oriented initiatives for areas of prime importance such as: (a) The development of a modern regulatory and legal framework (especially regarding infrastructures and services); (b) the protection of Intellectual Property Rights (IPR) and of privacy; (c) the support of applied policies and business initiatives to accelerate growth and use of networks, basic services/applications and content, and; (d) the support of the information society.

The essential principles affecting the expansion of the applicability of the most recent European regulatory initiatives (European Parliament and Council of the European Union, 2002c) were: (a) The effective separation of regulatory approaches for transmission and content; (b) the support of competition aspects for transmission infrastructure and services; (c) the "designation" of public interest objectives for the distribution and/or delivery of various converged forms of content; (d) the endorsement of regulatory measures only when and where is necessary—*according to the principle of proportionality amongst market players*—and to roll-back regulation once competition becomes effective in the market; (e) specific enforcement of the perspectives for self-regulation and/or co-regulation (Shoniregun, et al., 2004), particularly for content-related issues; (f) appliance of the principle of proportionality and assurance of legal certainty conditions for market players and investors, and; (g) the promotion of "technological neutrality" options, to ensure interoperability of services/infrastructure and to guarantee converged user choices.

The European Commission dynamically recommended the separation of infrastructure and content regulation. This implied, with regard to infrastructure regulation, the need to safeguard the access of the public to a wide variety of media content (Open Network Provision (ONP) Committee, 2002). Such separation implicates, with regard to content regulation:

- Considering the particular characteristics of the audiovisual sector (especially through a vertical and sectoral approach where necessary) and building on current regulatory structures with the public policy objectives.
- Establishment of a "fitting" regulatory regime for new appearing services, *after due consultation and market feedback*, recognizing the variableness of the marketplace and the requirement for significant initial investments while, at the same time, ensuring options like the protection of minors, consumer safeguards and other important public interests.
- Self-regulation can complement regulation and support the realization of the right balance between facilitating the development of

open and competitive markets and securing public interest objectives.

More specifically, the European Commission proposes a new strategic framework (i.e., the so-called "i2010—European Information Society 2010" initiative), laying out broad policy orientations (European Commission, 2005b). This promotes an "open and competitive digital economy" and emphasises various communications platforms as a "driver" of inclusion and quality of life. A key-element of this initiative will build towards an integrated approach to information society and audio-visual media policies in the EU.

THE MODERN EUROPEAN REGULATORY APPROACH FOR CONVERGED ELECTRONIC COMMUNICATIONS

The new European electronic communications regulation introduces a common, horizontal regulatory framework covering all networks (Ovum, 2001; Chochliouros & Spiliopoulou-Chochliourou, 2003c). As convergence is now a reality, a "horizontal" approach is crucial for a level playing field between all possible infrastructures and platforms. Competition between networks is a pre-condition if the EU is to realize the convergence's objectives (European Commission, 2001a), i.e., *"to become the world's most dynamic and competitive knowledge-based economy,"* and so to allow citizens to share the opportunities offered by the new electronic media.

Consequently, market actors can have gains from a broader selection among networks and terminals. Broadband networks are already dispersed in the EU (Chochliouros & Spiliopoulou-Chochliourou, 2003b). Such an option proposes a proper "return path" for interactive television and can allow television distribution next to traditional mechanisms (like satellite and terrestrial) offering remarkable flexibility for distributing Internet-based and multimedia services (Neale, Green, & Landovskis, 2001). To this scope, interactive television has a large market potential. Nevertheless, as there is no specific initiative to impose Internet on TV, regulation and promotional policies are separate. Some of the most exciting potential lies in delivering appropriately designed information-society services. However, the longer-term interest of market players lies in operating in a competitive network sector. The recent regulatory framework considers the links between transmission and content regulation. These links mainly emphasize on the following distinct sectors: authorisation of networks and services; allocation and assignment of radio spectrum (Chochliouros & Spiliopoulou-Chochliourou, 2003a); must-carry; access to networks and associated facilities, including access to application program interfaces (APIs) and electronic program guides (EPGs) for interactive digital television.

The latest "Framework" Directive (European Parliament and Council of the European Union, 2002c) supports the establishment of a harmonized regulatory framework across the EU. Actually, it responds to the convergence phenomenon by covering all electronic communications networks and services within its thematic scope. The Directive introduces a wider perception of the *"network notion"* as *"any system of sending signals"* while a service can be considered, generally, as any form of *"transmission and routing of signals."* In any case, considering the technological complexities, the Directive excludes services providing or exercising editorial control over content. Regulation of content broadcast over electronic communications networks (e.g., radio and television programs or TV bouquets) remains outside the scope of the framework, which is without prejudice to EU or national broadcast content regulation, adopted in conformity with the European law.

The latest "Authorization" Directive (European Parliament and Council of the European Union, 2002b) defines the new system for licensing and frequency assignment. The measure supports the full replacement of previously existing (telecommunications) licenses by more flexible "general authorizations" for transmission. In such a context, single licenses for transmission and content provision will no longer be possible. EU Member States still have the right to require certain content to be transmitted on certain frequencies, but transmission service has to be assigned according to open and fully transparent procedures. Any relevant "player" can exploit broadcast networks and provide transmission services without prior (strict) regulatory approval. This facilitates market entry and, hence, benefits network users and broadcasters.

As for the so-called "must-carry" obligation (European Parliament and Council of the European Union, 2002d), networks may be subject to relevant rules to realize public interest objectives. The reasons invoked are normally the widespread accessibility of certain radio and television programs and the requirement to assure a pluralistic offer to the public. Must-carry rules usually benefit broadcasters (public and private) with a public service remit. Occasionally, such prerequisites may constitute a "strict" obligation, especially for some network operators, content providers or both. Proportionate and transparent "must-carry" commitments can become effective for the transmission of specified radio and television broadcast channels and services, where the latter are necessary to perform general interest objectives.

Finally, the recent "Access Directive" (European Parliament and Council of the European Union, 2002a) defines instruments for the deployment of competitive and non-discriminatory access maintained for CA systems (European Parliament and Council of the European Union, 1995). Primarily, it establishes a specific set of conditions for access to digital television and radio services broadcast to viewers and listeners. In particular, the Directive examines the possibility to extend access conditions to APIs and EPGs, if necessary, for the promotion of content-based facilities.

THE MODERN APPROACH FOR CONTENT REGULATION

The major objectives for the new European content regulation intend to satisfy: (a) the freedom of expression and pluralism; (b) the cultural and linguistic diversity in the EU, in the scope of social inclusion; (c) the protection of minors and of public order; and (d) consumer protection issues.

Freedom of Expression and Pluralism

European policies recognize that content, services and applications are "vital" factors to make citizens improve their living standards. In particular, the basic relevant provisions of the Treaty about pluralism have to be estimated as "critical" guidelines for any future development, to avoid any potential restriction, while promoting the need for diligent and conforming application of competition law. It should be noted that the new regulatory regime is a more "liberal" one, maintaining choice to provide both television and electronic content services. It is important to ensure the avoidance of any acts which may prove harmful to the "freedom of movement and trade" in TV programs or which may support the creation of "abuse dominant positions" in the marketplace, leading to probable restrictions on pluralism and freedom of televised information and of the information sector as a whole.

Cultural and Linguistic Diversity

The EU has recognized that cultural policy objectives constitute public interest objectives that a Member State may legitimately pursue, especially in the scope of public service broadcasting (that has historically been a "means" for achieving

this priority). A number of European announcements (Council of the European Union, 1999) have highlighted the fact that the system of public broadcasting is directly related to the democratic, social and cultural needs of each society and to the need to preserve media pluralism. Public access to various channels and services, without discriminations and on the basis of equivalent opportunities, is a necessary precondition for offering citizens the benefits of the new audiovisual and information services (DigiCULT Project, 2002). In particular, Article 128 of the Treaty provides that the European Community *"shall contribute to the flowering of the cultures of the Member States"* including in the audiovisual and information sector, and that it shall also *"take cultural aspects into account in its action under other provisions of the Treaty."* Thus, the competence of broadcasting to offer quality programming (and services) to the public has to be preserved and enhanced. The new regulatory perspectives aim to minimise existing access restrictions and to offer a more extended variety of sources to the end-users. The market has to be developed freely, without affecting any trading conditions and/or options for competition; however, backing mechanisms have to be ready and available for use, whenever any market failure takes place.

Protection of Minors and Public Order

Public interest objectives relating to the protection of minors and public order have traditionally been recognized at national and Community levels (Council of the European Union, 1989). However, the transactional nature of some convergent services implies various modifications in the underlying means whereby such objectives are met, to ensure due respect for the principle of proportionality. Additionally, the complexity of imposing safeguards in the context of harmful, illegal and undesirable content and conduct on the Internet, PC, TV-set or home-cinema provides one more example of how market and technical development is challenging traditional regulatory approaches to implementation, while not invalidating the principle that rules are seeking to protect. New challenges appear both in quantitative terms (more "illegal" content) and qualitative terms (new platforms and new products). As the processing power and the storage capacity of information systems increase with fast rates, the requirement for enhanced safety becomes more and more important, especially due to the possibility of distributing content via emerging broadband solutions (such as video on 3G-mobile handsets). The overall characteristic and the complexity of exercising control within a given European State are currently leading to solutions that promote self-regulatory practices (Shoniregun, et al., 2004) by the industry sector rather than on formal regulation, in parallel with appropriate technological solutions (e.g., for parental guidance). It is against this background that recent measures (European Parliament and Council of the European Union, 2004) intend to support common guidelines for the applicability of a relevant framework in audiovisual and information services, whatever the means of conveyance, through a coherent cross-media approach.

Consumer Protection Issues

Consumer protection was always among the fundamental European policy targets (European Commission, 2001b). The basic approach aimed to make applicable compulsory requirements for the adequate protection of consumers, the impartiality of commercial transactions and the strengthening of competition. The launch of modern services has to consider the demand and the consumer viewpoints. An important issue in the process of the take-up of services is the penetration of PCs in the home, and particularly for the support of multimedia and Internet. Aware of the changing patterns of consumption, the television and computing industries are fighting for viewers'

attention. Broadcasters and TV-manufacturers are continuously enhancing the interactive capabilities of their services and equipment. Currently offered digital television set-top boxes (STBs) can combine television and telecommunication functionality in a very effective manner. TV-sets can already double as monitors, especially when connected to low cost Internet facilities/appliances. Many in the consumer electronics industry predict that TV-sets with built-in PC capability, including Internet access, will become an imperative element of the consumer market in the near future.

The multi-channel broadcast environment itself competes with packaged media (such as those played on video recorders and video-game consoles) and with computers and other informative online systems offering Internet access. It is expected that the consumer's "home platform" should be very rapidly evolved (European Telecommunications Standards Institute, 2003) over the next few years, especially via a sustainable commercial launch of innovative technical (Internet-based) solutions. Yet at the same time and in parallel, consumer demands and needs for enhanced access to information will consider convergence of the relevant electronic communications and media products (and services) that serve various public interest domains (such as education, health, environment and transport). Interactive digital television brings benefits and promotes interoperability options in a broader context at various levels (Chochliouros, et al., 2006), especially by adding other layers beyond the simple transmission and reception of video (i.e., options for e-Commerce and Internet-based services).

TELEVISION CONTENT DISTRIBUTION IN THE EUROPEAN MARKETS

The TVWF Directive was initially adopted in 1989 and was revised several times to take account of various technological and market developments (Council of the European Union, 1989). Since its inception, it influences the gradual development and builds the legal "framework of basis" for the free movement of television broadcasting services. It intends to promote the growth of a European market in broadcasting (and related activities), such as television advertising and the production of audiovisual programs. To this end, it provides for the European Community coordination of national legislation in the following areas, all dealing with fundamental issues:

Law Applicable to Television Broadcasts

The Directive provides a definition of *"what constitutes a broadcaster"* and defines which Member State's jurisdiction television broadcasters' fall; this is determined, mainly, by where their central administration is situated and where management decisions concerning programming are taken.

Support of the Production and Distribution of European Works in the Audiovisual Sector

This can include promotion of cinema and TV program works, via suitable methods and schemes, so that to explain possible aspects under which state aid to support audiovisual production may be compatible with the European Treaty, in parallel with full competition criteria originating from the liberalised market (Council of the European Union, 2000).

Access of Citizens to "Major" Events (Particularly Sport Events)

This constitutes a very critical issue and should be evaluated very carefully, especially within the framework of special business activities. States may each draw up a list of events, which must be broadcast unencrypted even if pay-television

stations have bought exclusive rights. The corresponding events may be national or international (such as the Olympic Games, the World Cup or the European Football Championship). The objective is to avoid danger of social exclusion or "digital divide" for people, via the availability of events of "major" importance on free television.

Television Advertising and Sponsorship

As digital technology create a series of multiple advertising and marketing techniques, the target is to continue to protect the interests of television viewers, in parallel with the prime "integrity value" of audiovisual works and their editorial independence. The Directive establishes terms and conditions for proper advertising, sponsorship and teleshopping.

Freedom of Reception and Retransmission

The European Member States have to certify the freedom of reception and they must not restrict the retransmission, on their territories, of television broadcasts from other Member States. This statement has the value of a general obligatory rule.

Protection of Minors and Public Order

The great dispersion of (digital) content necessitates measures for the protection of citizens (especially for the minors, as already discussed). To this aim, the Directive supports codes of conduct and self-regulatory measures, for greater flexibility and adaptability in the market.

Right of Reply

The right of reply has to be applicable to all possible media. The law applicable or corresponding measures shall be the law of the country in which the broadcaster is established.

Although technological and/or market-business evolution may necessitate revisions to its provisions, the Directive still remains an effective "means" for point-to-multipoint communication and it is well-adapted to the current market needs while, *simultaneously*, it is widely adopted in the EU. It remains an active tool, which serves both the interest of the European audiovisual sector and cultural diversity. The European Authorities periodically re-examine the Directive (European Commission, 2002b), in order to assess its impact on market development and evolution (particularly under the framework of the competitiveness of the European program industry). The basic philosophy aim is: (a) to make sure the free movement of television broadcasting services continues on the basis of the "country-of-origin" principle; (b) to encourage cultural and linguistic diversity, and; (c) to reinforce the central role of television broadcasting in the democratic, social and cultural life of society. In May 2002, the relevant authorities decided that the Directive should undergo an in-depth review, and this was followed in 2003 by series of discussion papers and public hearings (Directorate General Information Society of the European Commission, 2002). In response to the consultation process, the European Commission announced several policies on the subject, and has proposed a "two-step" approach to reviewing the overall context. In the short term, it will provide more clarity on the application of the Directive to new advertising techniques and an update of its definitions. In the medium term, while noting that no information society service had reached the importance and impact of television broadcasting services, the European Commission nevertheless considered that a thorough revision of the entire text might be necessary to include technological developments and changes in the audiovisual market. The key question in such an effort is whether the provisions should be extended to cover new audiovisual services. To provide a better basis for assessing this issue, several studies have been performed (Ofcom, 2004), concerning the impact of controls on advertising and measures to promote European TV production, and the application of co-regulatory measures (Shoniregun, et al., 2004).

ENSURING PRIVACY AND DATA PROTECTION

An essential precondition for the immediate growth and dispersion of several digital facilities is based on the assurance and the efficient protection of citizens' privacy, when users are able to access various forms of content. Users want (and require) to have confidence in the security of data circulated over the networks (or the platforms) they use, especially when they manage content (Kaufman, 2002). Modern applications (such as video-on-demand and interactive television facilities) can have a successful penetration in the international market(s), together with other "converged" services, if users are strongly convinced that their privacy is secure. The continuous deployment of publicly available electronic communications services over a variety of Internet-based facilities, creates significant market potential and opens new possibilities for users. However, despite the many and obvious benefits, it has also brought with it the worrying threat of intentional attacks against information systems and network platforms/infrastructures. As cyberspace gets more and more complex and its components more sophisticated, especially due to the fast development and evolution of Internet-based platforms (Crandall & Jackson, 2001), new and unforeseen vulnerabilities may emerge. This implies new challenges for personal data and privacy.

In the case of public telecommunications networks, specific legislation has been gradually promoted (European Parliament and Council of the European Union, 2002e) to "defend" fundamental rights of all (legal and natural) persons concerned, so that personal information should only be collected legitimately and for specific purposes; in particular, it may only be used in a manner compatible with the purpose of the collection. Personal data are to be *"adequate, relevant and not excessive in relation to the purposes for which they are collected and/or further processed."* In addition, the recent European framework has supported the "creation" of special protection requirements for "sensitive" data, implying the establishment of greater examination and protection for certain types of information (like those dealing with health or political beliefs). Yet, the creation of special protection is also understood as requiring attention not only to whether information identifies particular aspects of a person's life that are sensitive, but how data will actually be used. The ability of information technology to combine (and share) data makes impossible any abstract, non-contextual evaluation of the impact of disclosing a given piece of personal information. The impact of bureaucratic use of personal information, whether merely personal or highly sensitive, depends on the means of processing, the kinds of databases linked together and the ends to which information will be used. The latest e-Privacy Directive (European Parliament and Council of the European Union, 2002e) has become valid to provide an "equal level" of protection of personal data and privacy for all potential users, regardless of the technologies used. It also focuses on challenging issues of important sensitivity, such as the conservation of connection data by Member States for surveillance purposes (i.e., data retention), the sending of unsolicited electronic messages and the inclusion of personal data in public directories. Service providers offering publicly available electronic communications services over the Internet have to inform users of measures they intend to apply to protect security of communications (Sieber, 1998), e.g., by using specific types of software or "proper" encryp-

tion technologies. Measures have to be taken to prevent unauthorised access to communications and to protect confidentiality.

INTELLECTUAL PROPERTY RIGHTS, COPYRIGHT AND RELATED RIGHTS

Intellectual Property Rights

Content providers and platform (or services) operators agree to make content available if their IPR are satisfactorily protected. Correspondingly, these "actors" do invest in modern services if they are convinced that the new platforms of delivering information guarantee a plentiful "level" of protection for the intellectual and industrial effort of their organizations. Inadequate IPR protection is already a serious barrier for *off-line* electronic content, and this could project into the *on-line* world (Arnold, Schmucker, & Wolthusen, 2003). Within this specific framework, the European official concern was that high quality content would indeed only be made available if rights of content providers are adequately protected in the global digital environment (European Parliament and Council of the European Union, 2003a). However, practical problems appear when content becomes available for network use. To this aim, protection is required to ensure that content offered will not be copied, transformed or exploited without the knowledge and the agreement of the right-holders. The current framework has also examined other specific rights, applicable to different types of digital transmission, and provided opportunities for the distinction between a digital transmission right and a digital broadcasting right. In any case, copyright and related rights have to be considered in the wider context of the international legal framework: The approach offered by the single market legislation shows the way forward for Information Society policy.

Copyright and Related Rights

Copyright and related rights realize an important activity to protect and encourage the development and marketing of new products and services and both design and exploitation of "creative" content. The EU has validated suitable policy measures, the most recent of which was a relevant Directive (European Parliament and Council of the European Union, 2001), dealing with harmonization of rights of reproduction, distribution, communication to the public, legal protection of anti-copying devices and rights' management systems. This enhances incentives for creativity and investment in multimedia products and services (like "on-demand" services), software, performances and broadcasts, while also taking into account the interest of users, intermediaries and consumers. This is seen as complementary to the European e-Commerce Directive (European Parliament and Council of the European Union, 2000) to encourage the development of information society. A harmonized legal framework on copyright and related rights, through increased legal certainty, will foster substantial investment in creativity and innovation, especially for further network infrastructure, and lead in turn to growth and competitiveness of European industry (both for content provision and information technology), and more generally across a wide range of industrial and cultural sectors. This will safeguard employment and encourage new job creation. Relevant harmonization measures will help to implement the freedoms of property, including intellectual property, and freedom of expression and the public interest.

INTERACTIVE TELEVISION, INTERNET, AND SOCIAL INCLUSION

The *e*Europe Action Plan has become a main pillar of the strategy for the promotion of the information society. Decision-making in key areas (such as telecommunications and e-Commerce, network security, other initiatives for ensuring trust and confidence in cyberspace) has been accelerated (Shoniregun, et al., 2004), in parallel with measures for the promotion of attractive content, services and applications for all Europeans (European Commission, 2002a). Digital technologies create imperative social, cultural and educational changes and will bring about even greater changes in the future (DigiCULT Project, 2002). Digital technology allows (new) market operators to participate in the production and the distribution of content and information at a global level. Thus, telecommunications operators will offer broadband customers TV services over an IP network (ePanorama.net, 2004) where the servers are located close enough to the customer to avoid congestion and allow delivery of broadcast quality video services (European Commission,2005a).

Interactive digital television (iDTV) offers the vision of the Internet on television and extends Internet penetration beyond users possessing only computers. In fact, interactive television and 3G mobile terminals closely fit the lifestyle of many people who are not PC-oriented, and so offer possibilities to make use both of online public services and of attractive interactive content (European Commission, 2004a) provided by the private sector. The iDTV is currently subject to considerable debate across Europe, not only on a political level, but also within the industry. This debate focuses on how to encourage consumer take-up of digital interactive services, and how to boost overall digital TV penetration (Chochliouros, et al., 2006). Many people easily become excited by new technologies, but are quick to tire when their hopes are not immediately realized. Typically, commentators exaggerate short-term potential and underestimate long-term impacts. Even some market players have exaggerated the short-term interactive TV and are scaling back their expectations. In any case, developing technology is a crucial matter, but getting the public to accept new technologies is quite a different challenge. Indeed, consumers will need time to become accustomed to interactive television.

But the longer term looks promising (European Commission, 2003a) for Internet on TV: Broadcasters will increasingly be using Internet protocol in their transmissions over the next few years; consumers will be buying many new innovations that could help promote the Internet on television. High capacity hard disk drives that act as personal video recorders are an example. The Internet now offers a wide range of both linear and non-linear audiovisual services (Oxford Economic Research Associates Ltd., 2003). A "linear service" means services where the content service provider decides upon the moment in time when a specific program is offered and the composition of program schedules. These include, among others, (a) video streaming of live events (e.g., live feeds from television programs such as "Big Brother"); (b) streaming of radio programs over the Internet, including new free and subscription radio services, and existing free services that could be of particular interest to listeners who cannot receive the programme by terrestrial transmission; and (c) new services such as "Launchcast," where personalised linear music radio programmes are streamed to the listener. Related non-linear services include: (a) downloads of TV programs and films to personal computers (or video recorders); (b) downloads of radio programs for immediate listening or storage for replay on an (interactive) MP3 player, allowing viewers to catch up on TV and radio programs they may have missed up to several days after they have been broadcast; (c) music downloads for a fee; and (d) the so-called "PODcasts," where an Internet user browses sites offering content and subscribes to those of interest; the relevant software searches the subscribed sites on a regular basis and downloads new content to the PC for subsequent listening or viewing. (Current activities are restricted mainly to talk-based radio content, where the download times are short and there are no digital rights issues. But, once

Digital Rights Management (DRM) systems and payment mechanisms are established, these could extend to films, music and TV programs).

BACKING OF CONTENT THROUGH MODERN SERVICES AND APPLICATIONS

Prior European measures have mainly emphasized technology and regulation. Despite the fact that the decisive ambition was to serve users, the latter were not always and obviously at the center. This is, in fact, one of the basic viewpoints to be supported within the framework of the new European legislation, together with other measures, like the firm promotion of business partnerships (between operators from the public and the private sector), especially to boost innovative services and applications.

Among the aims of contemporary European initiatives is the "structuring" of policies around users so that technology can really appeal to them. This perspective makes it clear that content, services and applications are "decisive" factors to enable citizens to improve their lives. These factors have to be localized to reflect Europe with its diversity of cultures and languages, artistic freedom, creativity and innovation (Council of the European Union, 2002). The basic features in this area are both "personalization" and "localization." A key part of personalization involves use of language: For example, the Web today is English dominated (over three quarters of the pages on the World Wide Web are in English). Nevertheless, currently there is a trend to use local European languages. The Internet can reach all European populations if there is an important amount of content to be offered in mother tongues. Equally, content must be available on all existing terminals (e.g., the personal computer, the digital assistant, the mobile phone and digital television), to gather the diversity of uses and situations via appropriate measures to advance complementarity and synergy between the market players. Regarding localization, both governments and local authorities are the most important players in this scope. They own a large amount of high quality content (legal information, company information and geographical information-maps are good examples). The possibility to re-use the public content is critical. Content development primarily depends on market trends (European Commission, 2005b), to cover both the existing and the expected/estimated needs; however the public sector can provide significant contributions for further development, as it is practically the largest holder and producer of content in Europe (European Parliament and Council of the European Union, 2003b). There is huge potential in the re-use of public sector information for added value services, which governments shall facilitate and support. Another important aspect is that national, local and regional administrations shall also seek to advance the accessibility of their Web pages and discover new ways to deliver Web content and services.

A healthy, fair and competitive market is the best guarantee of consumer access to information society services. Public policy needs to emphasize users and supporting new content, services and applications. This mainly depends on the market development; however the State can help evolution by promoting the online use of public services, either by using its leverage power as "large" holder and producer of content in Europe or by promoting DRM solutions (European Commission, 2004b). An effective regime for digital rights management systems (DRMS) is undoubtedly an important feature of a developing market and interested parties shall continue to support the efforts of industry and consumer stakeholders to find internationally workable solutions. DRM systems and services are very much related to consumers' perception of "freedom of choice" in accessing information society services. The backing of "open," flexible and interoperable DRM systems is among the guiding EU policies. In particular, the European

Commission seeks to establish a more comprehensive approach for effective and interoperable DRM, especially to confront international challenges due to the fast (either current or expected) penetration of broadband mobile, wireless local and wide area networks (WiFi & WiMax) and digital TV (Reimers, 2000; Communications Committee, 2005).

Furthermore, rich media content is becoming available in new, diverse formats and can be delivered independent of location or time, personalised to individual citizens' preferences or requirements. In any case, all probable and relevant measures shall be "appropriate" both to provide an increased legal (and economic) certainty and to encourage new services and online content. In technical terms, communication networks, media, content, services and devices are undergoing a rapid digital convergence. Improvements in networks, combined with new compression techniques, create new and faster distribution channels and trigger new content formats and services (e.g., Voice over IP, Web-TV and online music). Two additional core issues are those referred to interoperability and security (Centeno, 2002): the former aims to investigate (and to promote) measures to enhance devices and platforms "talking to one another" and to forward services that are portable from platform to platform; the latter intends to support measures for making infrastructures and applications from fraudsters, harmful content and technology failures to increase trust amongst investors and consumers.

CONCLUSION

Information society has significant potential to offer to improve productivity and quality of life (European Commission, 2001a), especially if taking into account perspectives originating from the audiovisual and the innovative electronic communications sectors. Modern technologies penetrate the markets and affect expansion. The corresponding "potential" is particularly growing, especially due to technological developments of broadband access (Communications Committee, 2005) and of multi-platform access. More specifically, interactive media can perform a "critical" role for individual entertainment, innovation in the public and private sector and cultural diversity. In addition, the audiovisual sector, due to its particular nature, constitutes a fully competitive business area, able to affect further evolution. The convergence of voice, data and images is the new commercial reality. Voice over IP is ascendant. Television and radio programmes, movies, games, music and books are already available on both fixed and mobile platforms. Consequently, triple-play offers are now becoming increasingly widespread. In fact, telecommunications operators can offer broadcasting TV, while broadcasters can provide Internet services and telephony.

Content is a "decisive" factor in the digital economy, although it also plays a keyrole both on the economic and the social side (DigiCULT Project, 2002). Digital content can be seen as the core "fuel" of the Internet (or even of all digital delivery mechanisms). Applications and (interactive media) content are major features to ensure development of both audiovisual and innovative Internet-based applications, hence formulating an imperative and fast developing market (European Commission, 2005b). Attracting people to use converged devices (e.g., TV sets, computers and mobile handsets) depends on the variety of services offered and on the content available. The Internet offers access to an amount of electronic content which is infinite and potentially accessible from any point in the world, and (gradually) at low competitive costs. Such perspectives become more important, especially due to the penetration of the broadband challenges (Fenger & Elwood-Smith, 2000). Content includes audiovisual and software, but also an intense variety of facilities like online entertainment, video games, e-Commerce applications, publishing, education and public sector

information. Public interest applications (such as e-Government, e-Learning and e-Health) can create supplementary motivation for people to use new (converged) technologies, contributing to the viability of new business models and providing the basis for enhanced productivity. More than ever, the audiovisual sector is experiencing major challenges as a result of the introduction (and the adoption) of digital technologies. These changes necessitate the validation of a "compacted" regulatory framework (Open Network Provision (ONP) Committee, 2002) as well as the establishment of proper support mechanisms in the corresponding sector(s). As a consequence, it is quite significant for market players to "benefit" from a clear and predictable environment, where they can plan investment and finance and can develop strategies for their businesses. Furthermore, this option also plays an essential role in the functioning of modern democratic societies and the implementation of social values (DigiCULT Project, 2002), mainly via the free flow of information.

The new European regulatory framework for the converged electronic communications sector (Ovum, 2001) provides separate regulation for content and infrastructure. It promotes an effective "horizontal" approach, covering all electronic communications networks, associated facilities and related services, including those used to carry broadcasting content (such as cable television networks, terrestrial broadcasting networks and satellite broadcasting networks). It is a clear example of the full applicability of the "technological neutrality" principle. However, regulation of content broadcast over electronic communications networks (like radio and television programs or TV bouquets) remains outside the scope of the above regulation. The framework is without prejudice to EU or national broadcast content regulation adopted in conformity with European measures. In addition, the European electronic communications regulatory framework (in force since 2003) is a good example of best practice: Where it has been implemented consistently and effectively, it has opened up competition, encouraging lower prices and investment (Chochliouros & Spiliopoulou-Chochliourou, 2003c). The framework considers the links between transmission and content regulation, mainly covering: authorisation of networks and services, allocation and assignment of radio spectrum, "must-carry" obligations, access to networks and associated facilities (including access to APIs and EPGs for iDTV). One important alternative affecting the development of a "successful" content industry is the interoperability option with the right technical conditions (Oxford Economic Research Associates Ltd., 2003). Consequently, open standards are basic components as they provide new options for Internet connection and constitute new "interfaces" with the mobile and/or the advanced TV world.

As for more content-oriented characteristics, there are distinct regulatory provisions applicable, like the TVWF Directive and the e-Commerce Directive. The former is the basic legislative instrument in the European area for audiovisual services' provision and applies to television broadcasting services. It is intended to promote freedom of transmission in broadcasting by setting down "minimum rules" for the regulation of the content of television broadcasts. The rules are also intended to ensure that the interests of television viewers are fully and properly protected and to promote European and independent production. The e-Commerce Directive is an "alternative" issue, especially to clarify some legal concepts and harmonisation on certain aspects enabling information society services to benefit fully from internal market principles. In terms of future challenges, there will be significant activity with the challenge for digital rights management: The relevant DRM systems are expected to be essential to permit digital content delivery expansion, in particular within the context of the parallel broadband development (Fenger, & Elwood-Smith, 2000). The challenge will be to achieve the right balance between attractive business models, protection for rights' holders and user's

rights to sufficiently enjoy content and to enable the massive potential of the sector, via appropriate legal rules for the distribution of content over platforms and networks.

ACKNOWLEDGMENTS

The major author of the present work, Dr. Ioannis P. Chochliouros, would like to express his profound gratitude to the co-authors for their valuable contributions for the full completion of the exposed work. Furthermore, both Dr. Ioannis P. Chochliouros and Dr. Stegios P. Chochliouros would like to dedicate the present effort to the memory of their father Panagiotis, who was always an active inspiration for their activities.

REFERENCES

Arnold, M., Schmucker, M., & Wolthusen, S.D. (2003). *Digital watermarking and content protection: Techniques and applications.* Norwood, MA, USA: Artech House.

Centeno, C. (2002). Securing Internet payments: The potential of public key cryptography, Public Key Infrastructure and Digital Signatures. *ePSO Background Paper No.6.* Seville, Spain: Institute for Prospective Technological Studies. Retrieved August 9, 2005 from, http://epso.jrc.es/backgrnd.html

Chochliouros, I. P., & Spiliopoulou-Chochliourou, A. S. (2003a). Modern radio spectrum management and monitoring challenges within the context of the recent European regulation. In Oficyna Wydawnicza, Politechniki Wroclawskiej (Eds.), *EMC-2004, 17ʰ International Wroclaw Symposium and Exhibition on Electromagnetic Compatibility, Wroclaw, 29 June-1 July 2004* (pp. 525-530). Wroclaw, Poland: Wroclaw University of Technology, Institute of Telecommunication and Acoustics.

Chochliouros, I. P., & Spiliopoulou-Chochliourou, A. S. (2003b). The challenge from the development of innovative broadband access service and infrastructures. In EURESCOM GmbH & VDE Verlag (Eds.), *EURESCOM SUMMIT 2003—Evolution of Broadband Services—Satisfying User and Market Needs,* September 29-October 1, 2003 (pp. 221-229). Heidelberg, Germany: EURESCOM.

Chochliouros, I. P., & Spiliopoulou-Chochliourou, A. S. (2003c). Innovative horizons for Europe: The new European telecom framework for the development of modern electronic networks and services. *The Journal of The Communications Network (TCN), 2*(4), 53-62.

Chochliouros, I. P., Spiliopoulou-Chochliourou, A. S., Chochliouros, S. P., & Kaloxylos, A. (2006). Interactive digital television (iDTV) in the context of modern European policies and priorities. Investigating potential development in the European market. In AUEB (Ed.), *EuroITV2006: Beyond Usability, Broadcast, and TV,* May 25-26, 2006 (pp. 507-513). Athens, Greece: Athens University of Economics and Business (AUEB).

Communications Committee (2005). *Broadband access in the EU: Situation at 1 January 2005. COCOM 05-12, June 2005.* Brussels, Belgium: European Commission.

Council of the European Union (1989). *Council Directive 89/552/EEC of 3 October 1989 on the coordination of certain provisions laid down by law, regulation or administrative action in member states concerning the pursuit of television broadcasting activities (OJ L298, 17.10.1998, p.23)* [as amended by the Directive 97/36/EC (OJ L202, 30.07.1997, pp.60-70)]. Brussels, Belgium: Council of the European Union.

Council of the European Union (1999). *Resolution of 25 January 1999, concerning public service broadcasting (1999/C30/01) (OJ C30, 05.02.1999, p.1).* Brussels, Belgium: Council of the European Union.

Council of the European Union (2002). *Council resolution of 19 December 2002, on interactive media content in Europe (OJ C13, 18.01.2003, pp.08-09).* Brussels, Belgium: Council of the European Union.

Crandall, R. W., & Jackson, Ch. L. (2001). The $500 billion opportunity: The potential economic benefit of widespead diffusion of broadband Internet access. In A.L. Shampine, (Ed.), *Down to the wire: Studies in the diffusion and regulation of telecommunications technologies.* Haupaugge, NY, USA: Nova Science Press.

DigiCULT Project (2002). *Technological landscapes for tomorrow's cultural economy. Unlocking the value of cultural heritage. Full Report.* Brussels, Belgium: European Commission, Directorate General for the Information Society. Retrieved June 15, 2005, from http://www.digicult.info/pages/report.php

Directorate General Information Society of the European Commission (2002). *Digital switchover in broadcasting: A BIPE consulting study for the European commission, Final Report, April 12, 2002.* Brussels, Belgium: European Commission.

ePanorama.net (2004). *Internet protocol (IP) page—System and network administration & security.* Retrieved October 28, 2005 from, http://www.epanorama.net/links/ip.html

European Commission (1997). *Green paper on the convergence of the telecommunications, media and information technology services and the implications for regulation towards an information society approach [COM(97) 623, 03.12.1997].* Brussels, Belgium: European Commission.

European Commission (1999). *Communication on review of the telecommunications regulatory framework. [COM(1999) 539 final, 10.11.1999].* Brussels, Belgium: European Commission.

European Commission (2001a). *Communication on realising the European union's potential: Consolidating and wxtending the Lisbon atrategy [COM (2001) 79 final, 07.02.2001].* Brussels, Belgium: European Commission.

European Commission (2001b). *Green paper on European union consumer protection [COM(2001) 531 final, 02.10.2001].* Brussels, Belgium: European Commission.

European Commission (2002a). *Communication on eEurope 2005: An information society for all [COM(2002) 263 final, 28.05.2002].* Brussels, Belgium: European Commission.

European Commission (2002b). *Fourth report on the application of Directive 89/552/EEC [COM(2002) 778 final, 01.06.2003].* Brussels, Belgium: European Commission.

European Commission (2003a). *Communication on the transition from analogue to digital broadcasting [COM(2003) 541 final, 17.09.2003].* Brussels, Belgium: European Commission.

European Commission (2003b). *Communication on the future of European regulatory audiovisual policy [COM(2003) 784 final, December 2003].* Brussels, Belgium: European Commission.

European Commission (2004a). *Working paper on the interoperability of digital interactive television services [SEC(2004) 346, 18.03.2004].* Brussels, Belgium: European Commission.

European Commission (2004b). *Communication on the management of Copyright and Related Rights in the Internal Market [COM(2004) 261 final, 16.04.2004].* Brussels, Belgium: European Commission.

European Commission (2005a). *Communication on accelerating the transition from analogue to digital broadcasting [COM (2005) 204 final, May 2005].* Brussels, Belgium: European Commission.

European Commission (2005b). *Communication on i2010—A European information society for growth and development [COM(2005) 229 final, 01.06.2005].* Brussels, Belgium: European Commission.

European Parliament and Council of the European Union (1995). *Directive 95/47/EC of 24 October 1995, on the use of standards for the transmission of television signals (OJ L281, 23.11.1995, pp.51-54).* Brussels, Belgium: European Parliament and Council of the European Union.

European Parliament and Council of the European Union (2000). *Directive 2000/31/EC of 8 June 2000 on certain legal aspects of information society services, in particular electronic commerce, in the internal market (OJ L178, 17.07.2000, pp.01-16).* Brussels, Belgium: European Parliament and Council of the European Union.

European Parliament and Council of the European Union (2001). *Directive 2001/29/EC of 22 May 2001, on the harmonization of certain aspects of copyright and related rights in the information society (OJ L167, 22.06.2001, pp.10-19).* Brussels, Belgium: European Parliament and Council of the European Union.

European Parliament and Council of the European Union (2002a). *Directive 2002/19/EC of 7 March 2002 on access to, and interconnection of, electronic communications networks and associated facilities (OJ L108, 24.04.2002, pp.07-20).* Brussels, Belgium: European Parliament and Council of the European Union.

European Parliament and Council of the European Union (2002b). *Directive 2002/20/EC of 7 March 2002 on the authorisation of electronic communications networks and services (OJ L108, 24.04.2002, pp.21-32).* Brussels, Belgium: European Parliament and Council of the European Union.

European Parliament and Council of the European Union (2002c). *Directive 2002/21/EC of 7 March*

2002, on a common regulatory framework for electronic communications networks and services (OJ L108, 24.04.2002, pp.33-50). Brussels, Belgium: European Parliament and Council of the European Union.

European Parliament and Council of the European Union (2002d). *Directive 2002/22/EC of 7 March 2002 on universal service and user's rights relating to electronic communications networks and services (OJ L108, 24.04.2002, pp.51-77).* Brussels, Belgium: European Parliament and Council of the European Union.

European Parliament and Council of the European Union (2002e). *Directive 2002/58/EC of 12 July 2002, concerning the processing of personal data and the protection of privacy in the electronic communication sector (OJ L201, 31.07.2002, pp.37-47).* Brussels, Belgium: European Parliament and Council of the European Union.

European Parliament and Council of the European Union (2003a). *Proposal for a directive on measures and procedures to ensure the enforcement of intellectual property rights [COM(2003) 46 final, 30.01.2003].* Brussels, Belgium: European Parliament and Council of the European Union.

European Parliament and Council of the European Union (2003b). *Directive 2003/98/EC of 17 November 2003 on the re-use and commercial exploitation of public sector documents (OJ L345, 31.12.2003, pp.90-96).* Brussels, Belgium: European Parliament and Council of the European Union.

European Parliament and Council of the European Union (2004). *Proposal for a recommendation on the protection of minors and human dignity and the right of reply in relation to the competitiveness of the European audiovisual and information services industry [COM(2004) 341 final, 30.04.2004].* Brussels, Belgium: European Parliament and Council of the European Union.

European Telecommunications Standards Institute-ETSI (2003). *Technical specification (TS) 101 812: Digital video broadcasting (DVB); Multimedia home platform (MHP) specification 1.0.3.* Sophia-Antipolis, France: ETSI.

Fenger, C., & Elwood-Smith, M. (2000). *The fantastic broadband multimedia system.* Switzerland: The Fantastic Corporation.

Kaufman, C. (2002). *Network security: Private communication in a public world (2nd ed.),USA:* Prentice Hall.

Neale, J., Green, R., & Landovskis, L. (2001). Interactive channel for multimedia satellite networks, *IEEE Communications Magazine, 39*(3), 192-198.

Norcontel (Ireland) Ltd. (1997). *Economic implications of new communication technologies on the audio visual markets.* Final Report, NERA, Screen Digest, Stanbrook & Hooper.

Ofcom (2004). *Ofcom's review of public service television broadcasting—phase 2: Meeting the digital challenge.* London, UK: Office of Communications (Ofcom). Retrieved January 1, 2006, from www.ofcom.org.uk/consult/condocs/psb2/psb2/

Open Network Provision (ONP) Committee (2002). *Working Document—Subject: The 2003 regulatory framework for electronic communications-Implications for broadcasting, June 14, 2002.* Brussels, Belgium: Directorate-General Information Society of the European Commission.

Oxford Economic Research Associates Ltd (OXERA) (2003). *Study on interoperability, service diversity and business models in digital broadcasting services.* Oxford, UK: OXERA.

Ovum (2001). *Study on the development of competition for electronic communication access networks and services (OVUM Report to Euro-*

pean Commission, DG INFSO, February 2001). Brussels, Belgium: European Commission.

Reimers, U. (2000). *Digital video broadcasting, The international standard for digital television.* Berlin, Heidelberg and New York: Springer-Verlag.

Shoniregun, C. A., Chochliouros, I. P., Lapeche, B., Logvynovskiy, Ol., & Spiliopoulou-Chochliourou, A. S. (eds.). (2004). *Questioning the boundary issues of Internet security.* London, United Kingdom: e-Centre for Infonomics.

Sieber, U. (1998). *Legal aspects of computer-related crime in the information society (COM-CRIME Study).* University of Würzburg, Germany: European Commission, Legal Advisory Board. Retrieved, February 1, 2006 from, http://europa.eu.int/ISPO/legal/en/comcrime/sieber.html

UK's Consumers' Association (2001). *Turn on, tune in, switched off—Consumers attitudes to digital TV.* UK: Consumer's Association Report.

Chapter XI

Digital Convergence and IP Divergence:
Resolution of Potential IP Trade Wars and Establishment of Proper Digital Copyright Policies

YiJun Tian
University of Technology Sydney Law School, Australia

ABSTRACT

This chapter proposes a legal, political, and social framework for a nation to formulate proper copyright policy and minimize the risk of potential IP trade conflicts in the digital age. It examines the challenges that the Internet and digital technology present to the traditional copyright legal system. It reviews and compares the copyright history in the U.S. and China, and explores major rationales behind copyright policies of these two countries as well as the main reasons why they were able to avert potential IP trade wars in recent years. By drawing on their experiences, the author argues that the interest of a country is only best served by tailoring its IP regimes to its particular economic and social circumstances. The author believes a nation's copyright policy should always strike a sound balance of IP protection and social development, and makes some specific suggestions on how to achieve this in the digital age.

INTRODUCTION

In recent years, the application of Internet and digital technology has become increasingly "ubiquitous, embedded, and animated" in our society. The advent of the Internet, VoIP and digital TV has digitized the transmission of data, voice and TV contents in IP packets. As some commentators observed, the "digital convergence" has become a tendency (Knemeyer, 2004). "If the line between cyberspace and real space has grown increasingly difficult to draw, it may soon become impossible" (Kang & Cuff, 2005, p. 94). Ever-improving Internet technology and digital convergence have changed the traditional rules of information distribution and dissemination of information and copyrighted works. They enable users to more efficiently access and disseminate information online. However, they also facilitate copyright piracy, and enable unauthorized works to spread via various media.

Over the past two decades, a number of international Intellectual Property (IP) treaties have been established in order to address new digital challenges. In response to these treaties, many countries (particularly advanced copyright exporting nations) have adapted their domestic IP laws and tried to impose stronger protections to copyright products (even stronger than what international treaties required). Nevertheless, many other countries (particularly copyright importing countries) often hold opposite positions. They believe overly strong copyright protection would not only hurt their economic development, but also would harm public interests generally (such as limiting the public's rights to access and use digital works) (Okediji, 2004). Such divergence would, arguably, strengthen inherent conflicts of these two benefit groups in international copyright trades and international IP law/policy-making process. It might even increase the possibility of potential IP trade wars. Thus, how to establish a proper copyright policy in order to facilitate the resolution of potential international IP trade

conflicts and realize the harmony of social development and IP protection has become an importation issue that all countries have to face up to in the digital age.

An ancient book named *I Ching* (also known as the "Book of Change") which originated thousands of years ago among the courtly shaman-diviners of ancient China, may possibly give us some inspiration for dealing with current IP conflicts. The *I Ching* views "all of the changes" in the world as "an unfolding of the immutable laws and principles of existence," and contends "by explaining our present situation in terms of the natural laws that have given rise to it, we can know where we are headed and what the future is likely to be." This same principle might also be applicable to the resolution of the problems in the ever-changing Internet world. Many traditional problems still stay unchanged or unresolved in the digital age. Neither the Internet nor the development of digital technology has changed the conflict between copyright holders and copyright users, or weakened the link between trade and IP. Neither has conflict between copyright importing and exporting countries in the international trade arena been resolved. Nonetheless, these unresolved problems might constitute direct reasons for potential IP trade wars or sanctions. Based on the principle in *I Ching*, in order to cope with such problems and facilitate the resolution of potential IP trade conflicts, we should identify *"the natural laws"* that have given rise to them. Thus, it is necessary to review the history and examine how other countries have addressed similar issues.

This chapter will mainly focus on the situations in China and the United States. Specifically, Part II of this article will examine the impacts of the development of digital technology on international copyright protection and IP trade. It will also briefly review major legal responses that the US and international society have made, and the danger of potential IP trade wars in the digital age. Part III will review and compare the copyright history in both the U.S. and China, and try to identify the real reasons and rationales (identifying "the natural laws") behind copyright piracy, US-China IP trade conflicts and the copyright strategy/policy-making of these two countries. It will then try to explore the main reasons why these two countries have been able to successfully avoid potential IP wars, and why China's copyright policies have become increasingly positive in recent years. Based on this, Part IV of the article will summarize some experiences we could draw from China and the U.S., and provide some suggestions for IP importing nations to formulate proper copyright policies (such as by prioritizing/categorizing problem approach and coordinating copyright policy with development policy approach) in order to better coordinate the relation of IP protection and social economic development in the digital age.

TECHNOLOGY, COPYRIGHT PROTECTION, AND POTENTIAL IP TRADE WARS

Development of Digital Technology vs. Widespread Copyright Piracy

The *British Statute of Anne,* which was enacted in 1710, is often deemed the first formal statutory copyright law in the world. Yet the history of the fight against copyright piracy is even longer. It may be traced back to China's Song Dynasty (960-1127) when the earliest use of movable type in printing was invented (Tang, 2004). Over the past hundreds of years, with the dramatic development of printing and reproduction technology, copyright piracy became increasingly easy and widespread.

Up to the present, most of copyright works (books, videos, software, etc.) are available in the digital format. In comparison with traditional tangible format, digitalized copyright works are more vulnerable and easier to be pirated and diffused.

Traditionally, as copying a large printed copyright work (such as books and printed databases) was time consuming, copyright holders could enjoy natural "lead-time" with which to exploit their product and recoup their investment of research or development costs (McManis, 2001, p 23). But under the online environment, such "lead-time" does not exist any more. It is now possible for people to copy substantial amounts of material and nearly instantaneously disseminate them via the Internet using only their home computers—by a simple click of a mouse (Wald, 2002; Sullivan, 2001). As such, some commentators even called the Internet as "a global copy machine that is rife with possible (and probable) copyright infringement" (Fisher, 2002, paragraph 3).

Widespread copyright piracy has caused huge economic loss to copyright holders, especially producers of digital copyright products. According to a study conducted by the International Federation of the Phonographic Industry (IFPI), nearly 40% of physical recordings in the market are illegal, and the value of the pirated market for music had reached $4.6 billion in 2003 (*IACC*, 2005). The Business Software Alliance (BSA) reported 35% of software in use worldwide was pirated in 2004, representing a loss of nearly US$33 billion (BSA, 2004). In the U.S., as the biggest copyright exporting country in the world, the value of its software piracy losses was $6.6 billon in 2004 (ranked first in the world).

In addition, BSA studies indicated that software piracy in developed countries is "not much different from less developed countries" (Yu, 2003a, p. 139). For example, in 2002, nearly 25% of computer software used in the U.S. is pirated, costing the U.S. software industry $1.96 billion, just slightly lower than its total software revenue losses in China in the same year. In 2003, although the piracy rate in North America region (23%) was much lower than that of the Asia/Pacific region (53%), the losses of software industries in North America had gone beyond $7.2 billion, just slightly lower than their losses in the Asia/Pacific region

($ 7.5 billion). Thus, it is clear that in the digital age, piracy has become a global issue. It is not just a phenomenon for less developed countries, but also for developed ones.

Responses for Digital Challenges and Potential Trade Wars/Sanctions

In response to piracy challenges presented by digital technology, the World Intellectual Property Organization (WIPO) adopted two related treaties: the *WIPO Copyright Treaty (WCT)*, and the *WIPO Performances and Phonograms Treaty (WPPT)* in 1996. They are often referred to as the *"WIPO Internet Treaties"* (Ginsburg, 2003). These treaties extend copyright protection to "authors of literary and artistic works, copyright programmers and to compilations of data" (Okeiji, 2004, pp. 1-2), and try to ensure that traditional copyrights (such as reproduction rights) continue to apply in the digital environment.

At the domestic level in recent years, many developed countries have adapted their copyright law and policy to extend stronger copyright protection to copyright works, particularly the US. In 1998, the U.S. Congress passed the *Copyright Term Extension Act (CTEA)*, which extended the term of copyright protection to life of the author plus seventy years. In the same year, following the WIPO Internet treaties, the U.S. enacted the *Digital Millennium Copyright Act (DMCA)*. In addition, the U.S. constantly imposed pressures on other countries to strengthen their IP protection. Each year, the United States Trade Representative (USTR) issues its *Special 301 Report,* and always threatens potential Special 301 sanctions to certain countries they believe where serious IP problems exist. In its 2005 report, China, India, Ukraine, Brazil and many other developing countries was put into different categories of the Special 301 list (USTR, 2005). In addition to developing countries, some developed countries/entities (such as the European Union and Israel) have also been put on the Special 301 watch list. Thus, it is clear

that intense IP conflicts remain in the digital age, and might even trigger potential IP trader wars in certain circumstances.

HISTORICAL REVIEW: CHINA-U.S. IP CONFLICTS AND CHANGES OF THEIR COPYRIGHT POLICIES

The IP trade war is not a new scenario. In order to push China to strengthen protection for the U.S. copyright products and to open China's IP market, under constant pressures and lobbying efforts of the U.S. business community, the U.S. put China on the list of *Special 301* "priority foreign countries" (threatened potential IP trade wars) for three times between 1991 and 1996.

This chapter will next review and compare the copyright history in both the U.S. and China. It will try to explore the real reasons and rationales behind copyright piracy, U.S.-China IP trade conflicts, and copyright policy making in these two countries. It will then try to answer two questions: Why these two countries could successfully avoid potential trade wars in recent years? Why China's copyright policies become increasingly positive in terms of preventing piracy?

U.S. Copyright History: Protectionist Copyright Policies & Business Incentive Behind

Change of the U.S. Copyright Law/Policy: From Notorious Pirate to Dreadful Police

Reviewing the history, during the eighteenth and nineteenth centuries, the U.S. had been a major copyright importer and the biggest copyright pirating nation in the world (Griffin, 1998; Yu, 2003b). It is also a latecomer to the international copyright community, and its copyright law did not protect foreign copyrights until 1891 (Lessig, 2003).

By the end of the eighteenth century, the U.S. Congress enacted its first copyright statute—the *Copyright Act of 1790*. However, the Act (Section 5) explicitly stated "nothing in this act shall be construed to extend to prohibit the importation or vending, reprinting or publishing within the US, of any map, chart, book or books," produced by any non-U.S. citizen, in any place out of the U.S. jurisdiction. This provision naturally incurred huge criticisms from copyright exporting countries. In the nineteenth century, numerous government officials and authors in European countries constantly lobbied the U.S. government to provide the protection to foreign authors, but none of them succeeded (Yu, 2003b). As to the rationales of the U.S. copyright policy during this period, one commentator pointed out:

...Americans were suspicious about international copyright and feared that it meant exploitation and domination of their book trade. As a young nation the U.S. wanted the freedom to borrow literature as well as technology from any quarter of the globe... (Joffrains, 2001, p. 750)

Consequently, widespread piracy in the U.S. made book prices drop dramatically, and cheap books had flooded whole American market by the 1880s –the so-called "Cheap Book Movement" (Association of Research Libraries, 2005). However, with the flourish of U.S. domestic literature creations, the indigenous copyright holders gradually found their editions of American books had a hard time competing against cheap pirated books from EU. Moreover, they found an increasing amount of American literature had attracted readership in England and other European countries. But the U.S. copyright works could not be well protected in these countries because most countries extended copyright protection to foreign works based on the condition of reciprocity (Yu, 2003b). Under the strong pressures from domestic copyright industries, the U.S. Congress finally enacted the *International Copyright Act of*

March 3, 1891—"Chace Act", which for the first time granted reciprocal copyright protection to foreign authors. Nonetheless, the *Act* included a highly protectionist "manufacturing clause," and provided that the copyright protection was only available to authors who register the work before publication and "deposit two copies of the work" on or before the date of publication. And the "deposited copies" must be manufactured in the U.S. (Chace Act, Sec 3). Such provision arguably very much diminished the practical value of copyright protection to foreigners (DeWolf, 1925). Some commentators criticized that the clause was "not protection for authors" but was "protection of American labor from the effects of foreign importation" (Spoo, 1998, p. 645).

Generally speaking, the U.S.'s steps to become a member of the international IP community were very slow. Although the U.S. made some substantial revisions of its copyright law in 1909 and in 1976, the highly protectionist "manufacturing clause" was not formally abolished till 1986. And the U.S. did not become a formal signatory of Berne Convention till 1988 (Spoo, 1998). However, over the recent two decades, the U.S.'s copyright policy became increasingly internationalized. This is mainly driven by following reasons. In the 1980s, the U.S. had become a "superpower" and a country with the most advanced technology in the world. In the 1990s, the dramatic development of digital technology in the U.S. further secured its leadership in high technology and Internet Economy, and made it one of the biggest IP net exporters in the world. As McCarthy (1995) observed, IP protection is now not just the business of other nations (such as copyright exporting countries in EU) but also the U.S.'s business. All this made the U.S. become one of the most aggressive advocators of strong IPR protection in the world. The U.S. urged putting IP on the international trade agenda, and directly influenced the introduction of the TRIPS agreement at the WTO conference in 1995. In order to strengthen the copyright protection under the

Internet environment, the U.S. worked actively and directly contributed to the enactment of the *1996 WIPO Internet Treaties.* Furthermore, as introduced above, it also constantly pressures other countries (such as China and Australia) to strengthen copyright law and import the U.S. digital legislative model.

In short, as Professor Yu (2003b, p. 353) pointed out, "within a hundred years, the U.S. has been transformed from the most notorious pirate to the most dreadful police."

Features of the U.S. Copyright Policy: "Internationalism" or "Protectionism"?

The U.S.'s highly protectionist copyright policies have been criticized by many commentators. Nevertheless, it is not hard to understand why the U.S. adopts highly "protectionist" copyright policies. After all, pursuing the maximization of the benefits of domestic enterprises has been one of important tasks of each government. Instead of providing more criticism, this article will next identify some general features of the U.S. copyright policy-making, and summarize some experiences other countries may draw on.

Put simply, these can be summarized into three aspects. First, it is internal pressure (from domestic copyright industries) rather than external pressure (from foreign countries) that drove the U.S. government to constantly adapt its copyright policies and revise its copyright legislation. In other words, the U.S. always tries to make its copyright and trade policies independently, and tries to minimize external impacts (such as pressures and criticisms from Europe countries) on its policy-making.

Second, the U.S. government always tries to adapt its copyright policy in line with its trade or development policy, and make them work collaboratively in order to enhance the development of domestic industries. For example, as introduced above, the "manufacture clause" of *the 1891 Act* was not only designed for securing advantageous

situations of the U.S. copyright industries in international competition but also for reserving and creating more employ opportunities in U.S. printing industries.

Third, the U.S. always tries to make timely adaptations to its copyright policy according to its role in the global economy and the development status of its copyright industries in different periods. When it was a copyright net importer, the U.S. government did not provide much protection (or even no protection) to foreign copyright works. After becoming a copyright exporting country, it started to adopt a strong copyright protection policy. It even tried to influence international copyright regime and force other countries to adapt stronger copyright laws or policies (i.e., through free trade agreements). It is clear that the U.S. government isdevoted to creating an effective business and legal environment for its domestic enterprises to participate in international competition.

In summary, although in recent years the U.S. copyright policy became increasingly internationalized, some core features of its policy-making remain unchanged, and its copyright policy has been economically highly self-interest centered. In the last two decades, the U.S., to this extent, only transformed its copyright policy from a "traditional protectionist" form to an "internationalized protectionist" fashion. All these dictate that the U.S. will have unavoidable conflicts with other countries, particularly copyright importing nations, in copyright protection and IP trade areas. With the growth of Information economy, these conflicts will become more prominent.

Economic Reasons behind Copyright Piracy and China's Current Policy Options

A review of the U.S. copyright history might also be helpful to understand the situation in China. Like the U.S., the economic element (business incentive) plays a significant role in explaining copyright piracy problems and social resistance against IPR in China.

China's economic reforms and its "open door" policy since 1980 greatly enhanced its economic modernization. The economic modernization further prompted the people's desire for culture modernization—it increased the people's need for cultural products. But China is still a developing country. Most of people could not afford expensive foreign copyright products. Consequently, as one commentator pointed out, the public began to tolerate piracy because the pirates "make certain foreign goods affordable which would not otherwise be" (Hu, 1996, p 105).

In fact, China's situation (particularly in the early 1990s) is quite similar with those of the U.S. in the nineteenth century. As introduced above, the Cheap Book Movement made pirated EU literature extensively available throughout the U.S., and partially stimulated the flourish of the U.S. domestic creation. Similar things also happened in China. Since the early 1990s, unauthorized foreign copyright products (particularly software) had been spread throughout the whole country. The public enjoyed benefits from free riding on the foreign works, and some people openly argued software piracy would "speed the nation's modernization at little or no cost" (Cox, 1995, p2B), and IPR would only impose a substantial burden on the nation. Therefore, some western commentators concluded "as a developing country, China really has no incentive to cease its piracy activities" (Neigel, 2000, p403). Indeed, there seems to be no reason for a copyright importing country to actively implement a strong copyright protection regime, which is obviously in favor of copyright exporting countries.

Nonetheless, current international economic environments have decided that China is not able to adopt an "isolationism" or "economic self-interest" copyright policy (traditional protectionist copyright policy) which the U.S. adopted in the nineteenth century any more. First, globalization and free trade have become an international tendency (Okediji, 1999). The world economy has become increasingly interdependent, and "isolationism" is not an effective economic strategy in the current world any more. Second, technologically advanced nations will not allow China to adopt an isolationism or protectionist copyright policy either. In fact, since the early twentieth century, major western countries (such as the U.S.) have never stopped pushing China to internationalize its copyright law and open its copyright market. In the nineteenth century, the U.S. might be able to completely ignore the criticisms from EU countries (and take advantage from its own highly protectionist copyright policies). But under the current globalized economic environment (particularly under the WTO framework) China cannot ignore foreign criticisms. China has to deal with external pressures (i.e., threatened trade wars) imposed by the U.S. and other countries seriously, and try to find new economic strategies to defense its own rights in international IP trade.

This article will next review the developmental history of China's copyright laws and policies since 1903. It will focus on examining how external pressures (especially the pressures from the U.S.) influenced the reform of China's copyright protection regime.

China Copyright History: The Development of Copyright Laws and Impacts of External Pressures

Although the preliminary form of copyright protection (for both publishers and authors) in China could be traced back 1000 years ago—North Song Dynasty (960-1127)—China did not have formal copyright law until the twentieth century. The development of copyright protection in ancient China might still have some spontaneous/indigenous nature, but the development of China's copyright laws over the past century was full of the pressures/interventions from other countries.

The history of China's modern copyright law can be divided into four stages. The first stage was from 1903 to 1978—it was a beginning stage of China's formal copyright law. The Qing government enacted China's first copyright act *Author's Right in the Great Qing Empire*—in 1910 (one year before the Qing Dynasty was overthrown). Just three years after, some western countries had started to push China to reform copyright law and provide more protection for foreign works. In 1913 and 1920, the U.S., the UK and France had invited China to join *the Berne Convention*, and to conclude certain bilateral copyright treaties with them. However, the then Chinese government refused them on the ground of potential negative impacts on the Chinese economy and its education system (Zheng & Pendleton, 1987). After that, the interventions of a series of historical events, such as the World War II, the Chinese civil wars and the Cultural Revolution (Tang 2004; Zhou, 2002), significantly slowed down the development of China's copyright law.

The second stage was from 1979 to 1990—it was the formulation stage of the Chinese modern IP law framework. The "Open Door Policy" in the 1970s has been regarded as a significant step China made along the path toward stronger copyright law and the rule of law (Chynoweth, 2003; Wang, 2000). China and the U.S. established formal diplomatic relation in 1979. In the same year, they concluded the *1979 U.S.-China Bilateral Trade Agreement*, and both committed to reciprocity with regard to copyright, patent and trademark protection. Following this treaty, the China IPR systems experienced a dramatic development between 1980 and 1991. China enacted the *Trademark Law* in 1982, the *Patent Law* in 1984 and the *Copyright Law* in 1990. This legislation constitutes a framework of the IPR protection system, and indicated that the Chinese IP protection system had been basically established (Xue & Zheng, 2002). Also in this period, China became a signatory to the *Convention Establishing the World Intellectual Property Organization (WIPO)* in 1980. It joined the *Paris Convention for Protection of Industry Property (Paris Convention)* in 1985.

The third stage was from 1991 to 1996; in this stage, China was in a relatively passive position in its copyright law reform and copyright policy making. Although China had achieved remarkable progress on its IP legislation, it was still a long way from meeting the U.S.'s requirements. In order to force China to strengthen copyright protection and to open its IP market, the U.S. had put China on the list of *Special 301* "priority foreign countries" three times between 1991 and 1996. It also repeatedly threatened China with non-renewal of *Most-Favored-Nation status (MFN)*, and opposition to China's access to the WTO during this period (Xue, Zheng, 2002). Specifically, under constant pressures of the U.S. business community, the U.S.TR initiated its first "Special 301" action against China in May of 1991. It mainly focused on pushing China to provide stronger protection for foreign copyright works, especially computer software (Neigel, 2000). Lengthy negotiations led to the signing of the *Memorandum of Understanding on Intellectual Property Rights (1992 IP MOU)* in January 1992. In response to *the 1992 IP MOU*, China speeded up its steps to become a part of the international IPR community, and joined the *Berne Convention* and the *Universal Copyright Convention*, respectively, in 1992. China also promulgated a number of regulations to strengthen the protection for software, such as the *Regulations on the Protection of Computer Software 1991*. At the institutional level, considering the specialty of IP cases, since 1992 the government started to establish special "IP courts" in certain jurisdictions at both superior and intermediate levels of the court system (Hu, 1996). Despite China's progress in its implementation of the *1992 IP MOU*, the U.S. complained it felt frustrated with the China's lack of enforcement of its IP laws (Neigel, 2000), and criticized that China's judicial and administrative enforcement systems were too "young" and "to some extent ineffective" (Hu, 1996, p112). Consequently it initiated the second "Special 301" action on China in June of 1994. This time, the USTR was mainly aimed at pressuring China to resolve three problems: the rampant copyright piracy, the ineffective IPR enforcement system and the limited market access concerning U.S. copyrighted products. Although they threatened each other with trade sanctions, the two countries successfully averted the second IP trade war by concluding a last-minute agreement—*China-US Agreement Regarding Intellectual Property Rights (1995 IP Agreement)*. However, just one year after, the U.S. placed China on the "Special 301 Priority Foreign Country" list for the third time, due to dissatisfaction with China's implementation of the *1995 IP Agreement*. Again, both nations successfully averted trade war by reaching *the IP Agreement 1996*. China then took more effective measures in combating copyright piracy. At the administrative level, Chinese authorities raided and closed 39 factories that made unauthorized copies of U.S. music, movies or software, and they arrested more than 250 individuals who sold or made unauthorized copies (Neigel, 2000). At the legislative level, China amended the *Criminal Law* in 1997, and Articles 217-218 of the law explicitly codify that certain acts of copyright infringement constitute crimes.

The fourth stage is from 1997 to the present. In this stage, China's copyright law reform is significantly influenced by its WTO accession, and its copyright policy has become increasingly positive. As part of the WTO accession, China agreed to the *TRIPS Agreement* in 1999, and then extensively modified its three major IP laws (Chynoweth, 2003; Xue & Zheng, 2002). The government amended *patent law* in 2000, and amended both *copyright law* and *trademark law* in 2001 (Zhou, 2002). After successfully accessing the WTO in December of 2001, China started to pay more attention to the IPR enforcement issues. In order to facilitate the enforcement of IP law TRIPS, China enacted a number of related imple-

menting rules/regulations and Supreme People's Court (SPC) judicial interpretations, such as the *Interpretation of the SPC Concerning Several Issues on Application of Law in Hearing Correctly the Civil Copyright Cases,* and *Interpretation by the SPC in Handling Criminal Cases of Infringing IP* in 2004. Moreover, at the governmental level, in recent years the Chinese government started to work more collaboratively with the U.S. to address IPR and WTO compliance issues – through a series of constructive intergovernmental dialogs/negotiations. It also tries to adopt various avenues to educate the public the importance of IPR enforcement.

Reasons for Successfully Avoiding IP Trade Wars and China's Positive Post-WTO Copyright Policy

How could the U.S. and China could avoid three potential trade wars? Why did China's copyright policy become increasingly positive in recent years? The answers to these questions would arguably be helpful for other nations to formulate proper copyright policies, and facilitate the resolution of potential IP trade conflicts.

Reasons for the Peaceful resolutions of Potential IP Trade War

After comparison with the U.S. copyright history, and particularly after reviewing the history of China's economic development and copyright reform over the past few years, we find the main reasons that the two countries were able to resolve potential IP conflicts in a relatively peaceful and constructive manner may include following aspects:

1. **Growth of Economic Power of China and Increased Ability to Cope with Threatened Trade Sanctions**

With the growth of economic power, China has increased its capability of coping with threatened trade sanctions. China's economic reform and "open door policy" since 1979 greatly enhanced its economic development. In fact, China has never given up its efforts and attempts to apply its economic powers to respond to external pressures from foreign states. For example, when the USTR threatened its second Special 301 trade sanctions worth $1.08 billion on Chinese products in 1994, besides condemning the U.S. for ignoring China's diligent efforts on improving its copyright system, China retaliated by threatening its own trade sanctions against the U.S. products. The same thing also happened in 1996. Only thirty minutes after the U.S. initiated the third *Special 301* action against China, the Chinese government issued its own list of U.S. products that would be subject to 100% tariffs (Cooper & Chen, 1996).

In recent years, China's economy has boomed. Based on the information provided by China State Council, China's total value of import and export in 2004 had reached 1,154.8 billion US dollars (up 35.7% over 2003) ranked third in the world. China's GDP rose to $1.833 trillion in 2005, and became the "second-largest economy in the world after the US"—measured on a purchasing power parity (PPP) basis (CIA, 2006). Thus, as some commentators pointed out, China has now become a "greater economic power" and is able to effectively "wield trade weapons against its economic opponents" (Neigel, 2000, p199). The threatened trade sanction does not seem an effective avenue for the U.S. to influence China's copyright policy any longer. The U.S. has to consider other relatively peaceful avenues to "keep its impacts on China" and to relieve its loss due to widespread copyright piracy.

2.   Growth of Bilateral Economic Collaboration and Change of U.S. Company Roles

With the growth of bilateral economic collaboration, many U.S. companies are starting to hold increasingly positive attitudes toward China. Over the past decade, particularly after China joined the WTO in 2001, the bilateral trade between the U.S. and China has increased dramatically. According to the information provide by the USTR, in 1986, total bilateral trade of the U.S. and China was only $7.9 billion. Whereas, in 2003, total bilateral trade was close to top $170 billion (GTW Associates, 2003). Four years after China joined the WTO, China has become the U.S.'s third largest trading partner and the fourth largest export market. The USTR (2006, p. 3) found that the U.S.'s exports to China have increased five times faster than its exports to the rest of the world since 2001, and market forces are continuing to "drive broader and deeper economic ties" between the two countries.

With the growth of bilateral trade, many U.S. enterprises have changed their attitudes to China dramatically. These enterprises were triggers for potential trade wars, and three Special 301 actions mainly resulted from their endless lobbying and pressures imposed on the U.S. Congress. But now, increasingly, a number of U.S. companies have started to hold optimistic views about the U.S.-China trade relation. For example, at the 2003 USTR-chaired public hearing on China's implementation of its WTO commitments, one witness of an association representing many U.S. businesses operating in China stated:

Business is good. And, if you ask many American companies, if not most American companies, even the ones who are most exercised about apparent WTO lapses on the part of the Chinese whether 2003 is going to be better than 2002, most will say "yes." They [also] expect 2004 to be better than 2003. (GTW Associates, 2003, paragraph 3)

Such predictions proved to be correct. The USTR, in its *2004 Report to Congress on China's WTO Compliance,* cited the words in a written submission of two U.S. trade associations, and stated "[i]t has been a good year for American companies in China... .We believe China is now substantially in compliance with its [WTO] obligations—a marked improvement over last year" (USTR, 2004a).

Increased bilateral trades and dramatic increase of the U.S. corporate investment and operation in China have resulted in economic benefits for both countries (Government Accountability Office, 2004). Trade sanctions would not only hurt China, but also hurt the U.S., especially the U.S. companies operating in China. All of these push U.S. companies to play increasingly positive roles in the U.S. Congress/USTR Hearing in terms of facilitating the resolution of potential trade conflicts.

3. International Trend: Globalization and Economic Focus

Globalization has become a current trend. For China, adoption of an "open door" policy makes the focus of government work more on economic issues. "Maintaining steady and rapid economic development" has been regarded as "an important issue that the Chinese government must successfully handle" (*The Report on the Work of the Government*, 2005). Two decades of economic reform have transformed China's economy from a strict command economy (planned economy) towards a market economy country (USTR, 2004a).

The trend of economic globalization and China's continual economic reform are also gradually pushing the U.S. to adjust its foreign policy towards China. For example, in 1994, the Clinton Government not only approved a renewal of the China's most-favored-nation (MFN) trade status, but also decided to formally de-link China's MFN from human rights conditions (Hu, 1996). Many facts demonstrate that although political conflicts remain intense in certain circumstances, both countries have realized the importance of improving and maintaining constructive bilateral

economic relations (USTR, 2006). Improvement of economic relations further enhances improvement of political relations between two countries. Collectively, these factors create an effective foundation for both countries to peacefully resolve potential economic conflicts and avert potential IP trade wars.

4. Improved Legislative Systems of China and Positive Attitudes of China Government

At the legislative level, China has made remarkable progress in improving its copyright legislation in the past decade. As discussed above, in addition to modifying its three major IP laws to meet the TRIPS requirements, the SPC also enacted numerous specific regulations and judicial interpretations in order to facilitate and enhance the enforcement of the copyright laws. These legislative efforts have also been recognized by the U.S. government. The USTR, in its *2004 Report to Congress on China's WTO Compliance* (2004a, p. 5), stated:

China has undertaken substantial efforts in this regard, as it has revised or adopted a wide range of laws, regulations and other measures. While some problems remain, China did a relatively good job of overhauling its legal regime ...

At the government level, in recent years the Chinese government seems to have adopted a more positive and practical attitude to approach China-U.S. IP conflicts. A typical example may be China's Premier Wen Jiabao's visit to the U.S. in December 2003. In response to the U.S. claims on IP protection and other trade issues, Wen's suggestions were that both countries upgrade the level of economic interaction, and "undertake an intensive program of bilateral interaction" to resolve the U.S.-China bilateral trade problems (USTR, 2004, p. 4). The following annual U.S.-China Joint Commission on Commerce and Trade

(JCCT) meeting in April 2004 was deemed to be "highly constructive." Within three days' negotiations, both countries achieved the resolution of "no fewer than seven potential disputes over China's WTO compliance" (Zoellick, 2005). As to IP issues, in the JCCT meeting, China presented a detailed IPR action plan to address the piracy and counterfeiting of American ideas and innovations, and committed to apply criminal penalties for IPR violators, including imposing criminal sanctions to online piracy (USTR, 2004b). China also committed to improve protection of "electronic data" by ratifying *the WIPO Internet Treaties* as soon as possible. Moreover, in order to facilitate the implementation of the IPR action plan, the Chinese government established a special "IPR working group" under the JCCT, and noted that they hope the U.S. and the Chinese trade, judicial and law enforcement authorities will work together to enhance IPR enforcement in China. The USTR, in its recent report on U.S.-China Trade Relations (USTR, 2006) also reemphasized that the U.S. will expand trade policy and negotiating capacity in China, and increase effectiveness of high-level meetings between the two countries, including IPR issues.

Thus, it is clear that instead of threatening/ blaming each other (in the 1990s), both countries are now trying to adopt more constructive and practical attitudes/approaches to resolve potential disputes. China's copyright policy is getting increasingly active and collaborative.

Reasons for China's Positive Copyright Policy in Recent Years

How couldChina achieve such rapid progresses on its copyright legislation in recent years? Why has China's copyright policy become increasingly positive? On the one hand, it is due to external pressures from other countries, especially the U.S. (as introduced above). On the other hand, it is mainly due to internal pressures, especially the growth of domestic copyright industries in China.

1. **The growth of Domestic Copyright Industry in China**

Many data and facts demonstrate that China's copyright industry has experienced remarkable growth in recent years. Using the publishing industry as an example, with business steadily up each year, China has become an important international center for book publishing. The number of published book categories increased from 92,972 in 1991 to 110,283 in 1996(Li, 2002, p 89.). In 2002, the number went beyond 178,900 (up by 12% over 2001).

The growth of China's software industry is even faster. Although the Chinese software companies only appeared in the late 1980s, they grew up dramatically in the 1990s. In 1997 alone, they provided 61,346 jobs and contributed US$219.8 million in tax revenues (Li, 2002). Based on statistics, the average annual growth rate of the whole industry was over 30% between 1992 and 2000 (albeit from a very small base). The International Data Corporation (IDC) estimated China's software market would keep the same annual growth rate (over 30%) between 2000 and 2005. Moreover, based on the information provided by the Ministry of Information Industry of China, the scale of China's software industry surpassedits counterparts of India and Korea by 2004. The total value of China's software exports rose from US $ 400 million in 2000 to US $ 2.8 billion in 2004 (Xinhua News Agency, 2005).

In addition, many commentators believe China has a huge potential market for movies and broadcasting. China's movie industry had generated 4.1 billion yuan RMB (about US $500 million) revenue in 2004 (People Daily Online, 2005). And it was estimated the figure would exceed 10 billion (about US$1.2 billion) by 2007.

2. **Copyright Piracy vs. Growth of Domestic Copyright Industries**

As introduced above, the U.S. "*Cheap Book Movement*" in the nineteenth century not only harmed the benefits of EU copyright holders, but eventually also made the U.S. book publishers suffer. Inadequate copyright protection for foreign authors caused the dramatic growth of cheap book imports, and made pirated foreign works (sold with extremely low prices) "compete unfairly and directly against works written by indigenous authors" (Yu, 2003b, p. 345). The same thing seems to happen in China also, particularly in software industries. As Professor Li (2002, p. 92.) pointed out, the rampant software piracy could harm the Chinese software industry as much as foreign software producers, because "piracy of foreign software may help to increase the market share of foreign software firms and makes it more difficult for local competitors [China's software companies] to establish themselves." Since the pirated foreign software is available anywhere in a very low price, few people would have incentive to buy expensive software designed by indigenous software producers. Consequently, software companies could not recoup their investment. Both domestic and foreign investors would lose their incentives to make continuous investments in developing new software products in China. Thus, software piracy has become a significant factor obstructing the development of China's domestic software industry. As a result, preventing copyright piracy is now not only important for protecting foreign copyright holders, but also important for protecting China's indigenous copyright industries. Like the U.S. situation in the nineteenth century, the dramatic growth of domestic copyright industries arguably constitutes an important internal reason for China to adopt a positive copyright policy and constantly strengthening its enforcement of copyright laws.

In conclusion, the internal and external reasons previously discussed work in harmony in order to increase the possibility that China and U.S. may resolve potential IP trade disputes in a relatively peaceful fashion.

ESTABLISHMENT OF PROPER COPYRIGHT POLICY: COPYRIGHT & DEVELOPMENT

After reviewing the copyright history of the U.S. and China and exploring the main reasons why the two countries can resolve their IP trade conflicts in a relatively peaceful fashion, this article will next provide some general principles, or suggestions, for a nation (especially a copyright importing country) to formulate proper copyright policies in the digital age.

Classifying and Prioritizing Problems

In order to formulate a property copyright policy, we should first identify major copyright problems that we need to cope with. Obviously, widespread copyright piracy is one of most fundamental issues that each nation has to face up to. Piracy will not only greatly reduce the incentives of copyright holders to make further creation or investments, but also might trigger bilateral IP-trade wars. However, after reviewing copyright history in China and the U.S., we found that, behind this fundamental problem of widespread copyright piracy, there are many related sub-problems. And to some degree, it is these sub-problems that collectively result in the widespread copyright piracy.

These problems mainly include: (1) social resistance problems, such as lack of public support for IPR enforcement; (2) legislative problems, such as lack of strong copyright legislation; (3) law enforcement problems, such as inadequate public/government/administrative supports; (4) institutional problems, such as lack of transparency of court systems, local protectionism and inadequately trained legal personal; (5) economic problems, such as conflicts of benefits between copyright importing and exporting countries, and conflicts between strong copyright protection and the growth of domestic copyright industries; (6) public interest problems, such as the conflict between strong copyright protection and effective technology transfers, and the conflict between strong copyright protection and the public's right to access information. In order to seek effective resolutions, it is necessary to make a classification and prioritization of proposed problems, and try to decide: Which problems could be resolved in a relatively short period? Which problems have to be resolved in a long period? Which problems are not copyright problems? How do they relate to each other?

As for the social resistance problem, it has been one of biggest obstacles for IPR enforcement. It is a complex issue, and there are many social, political and economic elements involved (Hu, 1996). Educating the public (both consumers and copyright holders) to understand the significance of IPR protection is important to effectively prevent pirates (Li, 2002). However, the improvement of the public's knowledge on IPR can not be completed overnight. Thus, this problem naturally falls into the category of problems which should be resolved in the long term.

As to the legislative problem, strong and complete copyright legislation is clearly an effective weapon to fight against copyright piracy. China's remarkable legislative progress in the 1990s demonstrated that it is possible to establish a model copyright legislative framework in a relatively short time. Thus, it may belong to a problem which could be resolved in a relatively short period.

Regarding the law enforcement problem, as introduced above, this has been one of most controversial issues bothering U.S.-China relations. The effective enforcement of copyright law needs strong and constant support from the domestic government. However, it does take time for a government (especially a government in a copyright importing country) to adapt its copyright policy in line with its economic and development agendas—to find an effective manner to strike a sound balance of copyright protection, technology transfers and the growth of domestic industries. Thus, it might also belong to a long-term problem that needs resolution.

As to institutional problems, many commentators criticized that the lack of transparency of court systems, local protectionism and inadequate legal personal are direct reasons causing the copyright piracy and ineffective IP law enforcement in China (Yonehara, 2002; Neigel, 2000). Nevertheless, it is noteworthy that that those institutional problems are not just limited to the IP law area. Some of them belong to inherent problems existing in the whole institutional system of China. These would be expected to be resolved gradually along with China's political reform in the future. Thus, they also belong to problems that need resolution in a relatively long period.

.Moreover, as to how to balance economic conflicts between different benefit groups (copyright holders, copyright users and copyright importing and exporting nations) and how to strike a balance between copyright protection and the public interest, these are inherent problems existing in copyright laws for hundreds of years, and may even be intensified due to the advance of digital technology (as introduced before). The resolutions of these problems require governments to constantly coordinate/adapt their copyright policies along with their technological, economic and other public policies. The resolutions of these problems need continuous efforts of each nation in the world. Again, they cannot be resolved in a short period.

Obviously, there are overlaps between the problems discussed above, such as social resistance and law enforcement problems. These problems influence each other and this makes the resolution of copyright piracy problems more complicated. It is clear that those problems cannot be resolved only through the copyright law. The article will next try to provide some general principles for a nation to formulate proper copyright policies in order to resolve the above problems more systematically.

Sustainable Copyright Protection: Copyright Policy and Development Policy

WIPO has incorporated "development" as an integral part of its major missions since 1974 (USINFO, 2005a). Thus, when making its copyright policy, an important principle that a nation has to bear in mind may be that it should align copyright and economic development policies in order to make copyright policy more systematic and sustainable, and particularly create a better development environment for its domestic copyright industries.

Like the U.S, in recent years it seems that China also started to pay more attention to coordinate its copyright policy with its development policy. The major goals of China's IP laws and policies were summarized by Professor Zheng Chengsi (Director of the IP Center of the Chinese Academy of Social Sciences) in three dimensions: (i) strengthening the protection of IP; (ii) increasing the amount of self-owned IP production; and (iii) accelerating the industrialization of IP production, i.e., making domestic IP production entering the market as soon as possible. Thus, it is clear that enhancing the development of domestic copyright industries and IP economy (goals (ii) and (iii)) has become one important component of China's current IP strategy. China has realized, under the current international IP regime, only copyright holders would become the biggest winners. And in order to obtain an advantageous position in international IP trade, a nation has to take all possible measures (not just copyright law) to enhance the development of domestic copyright industry.

A typical example of applying such a strategy may be China's reforms of copyright exporting policy in 2004. Before 2004, most domestic movie and sound recording companies in China did not have an export right, and only the administrative department of State Council had the authorization to approve and issue an export license. Under the new rule, any movie and sound recording company, whose registered capital is no less than 1 million RMB (about US $123, 000), is eligible to apply for an export license. Administrative departments at the provincial level would also have authorization to approve an export license on movie and sound recording products. The reformed copyright export policy arguably assists domestic copyright industries to explore the oversea markets, and it would contribute to the development of domestic copyright industries and China's IP economy in general. A similar approach might also be applicable to other countries (especially copyright importing countries). Governments should try to adopt various preferential policies to enhance the development of domestic copyright industries.

Another successful example can be found in Korea. Since the start of the millennium, the popularity of the Korean movie and drama series, such as Dae Jang Geum (A Jewel in the Palace) and Winter Sonata, has "fuelled a South Korean cultural fever that has gripped ...Asia– a Korea Wave" (Kositchotethana, 2006). The export of Korean movies not only attracted huge audiences and gave the world a greater understanding of Korean cultural heritage with thousands of years of history, but also allowed Korea to reap massive commercial success in various areas. The success of cultural export not only enhanced Korean brand value and increased the sales of audio-visual and electronic products, but also attracted more overseas consumers for other industries, such as food industry, tourism industry and even the plastic surgery industry (Osnos, 2005). The "Korea Wave" provides us a good example that how a nation successfully explores and applies its comparative advantages to open new niches of international market. Actually, the so-called pop culture exports (Korea Wave) has been substantially supported by the Korea government. In 1998, the Korean Culture Ministry set its first five-year plan to enhance the development of the domestic culture industry, and encouraged education institutes to open culture industry departments (Onishi, 2005). Moreover, in 2002 the ministry opened the Korea Culture and Content Agency (KOCCA), which is dedicated to encourage culture content exports and help Korean culture industry develop global marketing strategies. In addition, the Seoul government has also provided "substantially reduced taxes and credit guarantee facilities for South Korean film production projects" (Kositchotethana, 2006). To this extent, all these efforts worked collectively and resulted in the success of the Korea Wave.

In summary, governments should regard strengthening IP protection and enhancing the development of domestic IP economy as integral parts of their future economic, political and legal reforms. They should try to create more business incentives for the public and domestic industries to protect IPR, and try to realize harmony between copyright protection and the development of IP economy.

Failed Myth of Development: Copyright Policy versus Technology Policy

Another principle that a nation should pay attention to when making its copyright policy is establishing a relation between copyright policy and technology policy, and make them work collaboratively to enhance the improvement of a nation's self-innovation capability.

Over the past few years, advanced western countries have constantly advocated that "intellectual property is an important tool in economic, social and cultural development, and it encourages domestic innovation, investment and technology transfer" (USINFO, 2005). Copyright protections "allow artists to benefit from their creations" (Chynoweth, 2003, p. 5). These promises and IP success in western countries made many developing countries believed that "IP" and "technology transfer" are quick routes to modernization.

However, undesirable realities in most developing countries, especially in African countries, broke "the myth of development" that western countries promised. As Professor Ruth Gana observed:

Of all the various programs and policy ... none has been as detrimental to the development process in Africa as technology transfer from developed countries ...after three decades of experimenting with Western-styled IP laws and an inordinate emphasis on technology from developed countries as an agent of development, African countries remain mired in the trenches of underdevelopments (Gana, 1996, p. 315)

In fact, one of main reasons causing the failure of modernization in most African countries is not "technology transfer" itself, but the inherent problem in current "international IP systems" which were used to facilitate such "technology transfer." As Professor Gana (1996, p. 315.) further criticized, the current international IP system "enabled owners of intellectual goods in developed counties to control access by developing counties to technology while also exacting from these countries huge transaction costs and licensing fee." Obviously, such a system has not struck a good balance between the benefits for advanced IP exporting countries and less developed IP importing countries.

Another major reason causing the failure of "the myth of development" may be that some developing nations overly relied on IP and technology transfer, and ignored or failed to coordinate their IP policies in line with their technology and economic policies. In fact, the IP success in western civilization should be understood "in connection with a series of historical events" (Gana, 1996, p. 342). For example, the U.S.'s current technology advantage seems to owe more to its strategic deployments of government technological, economic and defensive policies after World War II, such as deploying defense-related research for commercial application, emphasizing applied science, transforming the reigning ideology that called for a separation of government and scientific endeavor and dramatically increasing government's support on research and domestic innovation. In comparison with its IP policy, these important policy deployments seemed to have more direct influences/contributions in securing the U.S.'s technological leadership in the world.

Actually, not only the U.S., but a number of developing nations with certain technological potential have also realized the significance of technology and self-innovation ability on their economic growth and modernization (Thurow, 1997; Gantz & Rochester 2005). For example, in a recent issued technology development agenda for the coming 15 years—*the guidelines on national medium- and long-term program for science and technology development (2006-2020)*, China places the improvement of national "*self-innovation ability*" in a very high strategic position (GOV.CN, 2006). In addition to reemphasizing the significance of IP protection in stimulating innovation, the guideline declares that China will conduct a series of strategic deployments to promote its scientific development, such as reforming the current scientific and technological management system, combining and coordinating the military and civilian research organizations, giving more support to innovation of enterprises and creating a better environment for listing of high-tech firms. Moreover, the guideline announced that China will raise the proportion of research and development expenditure to 2.5 percent of the GDP by 2020—this means China's annual investment in scientific research will go above 900 billion RMB (about 112.5 billion USD). Those deployments are arguably quite similar to the strategic deployment of the U.S. in the 1980s (introduced above).

As such, when a nation makes its copyright policy, it should always bear in mind that copyright law and IP policy cannot replace the role of technology policy in terms of enhancing a nation's technology development and modernization.

When a nation, especially a developing nation, imports a western IP regime and conducts technology transfers, it should always bear in mind that "IP alone cannot bring about development." It should always try to adapt copyright/IP policy in line with its economic, technological and other development policies.

More Systematic and Collaborative Copyright Policies

When dealing with international IP conflicts and IPR enforcement problems, the collaborative and practical attitudes of governments in different countries are very important. External pressures may push a nation to establish modern copyright legislation but cannot guarantee the enforcement of its copyright law, because the effective law enforcement requires supports of both domestic governments and the public.

Many examples demonstrate that a more systematic, constructive and collaborative copyright policy could significantly facilitate the solution of potential IP conflicts and enhance the development of domestic copyright industries. As introduced above, China's new copyright export rule in 2004 might be an example that a developing country attempts to apply economic policy to enhance the development of local copyright industries, and allow its domestic companies to directly benefit from existing international IP regime. At the bilateral level, the U.S.-China JCCT meeting in April 2004 might serve as an example how developing copyright importing countries and developed copyright exporting countries could work together, and more constructively and collaboratively resolve existing copyright problems and IP trade conflicts.

At the international level, it is noteworthy that the U.S. proposed a "Partnership Program" at the WIPO conference in April of 2005. In its proposal, the U.S. delegation suggested the UN establish a WIPO Partnership Database and a special WIPO Partnership Office in order to help each nation to seek out potential partners, funds and matches. They believe such a program will greatly facilitate international IP collaboration and benefit developing countries in particular. For example, this program can help a culture ministry in a developing country more effectively utilize its cultural assets by being "matched with proper museum experts, charitable organizations and a regional development bank" (USINFO, 2005, paragraph 7). Indeed, the establishment of international IP partnership would arguably serve as a good strategy for strengthening international IP protection and improving the utility of potential Intellectual assets in developing nations. To that extent, this might also contribute to improve the fairness and balance of benefits between developing and developed countries in current International IP systems.

On the other hand, it should be noted many inherent copyright problems and other IPR problems (at both domestic and international levels) may be resolved or weakened in the process of the development. For example, as introduced above, the growth of domestic copyright industries and the involvement of domestic benefit groups would significantly increase the government's incentive to strengthen IPR enforcement. The growth of China-U.S. trade and the U.S. investment in China not only greatly improved the U.S.-China relation but also facilitated the resolution of IP trade conflicts.

As such, when addressing the IP conflict problem, instead of unconstructive resistance, different countries should try to work collaboratively with each other, to try to resolve existing IP problems in the process of development to adopt a more comprehensive and constructive copyright policy.

Variety and Flexibility: Implementation of Policy Framework

This article has highlighted some principles for a nation to establish copyright policies. However,

it is noteworthy that there is no simple resolution that suits each nation. Even for the same nation, there may be a different priority plan on IP protection and development over different periods of time. As such, when a nation makes its copyright and development policies, it should always use it flexibility and base on the policies on its specific economic, social and legal circumstances.

For example, for nations with high technology potential (including both developing and developed nations), their policies may focus more on improving their capability of self-innovation. The governments may adopt certain preferential policies to stimulate innovation and technology transfer. For nations who have a long history and substantial culture heritages (such as China, Korea, India and Thailand), their policies may focus more on improving their capability of industrializing existing IP assets. Moreover, Korea's strategies in promoting culture exports (introduced above) may be flexibly applied to minority groups in other nations, such as indigenous groups in Australia and most African countries.

In a word, each country should learn to explore and make the most of its comparative advantages. A wise nation should use copyright law and policy as a powerful tool to enhance its self-innovation ability and the development of domestic copyright industries, rather than a tool to simply collect money for foreign copyright owners.

CONCLUSION

This article started with a brief introduction of the impacts of Internet technology on traditional business models and the copyright legal system, and the dangers of potential IP trade wars in the digital age. It then reviewed and compared the copyright history in the U.S. and China, and explored the main reasons causing copyright piracy and U.S.-China IP trade conflicts. The article further explored major rationales (business incentives) behind copyright policy making of these two countries, and the main reasons why they was able to successfully resolve potential IP trade conflicts in recent years. Based on this, the article summarized some general principles for a nation to formulate a proper copyright policy in the digital age.

In 1756, Voltaire said, "[T]he true conquerors are those who know how to make laws. Their power is stable; the others are torrents which pass." In the digital age, the dramatic development of digital technology not only brings great challenges to traditional business models and copyright protection systems, but also brings many opportunities for different nations to make new laws and polices. Yet, when making its copyright policy, a nation should always try to realize the harmony of IP protection and social development, and bear in mind that a nation's interest is "only best served by tailoring its IP regimes to its particular economic and social circumstances" (Tian, 2004, p. 217).

REFERENCES

Association of Research Libraries. TIMELINE: *A history of copyright in the United States*. Retrieved March 18, 2006 from, http://www.arl.org/info/frn/copy/timeline.html

Barnes, J.J. (1974*). Preface to authors, publishers and politicians*. Ohio: Ohio State University Press.

BSA. (2004, July). *First annual BSA and IDC global software piracy study*. Retrieved June 10, 2005 from, http://www.bsa.org/globalstudy/

CIA. (2006, January 10). *China. The world factbook*. Retrieved March 18, 2006 from, http://www.cia.gov/cia/publications/factbook/geos/ch.html

Chynoweth, G.J. (2003). Reality bites: How the biting reality of piracy in China is working to strengthen its copyright laws. *Duke Law & Technology Review*, February 11, p. 3.

Cooper, H., & Kathy Chen, K. (1996). U.S. and China announce tariff rargets as both nations step up trade rhetoric. *Wall Street Journal*, p. A3.

Cox, J. U.S. (1995, August 23). Firms: Piracy rhrives in China. *USA Today*, p. 2B.

DeWolf, R. (1925). *An outline of copyright law*. Boston: John W. Luce & Company.

Fisher, J.H. (2002). The 21st century Internet: A digital copy machine: Copyright analysis, issues, and possibilities. *Virginia Journal of Law & Technology*, 7, p. 7.

Gana, R. (1996). The myth of development, te progress of rights: Human rights to intellectual property and development, *Law & Policy*, 18, p. 315

Gantz, J., & Rochester, J. B. (2005). *Pirates of the digital millennium: How the intellectually property wars damage our personal freedoms, our jobs, and the world economy*. Upper Saddle River, NJ: Financial Times Prentice Hall.

Ginsburg, J. C. (2003). Book review: Achieving balance in international copyright law—The WIPO treaties 1996: The WIPO copyright treaty and the WIPO performances and phonograms treaty: Commentary and legal analysis. By Jörg Reinbothe and Silke von Lewinski, 2002. p.581. *Columbia Journal of Law & the Arts*, 26, p. 201.

GOV.CN. (2006, February 9). *China issues S&T development guidelines*. Retrieved March 16, 2006 from, http://english.gov.cn/2006-02/09/content_183426.htm

Government Accountability Office. (March 24, 2004). *World trade organization: U.S. companies' views on China's implementation of its commitments. GAO report* number GAO-04-508. Retrieved August 16, 2005 from, http://www.gao.gov/htext/d04508.html.

Griffin, E. M. (1998). Note: Stop relying on uncle sam!—A proactive approach to copyright protection in the People's Republic of China. *Texas Intellectual Property Law Journal, 6*, p. 169.

GTW Associates. (2003, December 11) *Executive summary of United States trade representative 2003 report to congress on China's WTO compliance.* Retrieved March 6, 2006 from, http://www.gtwassociates.com/answers/ChinaWTO.htm

Hu, P. H. (1996). "Mickey Mouse" in China: Legal and cultural implications in protecting U.S. copyrights. *Boston University International Law Journal, 14*(Spring), p. 81.

IACC. (2005, January). *IACC white paper.* Retrieved October 23, 2005 from, http://www.iacc.org/WhitePaper.pdf

Joffrain, (2001). T. deriving a (moral) right for creators. *Texas International Law Journal, 36,* p. 735.

Kang, J., & Cuff, D. (2005). Pervasive computing: Embedding the public sphere. *Washington. & Lee Law Review, 62,* p. 93.

Knemeyer, D. (2004, May 5). *Digital convergence: Insight into the future of web design.* Digital Web Magazine. Retrieved March 16, 2006 from, http://digital-web.com/articles/digital_convergence/

KOCCA, *Main objective of KOCCA actives.* Retrieved March 16, 2006 from, http://www.kocca.or.kr/e/act/1.jsp

Kositchotethana, B. (2006, January 11). A lesson from South Korea. *Bangkok Post.* Retrieved March 16, 2006 from, http://www.asiamedia.ucla.edu/article.asp?parentid=36936

Lessig, L. (2003). Dunwody distinguished lecture in law: The creative commons. *Florida Law Review, 55,* p. 763.

Li, Y.H. (2002). The wolf has come: Are China's intellectual property industries prepared for the WTO?. *UCLA Pacific Basin Law Journal, 77,* 20, p. 77.

McCarthy, T. (1995). Intellectual property—America's overlooked export. *University of Dayton Law Review, 20,* p. 809

McManis, C.R. (2001). Symposium—Information and electronic commerce law: Comparative perspectives: Database protection in the digital information age. *Roger Williams University Law Review, 7,* 7.

Neigel, C. (2000). Piracy in Russia and China: A different U.S. reaction. *Law and Contemporary Problems 63,* p. 179.

Okediji, R G. (1999). Copyright and public welfare in global perspective. *Indiana Journal of Global Legal Studies, 7*(1), pp. 117,119.

Okediji, R.L. (2004, May). Development in the information age. *UNCTAD-ICTSD Project on IPRs and Sustainable Development,* (Issue Paper No.9), p. 1.

Osnos, E. (2005, December 23). Asia rides wave of Korean pop culture invasion. *Chicago Tribune.* Retrieved March 13, 2006 from, http://www.chicagotribune.com/entertainment/music/chi-0512230216dec23,1,2801936.story?coll=chient_music-hed&ctrack=1&cset=true

People Daily Online. (2005, March 16*). Revenue of China's movie market to exceed 10 billion Yuan in three years.* Retrieved March 13, 2006 from, http://english.people.com.cn/200503/16/eng20050316_177098.html

Spoo, R. (1998). Copyright protectionism and its discontents: The case of the James Joyce's Ulysses in America. *Yale Law Journal, 108,* p. 633.

Sullivan, A. C. (2001). When the creative is the enemy of true: Database protection in the U.S. and abroad. *AIPLA Quarterly Journal, 29,* p. 317.

Tang, G. H. (2004). *A comparative study of copyright and the public interest in the United*

Kingdom and China. 1:2 SCRIPT-ed 319. Retrieved March 18, 2006 from, http://www.law. ed.ac.uk/ahrb/script-ed/issue2/china.asp

Thurow, L. C. (1997). Needed: A new system of intellectual property rights. *Harvard Business Review,* September-October.

Tian, Y. J., (2004). WIPO treaties, free trade agreement and implications for ISP safe harbour provisions—the role of ISP in australian copyright law. *Bond Law Review, 16*(1), 186-217. Gold Coast, Australia.

USINFO (2005a). *United States proposes intellectual-property partnerships.* Retrieved from: http://usinfo.state.gov/ei/Archive/2005/Apr/15-125293.html

United States Trade Representative (USTR), (2004a). *2004 USTR report to congress on China's WTO compliance.* Retrieved March 10, 2006from, http://www.ustr.gov/Document_Library/Reports_Publications/2004/asset_upload_file281_6986.pdf

USTR, (2004b, April 21*). Trade facts—The U.S.-China JCCT: Outcomes on major U.S. trade concerns.* Retrieved March 10, 2006 from, http://www.ustr.gov/assets/Document_Library/Fact_Sheets/2004/asset_upload_file225_5834.pdf [last visited April 13, 2005]

USTR, (2005) *2005 special 301 report.* Retrieved March 10, 2006 from, http://www.ustr.gov/Document_Library/Reports_Publications/2005/2005_Special_301/Section_Index.html

USTR. (2006, February). *U.S.-China trade relations: Entering a new phase of greater accountability and enforcement top-to-bottom review.* Retrieved March 10, 2006 from, http://www.ustr.gov/World_Regions/North_Asia/China/2006_Top-to-Bottom_Review/Section_Index.html

Voltaire, (1756). *Essai sur l'histoire Generale et sur les moeurs et l'Esprit des nation's, Tome 1,* Ch. 25, p. 390.

What is the I Ching?. Retrieved March 10, 2005 from, http://www.wholarts.com/psychic/iching.html

Wald, J. (2000). Note: legislating the golden rule: Achieving comparable rrotection under the european union database directive. *Fordham International Law Journal*, 25, p. 987.

Yonehara, B T. (2002). Comment: Enter the dragon: China's WTO accession, film piracy and prospects for the enforcement of copyright laws. *UCLA Entertainment Law Review,* 9, p. 389.

Yu, P. K. (2003a). Four common misconceptions about copyright piracy. *Loyola of Los Angeles International and Comparative Law Review,* 26, p.127.

Yu, P K. (2003b, November). The copyright divide. *Cardozo Law Review*, 25, p. 331

Xue, H., & Zheng, C.S. (2002). *Chinese intellectual property law in the 21st century.* Hong Kong: Sweet & Maxwell Asia.

Zheng, C.S., & Pendleton, M. (1987). *Chinese intellectual property & technology transfer law.* Hong Kong: Sweet & Maxwell Asia.

Zhou, J.J. (2002). Notes and comments: Trademark law & enforcement in China: A transnational perspective. *Wisconsin International Law Journal* 20, p. 415.

Zoellick, R.B. (2005). *Statement of U.S. trade representative Robert B. Zoellick on U.S.-China trade relation.* Retrieved April 13, 2005 from, http://www.ustr.gov/Document_Library/Press_Releases/2004/April/Statement_of_U.S._Trade_Representative_Robert_B._Zoellick_on_U.S.-China_Trade_Relations.html

Chapter XII
The Public Policy Environment of the Privacy–Security Conundrum/Complement

John W. Bagby
Pennsylvania State University, USA

ABSTRACT

Public policy constraints impact deployment of most technology underlying the convergence of digital technologies in telecommunications, e-commerce, and e-government. Networked computers increase the vulnerability of confidential data, transaction processing infrastructure and national security. Compliance regulation imposes complex constrains on data management by government, the private-sector and their personnel. Privacy and security are a balance between individual interests in secrecy/solitude and society's interests in security, order, and efficiency. This chapter explores the key political, legal, and regulatory methods for resolving conflicts between privacy rights and security methods to encourage convergence success. The "Privacy-Security Conundrum" is framed, then set against the more cross-dependant relationships of a "Privacy-Security Complement." Security law illustrates that the conundrum-complement dilemma serves to define convergence as constrained and induced by the legal and policy perspectives or privacy, intellectual property, technology transfer, electronic records management, torts, criminal law, fiduciary and contractual duties and professional ethics regulating privacy and security.

INTRODUCTION

Public policy constraints are likely to impact the deployment and continuing operation of nearly any technology, method or process designed to support counter-terrorism. Policy drives the traditional institutional efforts to maintain security. These have been focused on criminal enforcement and regulatory risks based on commonly-held understandings of burglary, theft, conversion and other protections of physical property. However, such a focus largely on physical security protections for tangible property is inconsistent with the proliferation of networked computers and their impact on the economy and key infrastructures (Exec. Order No. 13,231, 2001). The latter has vastly increased the vulnerability of confidential-private data, transaction processing and critical national security systems. At the heart of these challenges lies regulatory compliance with security and privacy laws. Such responsibility now falls much more clearly on all levels of government (local, state/provincial, national/federal and regional/international) as well as on the private-sector and on individuals. These complex new duties constrain organizations in the data management industry as well as suppliers and users of data and all participants in the information supply chain, a useful conceptual framework discussed in this chapter. Such participants include consultants, software suppliers, applications service providers, out-sources of maintenance and communications intermediaries.

Privacy and security will likely remain in a balance between individual interests in secrecy/solitude and society's interests in security, order and efficiency. Privacy is a fragmented, assortment of rights found in international law, constitutions, federal statutes and regulations, state statutes and regulations, common law precedents and private contracts. Many of these sources of law can simultaneously exhibit conflicts, complements and direct or indirect referencing. This Chapter frames the privacy rights debate in two ways: as a conundrum or tradeoff with security and alternatively as a complement between these two concepts. The conundrum/complement model provides insight for policy makers who constrain and enable the design of information and communications technologies (ICT). These policies inform the identification and resolution of policy concerns throughout the design and implementation process. These are policy analysis tools that can advance technology implementation by attenuating public surprise of privacy intrusions and thereby improve the opportunities for technological convergence.

This article explores the converging fields of privacy rights and security in light of legal duties and public policy under American and International laws. Several key factors are examined: public policies underlying regulation of privacy and security, insights into how society accommodates transition of existing laws to the unique vulnerabilities of government and the information economy, management of employment and independent contractor relations for privacy and security and the processes used at many government agencies to regulate privacy and security. There is an analysis of recurring privacy and security experience in some particular industry "sectors."

CONCEPTUAL PRIVACY AND PUBLIC POLICY

Privacy is understood more fully if seen through fundamental and enduring historical and social expectations. Privacy can be viewed from its Biblical origins. As early as the Garden of Eden, privacy concepts of shame and modesty signaled the inevitable imperfection of human decision-making and the will to avoid embarrassment. Abundant privacy lowers the human risk of public contempt or retribution. Similarly, modesty, shyness and prudent appearance discourage societal predators. Privacy is an enduring, nearly universal, but elusive aspiration:

Who could deny that privacy is a jewel? It has always been the mark of privilege. ... Out of the cave, the tribal tepee, the pueblo, the community fortress, man emerged to build himself a house of his own with a shelter in it for himself and his diversions. Every age has seen it so. The poor might have to huddle together ... [b]ut in each civilization, as it advanced, those who could afford it chose the luxury of a withdrawing-place. (McGinley, 1959)

Early American privacy rights protected citizens from intrusions by government, such as those suffered by early American colonists both as they left behind government oppression in their native lands and as colonists suffered under the tyranny of the English Crown. The American Founders incorporated forms of privacy into the U.S. Constitution as rights: religious freedom, limitations on search and seizure and the quartering of soldiers, freedom of speech, press and association as well as due process and equal protection rights. Privacy is a fundamental right for liberty isolating individuals from undue interference by government or from powerful private interests. Privacy promotes competition by allowing individuals or firms to exploit valuable secrets. As the American frontier was tamed, the industrial revolution emerged and the cities became more populous. This caused privacy concerns to shift from government intrusions to intrusions from private parties. High tech investigatory tools are now accessible to individuals and business firms that increasingly monitor customer, client and employee activities and performance. Nevertheless, government intrusions continue to stimulate pressures for privacy rights in 21st Century North America, Europe and the Middle East.

Privacy is becoming viewed by society as a fundamental right or civil liberty, essential to individual freedom, autonomy and dignity. Technological advances in data collection, storage, integration and secondary use contribute to a heightened public concern in the abuse of personally identifiable information (hereinafter PII). Computerized telecommunications and the increasing value of PII contribute to the commoditization of private information as PII becomes more easily shared, traded, sold and presumptively valued. The public is aware of industry expectations as once succinctly expressed by Sun Microsystem's CEO Scott McNealy: "You have zero privacy anyway. Get over it!" (Sprenger, 1999). Furthermore, PII is subject to data creep, that is, as PII is collected for one purpose it is eventually seen as useful for other, secondary and tertiary purposes. Consider how the function of social security numbers has expanded beyond the limited, original purpose of FICA payment record-keeping and Social Security benefit payments to become a primary individual information locator.

The American public's attitudes towards privacy are captured in research by Dr. Alan F. Westin, who claims the public is segmented into three fairly distinct groups in their privacy attitudes and expectations (Westin, A. F. 2000). Privacy fundamentalists, about 25% of the U.S. population, value privacy highly, summarily reject business and government claims that PII needs are legitimate, advocate that individuals should refuse to disclose PII and seek strong regulation of privacy rights. Privacy pragmatists, whose numbers have grown from 55% in 1990 to 63% by 2000, can be expected to balance their personal privacy with societal needs for PII, examine privacy policies and practices, disclose PII when economically rational, may support industry self-regulation of privacy and support privacy regulation when self-regulation fails. The privacy unconcerned, whose numbers have decreased from 20% in 1990 to 12 % by 2000, readily disclose PII, either trust in the benefits derived or are oblivious and are unlikely to engage in political efforts directed at strengthening privacy rights or regulation.

Privacy and security are terms now widely used but too often with imprecision. Privacy and security are not just technologies implementing privacy or security despite the insistence of some who argue that "encryption is privacy and security." Instead, privacy and security are broad, vague and complex terms that are too often misunderstood. Privacy includes several distinct interests and individual expectations that trigger legal rights which implicate duties in data processing practices. Katz v. U.S. (1967) synonyms for privacy provide some perspective: seclusion, solitude, retreat from intrusion, intimacy, isolation, secrecy, concealment and separateness. Dictionary definitions also illustrate these diverse interests.

- Privacy—Withdrawn from company or public view, secrecy, one's private life or personal affairs.

A definition useful in the counter-terrorism context is that privacy is the maintenance of secrecy over PII.

PRIVACY STANDARDS: FAIR INFORMATION PRACTICE PRINCIPLES

Many privacy laws and policies can be traced to five fair information practices: the **Fair Information Practice Principles** (**FIPP**) that originated from the U.S. Department of Health, Education and Welfare (HEW Report, 1973). FIPP amounts to informal standards followed in many privacy statutes, regulations and policies in the U.S. and other nations as well in self-regulatory programs. The five FIPP standards are discussed next and listed in Table 1.

The first FIPP standard is notice, recommending that subject individuals be given notice and/or have a clear awareness that their PII will be captured, processed and used for some purpose. That is, before collection of PII, there should be a reasonably adequate, conspicuous and compre-

hensible notification of the data capture practices. Without notice, a subject individual cannot make an informed choice. Therefore, notice enables counter-measures to protect privacy. Notice should provide all details to inform the choice, at least: (1) identify the data collector, (2) identify the data recipient, (3) describe the use of the data, (4) describe the data to be collected, (5) describe the means, methods or mechanisms used in data collection, (6) acknowledge if access or initiating a relationship with the collector is conditioned on the data collection and (7) describe the quality and security controls.

The second FIPP standard is choice, recommending that subject individuals must have a choice on whether and how their PII is collected and used. Choice is a clear and intentional manifestation of consent that extends to the primary uses of the information as necessary for the immediate transaction or purpose. Consent may also address secondary uses such as those beyond the immediate needs in the current transaction, such as an expected future transfer onward in a sale or barter. The form and significance of an opt-out consent versus an opt-in consent is detailed in a later section. It can be expected that the terms of privacy agreements will become more complex as there are advances in the methods of data col-

Table 1. Fair information practice principles (FIPP)

Fair Information Practice Principle	Suggested Implementation in Public Policy
Notice/Awareness	Subject individuals should be given notice of information processing practices before PII is collected, i.e., details about the data's collection, security and uses.
Choice/Consent	Subject individual should be given choice or consent to whether and how PII is collected, such as with opt-in or opt-out consents or as implied from conduct.
Access/ Participation	Subject individual should be given timely and inexpensive access to review their PII and a simple as well as an effective method to contest/correct inaccurate data.
Integrity/ Security	The PII collector should take reasonable steps to assure the accuracy of PII and also install and maintain administrative and technical security measures to prevent unauthorized access, disclosure, destruction or misuse of PII.
Enforcement/ Redress	There should be a mechanism(s) to enforce and remedy privacy malpractices, e.g., self-regulation, private rights of action, regulatory oversight and enforcement.

lection, archival, processing and uses. Parallel progress and complexity can be expected in the form of consent that allows the subject individual and the data collector to personalize their PII use agreement.

The third FIPP standard is access. Subject individuals should be enabled to review their PII files in a timely, accurate and inexpensive manner. There has been considerable experience with credit bureaus illustrating the pervasiveness of errors that can severely disadvantage subject individuals. For example, the financial fraud aspects of identity theft are becoming pervasive today. Database security is enhanced by the participation of subject individuals who have strong incentives to identify and correct disparaging errors. Simple and effective methods to contest and correct inaccurate data should be implemented.

The fourth FIPP standard is security. Owners and operators of PII databases should be charged with at least two major custodial duties: quality control of data processing and safeguarding from unauthorized alteration. PII data processors should continually devise and revise reasonable controls that assure the accuracy of PII. This includes the maintenance of administrative and technical security measures to inhibit unauthorized access, destruction, misuse or disclosure of PII. These approaches are largely preventive – intended to deter the intrusion and improve controls after vulnerabilities are discovered.

The fifth FIPP standard is enforcement. FIPP compliant procedures are costly, raising the probability of shirking by data processors. Without various forms of incentive to encourage persistent performance, the predictable result is lax security, which runs the risk of injury to subject individuals. For most of the 20th century, there has developed fairly broad public support to provide remedies to subject individuals following failures of preventative mechanisms. Despite the more Draconian efforts of tort reformers, when injuries appear preventable but irresponsibility and/or self-interest contribute substantially to the

injury, there persists a political preponderance of support for curative remedies such as liability for money damages for past, unprevented privacy violations. Further, there continues public support for punishment in egregious cases; punishment serves as a deterrent signaling the importance of the safeguarding duty. There are a variety of possible mechanisms to enforce privacy practices, including, self-regulation, government regulation and/or private rights of action for redress. As with other professional pursuits, a combination of these mechanisms is often deployed, including professional regulation of competence, government regulation of security controls to prevent future injuries and private suits to compensate past injuries resulting from data management malpractice.

SUPPLY CHAIN ARCHITECTURAL APPROACH TO REGULATION OF PRIVATE DATA MANAGEMENT

Information IS property (*Carpenter v. U.S.* (1987), *Ruckelshaus v. Monsanto Co.*, 1984). The basic organization of PII data management can be structured as a intangible distribution vertical for valuable information property similar to other supply chains. This organization provides policymakers with guidance for targeted imposition of privacy enhancing mechanisms. There are several major choke-points along the sequence of events typical to the PII data management process. The effectiveness of privacy regulations depends on a clear technical understanding of PII data management practices. Without such an understanding, subversive techniques are encouraged that might circumvent weak controls. Privacy regulations can discourage particular activities at any or at each stage during PII data management. As pictured in Figure 1, there are four basic steps revealing a supply chain of PII in most data management practices: (1) collection, (2) storage, (3) analysis and (4) use (Bagby & McCarty (2003)).

Figure 1. PII supply chain of custody and data management sequence

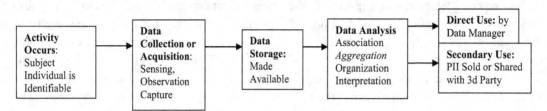

Data Acquisition is the first step in the PII Supply Chain. When some activity occurs, and if it is observed, the chain of custody is initiated and a data management sequence ensues. PII can then be collected and coded into data storage. Information flowing through networks can be captured during telecommunication from public wire lines, from public airwaves, within secured networks or at particular Web sites. Capture is the interception and storage of data during its creation, entry, discovery, detection or transmission. For example, information is directly observed as transactions are recorded, vendors and delivery services report transactions, loan payments or defaults are recorded by lenders or financial service intermediaries, Web sites are visited, hot links are clicked, PII is supplied to queries, data are derived from cookies or spyware and data from keyboard capture programs are made available. Privacy regulation can be directed to prohibit or limit such data acquisition.

Information analysis is the second step in the PII Supply Chain. Information analysis involves the organization, association, aggregation and interpretation of the data to create useful information. The analysis of PII often requires systematic handling and pragmatic evaluation before valid conclusions are drawn. Large scale and mechanized analysis makes up data warehousing. Impromptu, real time analysis is data mining. Innovative analysis can reveal important and useful relationships but can require considerable computing power and ready access

to large data sets, sometimes impractical for smaller firms or organizations. PII is captured by third party specialists, which gather PII from multiple sources then provide analysis for clients. Such service providers may combine PII about one or more subject individuals from multiple sources. The term aggregators—this term is a noun (suffix pronounced -gate)—is sometimes used to designate particular database management service providers that combine partial bits of PII data from various sources. These data can be assembled to form a profile or dossier about the subject individual potentially useful in making marketing, insurance, credit, employment decisions and security-risk assessments. An important and stark contrast should be drawn with an apparently related term—aggregate data; this term is an adjective (suffix pronounced: -git). Many privacy advocates urge data practices that anonymize collections of data about numerous individuals. These databases of anonymized, aggregate data are more likely to be compliant with strong privacy rights because of their removal or non-collection of personal identifiers.

Large databases can be made more useful with new and evolving methods of data organization, structuring, filtering, aggregation, association and analysis. Implications from such data analyses are often speculative conclusions based on theories and conjecture taken from many social science and natural science fields such as biology, psychology, sociology, economics or criminology. Such theories can also be based on generalizations from empirical testing. Advocates of strong privacy rights allege that too many recommendations of PII data analysis are based on faulty assumptions, erroneous calculations or premature generalizations without a scientific basis—some call this *junk science*. For example, lie detector evidence is generally inadmissible to disprove an alibi. Restrictions prohibiting the use of some data analysis methods seem likely as the public perceives the PII Supply Chain results in uses without a reasonable scientific basis. For example, genetic testing of human tissue samples to infer predisposition to disease, to deny costly health insurance, to infer dishonesty, criminality or mental instability are politically sensitive issues. Privacy advocates can be expected to demand that a very strong and reliable scientific consensus emerge that connects particular genetic markers with undesirable predispositions before any implementation is permissible for such generalizations in PII profiling.

Use of knowledge is the third step in the PII Supply Chain. Data is collected and analyzed to give it value that is realized as knowledge only when it is used or sold for re-use. The economic incentive to support PII Supply Chain activities recognizes that valuable and accurate knowledge is scarce and often critical to avoid adverse selection. The PII Supply Chain collects data and can produce useful knowledge for direct use by the data manager or for secondary use by third parties such as when sold to clients, shared with affiliates or bartered in return for other information.

The public policy focus on this third stage serves an important residual function. Regulation can prohibit uses of information considered socially unacceptable. This approach essentially acknowledges that PII collection and analysis may be inevitable. Indeed, subject individuals often suffer injury only with the actual use of PII. Use restrictions are a form of last resort for advocates of strong privacy rights because such restrictions preclude the privacy intrusion from causing injury to the subject individual. Privacy rights are often designed as use restrictions; consider some examples: (1) automobile insurance underwriters are often prohibited from considering moving violations after passage of a few years; (2) an individual's former bankruptcy cannot be considered by potential creditors in making credit decisions after several years pass; (3) financial and health care privacy rules require the subject individual's consent before the release or sale of private data; (4) law enforcement is prohibited from using a confession to prove guilt unless Miranda warnings were given.

When policy focuses on any or all three major functions in the PII Supply Chain, it arguably transforms into a *chain of custody*. Custody presumes subject individuals have rights, further legitimizing the constraints imposed by privacy regulation throughout the three basic stages of collection, analysis and use. Custodial responsibility likely includes duties of reasonable care and safeguarding by enabling the restrictions of privacy regulation to constrain the transfer, transmission, communication and/or receipt of PII. Furthermore, the chain of custody concept recognizes the vulnerability in flows of data further necessitating security duties.

The U.S. has no comprehensive privacy protection policy. Privacy laws are narrowly drawn to particular industry sectors, which can be called a **sectoral** approach to privacy regulation. Regulation of privacy generally arises in the U.S. after there is considerable experience with privacy abuses, an approach consistent with liberty, laissez-faire economics and common law precedents as the major approach to law making. As a result, U.S. privacy law is a hodgepodge, patchwork of sectoral protections, narrowly construed and derived from constitutional, statutory and regulatory provisions of international, federal and state law.

By contrast to the U.S.'s sectoral approach, consider the European *omnibus* approach that has deployed a comprehensive and uniform method granting strong privacy rights and thereby imposing strong privacy duties on most industries and on many government activities. Clearly, privacy advocates urge conformance with the European omnibus approach while many in the U.S., including sectors of government, business and the data management industries, prefer the sectoral approach. This sectoral versus omnibus debate pervades the discussion of privacy rights and security duties in the U.S. (Strauss & Rogerson , 2002)

THE PRIVACY-SECURITY CONUNDRUM

Law and economics provide an important perspective on the regulation of privacy because this approach helps in predicting the incentives and behaviors of subject individuals, data managers and data users. These behaviors may change as society continues to reset the balance of personal privacy rights against society's PII needs. There are at least three basic principles applicable to the economic analysis of privacy: (1) markets function best with complete information, (2) information is costly and often incomplete and (3) information often defies exclusive control making it difficult to maintain secrecy, control its use or prevent its misappropriation.

The perfect competition model presumes all transacting parties already possess perfect information concerning the subject matter, the parties and market conditions. Indeed, many economists still presume sufficient information is always freely available to inform all contracting parties. Further, efficient market theorists often extend their analysis of information economics to make additional presumptions that perfect information and rational action by contracting parties inevitably lead to predict efficient markets–prices, trading volumes and "goods" traded are correctly assessed resulting in information about true asset values. Completed transactions send information signals that communicate the preferences of consumers and capabilities of producers through these efficient markets. Rising consumer demand attracts optimal investment to produce products and services using the most promising technologies and businesses. Decreasing demand redirects investment away from less promising alternatives freeing up capital for more promising technologies, projects or industry sectors. Economists who presume perfect information and rational action conclude that Adam Smith's "invisible hand" produces optimal results for society.

Increasingly, behavioral economists admit the existence of market anomalies—market failures such as imperfect information, incompetent information analysis or the irrationality of buyers or sellers—and that anomalies lead to market inefficiency. Perhaps such imperfections help explain the increasing expenditure of resources to collect and assure the quality of information. Many policymakers have long recognized the imperfection of information and this has resulted in regulation. Such has also been the history of secrecy; law intervenes when society eventually discovers that secrecy is harmful. Consider the significant examples of mandatory corporate financial reporting, toxic chemical disclosures or Meagan's laws governing sex-offenders.

Information, as a form of intangible property, is seemingly inexhaustible—the original copy usually persists after numerous copies are made. This inexhaustibility is an illusion because there are narrow profit opportunities for information owners unless they maintain exclusive control over it. When information becomes available to the public, competitors, suppliers or customers, then its value steadily erodes to the owner; eventually the value is totally depleted. "Information wants to be free," a maxim recognizing the strong incentives to learn, purchase or sell information, makes it vulnerable to unauthorized communication and even unlawful misappropriation. Furthermore, after information is revealed, it cannot be easily or effectively withdrawn. Despite the development of e-mail recall technologies, important information will all too often become widely known.

Intellectual property (IP) is information, and long experience illustrates that IP almost defies exclusive possession without significant regulation and rights to remedies (trade secret misappropriation and infringement suits). Information is unlike tangible property because tangibles are susceptible to possession by just one person at a time. Even when the rightful owner of intangibles (IP) or a subject individual (PII) has no knowledge that copies were made or secrets revealed, nevertheless unauthorized copies can still exist even proliferate. The IP owner or subject individual may have further ignorance of who possesses copies or uses such copies. Consider the loss of profit-making opportunities to the rightful owner of IP such as data, software, music or video when serious potential buyers can obtain illegal copies. The owner's marginal revenue opportunities are largely lost for sales to buyers who would have purchased legitimate copies. There is a similar effect on PII which is information, and information is property. A subject individual's PII is a personal asset. When PII is used without the subject individual's consent or is misappropriated or used without the subject individual's understanding of the PII's value, this deprives the subject individual of personal advantages. Therefore, when outsiders trade in a subject individual's PII, the subject individual's personal advantages are siphoned off to others who benefit at the subject individual's expense.

This analysis suggests the basic economic conundrum of PII—who should capture the value of a subject individual's information, an intruder or the subject individual? Should vicarious experience belong to each person who perceives PII, making the finder of information its owner? Without the right to use perception, society would lose important incentives to capture, store, analyze and produce highly valuable information. This would result in many bad outcomes for society: lost economic efficiency and dangerous security

risks. An opposite theory argues that PII is the product of each subject individual's right of self-expression (thought, action and ingenuity).

Society cannot accommodate both of these extreme positions: the personal right to perceptual experience containing PII of others versus each subject individual's right to prevent others from appropriating any PII. Therefore, privacy and security may remain a balance, albeit continually tilted as society perceives the balance must be redrawn. That is, adjustments may be continually needed to accommodate societal interests in efficient markets, justice, security and social order while continuing to indulge in the individual liberty and autonomy of privacy that is so fundamental to liberty.

Key to both privacy and security are their relationships between these concepts: Some relationships are conflicting while other relationships are complementary. One line of reasoning holds that there are irreconcilable trade-offs between privacy and security. Under this conception, deploying optimal and effective public policies for both privacy and security is an impossible task because they represent a zero-sum game: Privacy gains diminish security while security gains come mainly at the expense of privacy losses. This conflict generally leads both advocates of strong privacy rights and advocates of strong national security to a similar set of public policy presumptions and then these presumptions typically lead these two groups to opposite public policy prescriptions.

Consider the conundrum example typified by the Chinese experience in limiting Chinese people from unlimited access to content that may be seen by the Chinese government as a potential threat to political stability. Privacy can be characterized as broadly encompassing more than access to PII, it also embraces liberty, freedom, autonomy and the right to access views. Internet censorship by the "Golden Shield" limits access to alternative political thought, cultural change advocacy or even sexually explicit content and is a privacy intrusion that many believe is intended to provide security to the current Chinese government's political stability (Deibert, 2002). These practices are worrisome as the Internet further intensifies as the point of convergence for reliable eCommerce because China blocks content by rerouting IP addressing and selectively deploying DNS poisoning when particular sites are requested, the so-called "Great Firewall." This has impact on Internet governance causing a potentially troublesome fragmentation of addressing. Essentially, the methods of Internet censorship used to implement national political security impacts privacy, and may also threaten Internet functionality the world over (Bagby, & Ruhnka, 2004).

A Conundrum in the European Union: Data Retention

The European Union's (EU) controversial Data Retention Directive has directly implicated the conundrum and trade-off between privacy and security (EU Directive (2002))It is intended to enhance law enforcement in EU nations when the legislature of each member state implements the Directive with compliant legislation. The EU Data Retention Directive does not enhance pre-trial discovery for civil litigation but instead permits legislation that would require data retention for law enforcement purposes such as national security, criminal investigations and prevention and the prosecution of criminal offenses, even without specific judicial authorization such as by subpoena or wiretap order.

The EU Data Retention Directive requires retention of various electronic records concerning traffic and location data of communications systems such as mobile phones, SMS, landlines, faxes, e-mails, chat rooms, Internet and other electronic communication devices. The Data Retention Directive explicitly permits EU national laws to compel Internet Service Providers (ISP) and telecommunications carriers (TelCo) to record, index and store communications data. Traffic

data includes all data generated by conveyance of communications on electronic communications networks. Location data indicates the geographic position of mobile phone user, similar to consumer proprietary network information (CPNI) in the U.S. Retention of the contents of messages is not required.

The EU Data Retention Directive is quite controversial and compliance by member state legislatures is incomplete. Only Belgium, France, Spain and the UK have enacted valid statutes. Indeed, in February of 2003, the Austrian Federal Constitutional Court held unconstitutional an Austrian statute compelling TelCos and ISPs to implement wiretapping measures at their own expense. Many TelCos and ISPs oppose the costs and likely customer mistrust of compliance, and most opposition is driven by individual privacy concerns and not by corporate confidentiality. Opposition to the EU Data Retention Directive is largely due to the perceived trade-off between increased security and diminished individual privacy (Statement of the European Data Protection Commissioners (2002)).

Arguments Opposing Strong Privacy Rights

Arguments advanced against strong privacy rights are initially based on the desire for PII to inform the evaluation of a counter-party before contract negotiations and performance. Strong privacy rights can lead to adverse selection if relevant information is withheld. Thus, under-informed parties, ignorant of critical information, cannot effectively evaluate the counter-party's ability to perform or reputation for satisfactory performances. Consider how insurers might underwrite bad risks or creditors might make risky loans if a customer could hide such relevant PII about their behavior or credit-worthiness. Higher premiums and credit costs would then be spread over all customers. Judge Posner refers to such PII that is derogatory about personal reputation as *deserv-*

edly discrediting information (Posner, 1986). Supporters of weakening privacy rights argue that deservedly discrediting information must remain available, otherwise society cannot effectively assess transaction risks or security risks.

Societal efficiency may be enhanced when the party with the lowest cost performs an activity: the *least cost provider* concept. Therefore, individuals should reveal personal PII that they already know because such disclosure is inexpensive, being derived from direct personal knowledge. This would permit a cumulative reduction of costs for investigations, data collection and analysis. However, if subject individuals more readily reveal discrediting information, the growth of new intermediary markets for PII could be inhibited. Markets for products produced in the mass customization model require significant PII. Perhaps consumers will demand much more precisely targeted marketing and view the result as a good use of their PII. However, such developments might be hindered if privacy laws are strengthened such as the recent increase in private, state and federal restrictions on spam, junk mail, telemarketing, spyware and ad tracking software. Weak privacy law encourages personal profiling and clickstream dossiers that may be essential to such marketing efficiencies because they reveal individual interests, purchasing habits, characteristics and judgments. Weak privacy law also may enable perfect price discrimination—the variable pricing of goods or services according to each individual customer's utility permitting precise customer ranking and encouraging sellers to charge more to customers who are more intently craving the product or better able to pay higher prices while charging less to others to achieve economies of scale (Choi, Stahl, & Whinston, 1997).

Much of the time, users of PII data clearly have rival interests to subject individuals. Data users will likely seek to collect any data perceived to be helpful in their business decision-making that has profit potential or might be useful to counter-terrorism. Despite users' immediate incentives to broadly collect and utilize PII, some data users can be expected to eventually respond to market pressures by providing some individual privacy. Many users will be pressured by privacy advocates to adopt privacy protection standards. These are most likely to be privately-orchestrated efforts that would be advanced to preempt pressures for further government privacy regulations. Such preclusive efforts may be implemented in various forms: vendor/users' unilateral adoption of privacy procedures, industry sponsored self-regulatory codes of conduct and/or third party privacy certification schemes. Users may bargain with individuals for the use of personal data. Users may either pay outright for some data or they may offer discounts or special services in exchange for particular data elements. In competitive markets, subject individuals might eventually have a choice to purchase products or services from vendors promising privacy or alternatively purchase more cheaply from other vendors that collect and use data. Presumably, different contracts would emerge for different terms of service and/or prices depending on the level of privacy desired or at least made available. However, such consumer choice depends directly on the existence of competitive markets in which there are several vendors available as alternatives. More realistically, during the early phases of this market development, it is less likely that there will be abundant competition among vendors of similar services or that several competitors would offer varying service packages, some with and some without privacy protections.

Several organizations are likely to fight strong privacy protections. Business trade associations have and can be expected to continue to protect their members' access to PII so long as the data seems useful. For example, credit bureaus have a substantial and lucrative business model that would be adversely impacted if privacy rights are strengthened significantly. Also data aggregators facilitate the collection, archiving and warehousing of PII and can be expected to advance their technologies both inside Cyberspace and from sources in traditional commerce. Law enforcement at all levels (local, state, federal, regulatory and self-regulation) is highly conscious of the useful insights possible from PII data warehousing.

The law enforcement community was one of the original focal points for strong privacy rights and counter-terrorism suggests their heightened interest in narrowing privacy rights. Among the most powerful Constitutional rights are those targeting the long history of government intrusions. The law enforcement community may intimately understand the potential for negative implications from political and public reaction from their long negative experience with public advocacy for weak privacy.

Opponents of strict privacy protections can be expected to lobby for weakness in privacy laws, undertake perfunctory industry efforts to protect privacy, be slow to invest or innovate in privacy protections and advocate broader definition of "business necessity" when needed to justify their data collection and use (Bagby & Gittings,1999). Data users that become convinced about the profitability of data warehousing can be expected to aggressively push new methods for refining, collecting and archiving data, to develop new uses for personal data and to resell or trade data whenever profitable. International laws creating barriers to cross-border data flows arguably inhibit the free flow of commerce (Swire & Litan, 1998). Data users and their trade associations can be expected to closely monitor the progress of privacy advocates. If subject individuals develop strong aversion to data warehousing, then data users may develop a further incentive to hide the data industry's practices of collection, warehousing and the sale and use of PII.

Arguments Favoring Strong Privacy Rights

Advocates of strong privacy rights counter the arguments above with several contentions. PII data management practices are imperfect and there are failures in the markets for PII because of the incentives stimulating practices in the data management industry. Data managers, but not subject individuals, "gain the full benefit of using the information in its own marketing or in the fee it receives when it sells information to third parties" and the data manager disclosing the information does not suffer any injury (Swire & Litan,1998). Furthermore, the data management industry seldom reveals fully the extent of PII concerning a subject individual, the use of the PII or the identity of the data purchaser or collector. Such secrecy generally prevents subject individuals from effectively monitoring the use of their PII or from correcting errors. While customers purchasing erroneous PII data could pressure the data manager to improve their service quality, the subject individual has the stronger, more personal and immediate incentive to assure accuracy. Finally, despite the emergence of many potential terms and conditions in the collection, processing and use of PII, there is remarkably little negotiation between subject individuals and data processing organizations. Furthermore, there is little likelihood of such bargaining, given the high transaction costs relative to the small value of most PII. Therefore, the data management industry captures most of the benefits of subject individuals' PII yet bears little responsibility for the data until required to do so either by competitive market conditions or privacy regulations.

Strong privacy rights are consistent with a property rights approach. Property rights recognize individuals' ownership and control over their PII, permitting PII to be used as a form of currency useful in accessing online content. A PII property rights perspective might be implemented with technical solutions that control PII use mechanically. For example, a *digital rights management* (DRM) system like those used to deter and track online copyright infringement or the misappropriation of electronic payments could be adapted to PII collection, aggregation use and resale. For example, meta-data, digital watermarks and third party Web services could be deployed to identify and track PII sources and uses to enforce the subject individual's rights and imposition of restrictions. Such a *digital privacy rights management* (DPRM) system might include the subject individual's profile of privacy preferences that would accompany digital copies of their PII and be interpreted and implemented by electronic agents. If the Platform for Privacy Preferences develops into an effective example of such technologies, DPRM may gain acceptance.

Subject individuals incentives for the preservation of confidentiality are generally defensive, suggesting they are likely to seek legal protection or even take defensive, self-help measures to protect their personal privacy and thwart the collection, archiving and use of such personal data (Bagby& Gittings,1999). This conduct will most likely include efforts to eliminate publication or use of false data or defamatory content. Privacy advocates may also likely seek to eliminate and conceal truthful data they view as damaging to their reputations or solitude. Some privacy advocates seek simply to avoid the "fishbowl exposure" of public revelation of highly private facts. Privacy advocates also worry such data archives are insecure and entirely too vulnerable to misuse of financial and personal safety data by electronic hackers or societal predators (e.g., extortion and stalking).

It is expected that privacy advocates will seek public policies to more narrowly define the legitimate uses of personal data. Privacy advocates will likely seek broad definitions for

the illegitimate, misuse of private data and seek imposition of severe sanctions for data misuse. Further, they will likely seek legal protections for personal privacy by constitutional provision or interpretation, statute, regulation and through provisions in private contracts. Privacy advocates may be expected to publicly expose the misuse of private information and seek public denunciation and censure of those seen to misuse private data.

DRAWING THE PRIVACY "BALANCE"

This Chapter repeatedly describes privacy as a balance between each individual's rights and society's rights set within the context of our long cultural and legal history. However, there is not much practical guidance on how that balance is drawn. This is because there is really no deterministic or formulaic balancing method. Instead, balancing is a compromise resulting from social, economic and political pressures as focused through available technology implementations. Experience with repeated privacy intrusions from government or by private entities leads society to evaluate two major factors: (1) the usefulness to society of the type of information acquired in the intrusion and (2) the repugnance of such intrusions. This balance has inspired various social pressures and legal responses. The extent of privacy protection depends on existing mores and society's legitimate needs for information to function properly. Society then chooses either to permit such intrusions, to regulate them or to prohibit them.

The famed jurist, Learned Hand, developed a public policy balancing framework for the imposition of tort law duties (*United States v. Carroll Towing Co.*, 1947). This framework is adapted by Judge Richard A. Posner to the limited privacy context of Fourth Amendment search and seizure, and is further adapted here to the privacy-security

Table 2. Privacy-security balancing formula

To adapt the Hand Formula to the privacy-security conundrum, assume the following:
B=intrusion costs
P=probability of discovering useful information
L=societal losses.

	Privacy vs. Security: The Impact on Legislation, Precedent or Regulation
B>P*L	Privacy interests outweigh Security interests
B<P*L	Security interests outweigh Privacy interests

conundrum (Posner, 1986). This model subsumes the conundrum—it would either protect privacy or alternatively enhance security depending on a balancing of: the usefulness to society of PII acquired from an intrusion against the repugnance of the intrusion.

The resulting relationship signals an optimal public policy balancing of privacy *against* security and/or security *against* privacy. Under the trade-off theory, a good society will "carefully balance individual rights and social responsibilities, autonomy and the common good, privacy and...public safety" (Etzioni, 1999). Much of the public policy debate recognizes this as the fundamental trade-off as society addresses the privacy-security conundrum surrounding the post-9/11 efforts at counter-terrorism, cyber-security and critical infrastructure protections.

The privacy-security conundrum is based on several related propositions. First, there is a focus on the externalities of strong privacy rights: Privacy compromises security because intruders and terrorists enjoy increasing anonymity as privacy protections shield them from scrutiny. Second, the corollary is similar as the focus changes to conditions conducive to strong security: Strong security requires privacy intrusions that require limited privacy rights because weak privacy better avails counter-terrorism forces of information potentially relevant to circumventing or apprehending the activities of intruders or terrorists. Third, intrusion and attack are deterred by limited privacy because would-be intruders who are seeking to evade detection suspect that notoriety of their intentions or preparations would trigger countermeasures and prevention. Fourth, security can be enhanced with limitations on the liberty of intruders and terrorists; weak privacy enhances the controls and disincentives that constrain their liberty.

THE PRIVACY-SECURITY COMPLEMENT

The security-privacy conundrum is overly simplistic and it ignores the basic public policy underlying the function of information assurance (IA) in privacy as well as the security benefits of privacy. First, liberty can provide security such as when flight averts injury. Second, and related, is that the privacy concept of isolation is useful for the protection of prey, that is, self-imposed seclusion, and its related anonymity, can be an effective preemption to many external threats. Third, restricting this isolation to PII, the benefits of privacy rights are diminished if PII becomes insecure because vulnerable physical and electronic collections of private data risk misuse. For example, insecure private and public databases have been used by predators to inform their stalking and identity theft activities—eventually prompting legislative, regulatory and judicial reaction (Attorney General's Cyberstalking Report, 1999; FTC Identity Theft Report, 2003). Finally, these propositions provide a segueway to the next Section in which data security is argued as essential to strong privacy, which in turn contributes greatly to individual security.

Consider the example of a data broker harvesting PII from public records. The courts in the U.S. are recognizing that the pressures for open government may cause privacy difficulties. PII is increasingly harvestable from court and other public records that are now seen as heightening the vulnerability of individuals to identity theft. Despite mandates to open government, closer regulation of access to court records is forthcoming in the U.S. better aligning privacy with the security of eGovernment records (Coyle, E-Government Act2002, 2006).

Security Component in Financial Privacy Regulation

Financial privacy and financial information security offer key, contemporary views of the resolution of the conundrum and complement. There is general recognition in the purposes of the major financial privacy laws and regulations of recent years that privacy rights are ineffective without an ongoing IA regime designed, evaluated and maintained to protect and defend PII and personally identifiable financial information (PIFI) and their supporting information systems. Modern financial information assurance regulations are traced to the *Fair Credit Reporting Act* (FCRA) as amended recently in the Fair and Accurate Credit Transactions Act (FACTA) (Fair Credit Reporting Act, 1970; Fair and Accurate Credit Transactions Act, 2003). The FCRA has IA rules that limit third party access to consumer credit reports except for legitimate purposes. FCRA bestows on the subject individual rights of access and redress, it promotes PII accuracy (e.g., revision/deletion of inaccurate or obsolete PII) and it authorizes

both civil and criminal enforcement mechanisms. FCRA enforcement is a strong incentive for PIFI security. Credit reporting agencies are subject to tort liability for negligent or intentional failure to install and maintain reasonable procedures to ensure accurate reports.

The Gramm-Leach-Bliley Act of 1999 (GLB) effectively eliminated the New Deal-era separations between the three major financial services sectors: commercial banking, investment banking and insurance (Financial Modernization Act,1999). The inevitable, perhaps intentional, consequence was a consolidation of financial services of theretofore separate financial records into more conveniently useful databases. Aggregated records containing customers' banking, brokerage and insurance PIFI are proliferating. GLB required the major federal regulators of financial services to coordinate their promulgation of new privacy regulations. GLB generally restricts the onward transfer of PIFI outside these affiliated firms. GLB requires an initial and annual delivery of privacy notices. GLB provides for an opt-out consent and imposes IA data security measures.

The GLB security provisions impose on every financial institution "an affirmative and continuing obligation to respect the privacy of its customers and to protect the security and confidentiality of those customers' nonpublic personal information." This policy is initially implemented through sectoral financial regulators, each of which is directed to "establish appropriate standards ... relating to administrative, technical, and physical safeguards to:

1. insure the security and confidentiality of customer records and information;
2. protect against any anticipated threats or hazards to the security or integrity of such records; and
3. protect against unauthorized access to or use of such records or information which could result in substantial harm or inconvenience to any customer."

During 2000, these "designated federal functional regulators" coordinated their GLB privacy rulemakings, resulting in cooperation and closely parallel GLB privacy rules. However, the detail and flexibility of the GLB security rules varies widely, particularly when compared with the detailed healthcare privacy rules promulgated by the Department of Health and Human Services (HHS) under the Health Insurance Portability and Accountability Act (HIPAA) or with the highly detailed guidance from the International Standards Organization as captured in ISO 17,799 (Health Insurance Portability and Accountability Act, 1996, ISO/IEC 17799 (2005)). In the remainder of this Section, a comparison follows of the IA regulations under GLB promulgated by the Securities and Exchange Commission (SEC) for the financial services under its regulatory control as compared with the IA regulations of the Federal Trade Commission (FTC) for other types of financial services firms.

The SEC's GLB privacy rule is Regulation S-P, which includes the SEC security/safeguard rule—a simple, straightforward and general, principles-based standard when compared with the extensive specifications found in the rules-based approach used in HHS's HIPAA rule (SEC Regulation S-P, 2000). Regulation S-P requires financial services firms to adopt policies and procedures that assure IA safeguards of customer records and information in three major areas: (1) administrative, (2) technical and (3) physical. Firms must use evaluation techniques to achieve a "reasonable" design that ensures security and confidentiality, protects against anticipated threats and hazards to the security or integrity of PIFI and protects against unauthorized access or use of PIFI if such could result in substantial harm or inconvenience to any subject individual (customer).

The guidance provided in the SEC security rule is vague; it allows considerable discretion on nearly every aspect of IA controls. For example, each regulated firm's selection or development of particular controls, their implementation and

monitoring and their evaluation are largely left to develop by industry custom, best practice or through evolution following regulatory inspections. It can be expected that some clarity and specificity may emerge as enforcement actions or private litigation scrutinize (1) the particular policies adopted pursuant to this rule, (2) the implementation of particular controls by regulated entities and (3) the effectiveness of remediation response to intrusion incidents. An evaluation framework and de facto standards may emerge, perhaps paralleling litigation over internal accounting controls.

The FTC has taken a somewhat more detailed approach in its implementation of the GLB security provision. The FTC's guidance is faithful to the GLB security requirement, yet is considerably more specific than the SEC safeguard rule by the FTC's mandate for an information security program, a risk assessment, the design and implementation process for information safeguards and the oversight of third party service providers. In addition, the FTC safeguard rule sets standards for program evaluation.

The most basic requirement is for the initial development of a written *information security program,* and this is followed with a continuing duty of execution through program implementation and maintenance. Several component elements are required: coordination, risk assessment and deployment of information safeguards. First, *coordination* responsibility for the information security program must lie with a designated employee or employees. Second, a *risk assessment* must be conducted to "identify reasonably foreseeable internal and external risks to the security, confidentiality, and integrity of customer information that could result in the unauthorized disclosure, misuse, alteration, destruction or other compromise of such information, and assess the sufficiency of any safeguards in place to control these risks." The risk assessment must focus on each relevant area of operations, including at a minimum, employee training and management, information systems, (e.g., network and software design, information processing, storage, transmission and disposal), and the development of appropriate *safeguards*—detection, preventing and responding to attacks, intrusions or other systems failures.

Third, the results of the risk assessment are needed to inform a *design and implementation* process that deploys the information safeguards. Fourth, each regulated entity must exercise *oversight of service provider(s)* (generally third parties) that may handle or supply software and hardware that processes customer PIFI. There are at least two aspects to third party oversightm including reasonable selection and retention of competent service providers and delegating the safeguards implementation and maintenance obligations, imposed under the service contract(s).

The FTC security rule envisions both an initial (at implementation) and (periodic) recurring evaluation of the information security program. An initial and (likely) most comprehensive evaluation is needed in the conduct of the risk assessment. The evaluation rigor is measured against the regulated entity's "size and complexity, the nature and scope of [its'] activities, and the sensitivity of any customer information at issue." The evaluation must be conducted "in light of the results of the [risk assessment's] testing and monitoring." This evaluation must inform the design and implementation of information safeguards that control the risks identified. Thereafter, and on an arguably regular basis, the effectiveness of the information safeguards' key controls, systems and procedures must be regularly monitored and tested. Furthermore, additional evaluation may become necessary in light of the results of the testing and monitoring, to "any material changes to your operations or business arrangements; or any other circumstances that you know or have reason to know may have a material impact on your information security program." In addition to the considerable detail in the FTC's security rule, plain language guidance has been made

available to sensitize regulated entities to other security resources throughout the public and private sectors. Commentators argue GLB has enhanced the security of the customer data held by financial institutions thereby complementing individual privacy (Swire, 2002).

CONCLUDING OBSERVATIONS

The relationship between public policy of privacy and security and the implementation of privacy and security is persistently misconstrued. Privacy and security public policies drive the deployment of technical solutions, tools and mechanisms. Furthermore, most technical solutions have policy impact and are likely to be acceptable or unacceptable as the relevant policy implications of such solutions become evident to various political groups. Therefore, it is critical for the successful deployment of any technical solution that the policy implications are thoroughly understood, otherwise there is significant risk of investment lost or costly revisions required for technologies unenlightened by policy constraints. For example, consider how security/privacy technologies such as encryption, firewalls, authentication, biometrics, third party certification and secret codes are generally considered tools useful to improving both privacy and security. However, these technologies are not "privacy" and these technologies are not the same as "security." This is true to the same extent that any tool used in the physical world to protect privacy (e.g., door locks/keys or curtains) is not the expectation of privacy itself, nor is it the condition of security itself.

This article argues that privacy is an expectation, a complex set of rights, a limitation on countervailing/reciprocal rights of observation and a condition descriptive of current circumstances. This is not to say that technology might not play an important role contributing to the enablement of privacy and to the protection or enhancement of privacy. However, privacy enhancing technologies usually play only a partial role in securing privacy. Privacy depends on a systems engineering approach that coordinates technologies with various other controls (governmental/regulatory, managerial/supervisory, monitoring and financial) to achieve satisfactory security protections.

A similar problem exists for security. Technologies are tools that can improve security when they are part of a systems engineering approach that integrates with governmental/regulatory, managerial/supervisory, monitoring and financial controls. Security tools can also be deployed to decrease or destroy privacy, recalibrate the privacy-security balance and contribute to a temporal resolution of the privacy-security conundrum. Of course, many security tools are privacy enhancing—the complement, when they are directed towards protection of the subject individuals. Consider such examples as biometrics, encryption, firewalls, authentication, biometrics, third party certification and secret codes. The privacy-security conundrum and complement fundamentally implicate security tools because they may both be intrusive and protective.

REFERENCES

Bagby, J. W., & Gittings, G. L. (1999). Litigation risk management for intelligent transportation systems (part two). *ITS-Quarterly, 7*(3) 60-67.

Bagby, J. W., & McCarty, F. W. (2003). *The legal and regulatory environment of e-business.* St.Paul MN: West Pub.

Bagby, J. W., & Ruhnka, J. C. (2004). *Merger of dns governance into trademark law.* Proceedings of the 32nd Telecommunications Policy Research Conference (online), http://web.si.umich.edu/tprc/papers/2004/378/TPRC-04-tmDomNaMerger-Final.htm

Carpenter v. U.S., 484 U.S. 19 (1987).

Choi, S-Y., Stahl, D. O., & Whinston, A. B. (1997). *The economics of electronic commerce.* Indianapolis: MacMillan Technical Pub. 344.

Coyle, M. (2006). Courts balancing privacy, access: U.S. judiciary must protect "e-records," *National Law Journal, 28*(25).

Cyberstalking: A new challenge for law enforcement and industry. Report of the U.S. Attorney General to the Vice President (1999).

Deibert, R. J. (2002). Dark guests and great firewalls: The Internet and chinese security policy. *Journal of Social Issues, 58*(1) 143-159.

Etzioni, A. (1999). *The limits of privacy.* Durham: Duke University Press, 184.

E-Government Act (2002), Pub. Law 107-347, 44 U.S.C., Ch 36.

EU Directive 2002/58/EC.

Exec. Order No. 13,231 (Oct.16, 2001).

Fair and Accurate Credit Transactions Act (2003). 117 STAT. 1954, Pub. Law 108-159, 15 U.S.C. §1601.

Fair Credit Reporting Act (1970). 84 Stat. 1128, Pub. L. 91-508, 15 U.S.C. §1681.

Federal Trade Commission (2004). *National and state trends in fraud & identity theft: January-December 2003.*

ISO/IEC 17799 (2005). *Information technology—Security techniques—Code of practice for information security management, International Standards Organization & International Electrotechnical Commission.*

Financial Modernization Act (1999), 113 Stat. 1443, Pub. L. 106-102, 15 U.S.C. § 6801-6809.

Health Insurance Portability and Accountability Act (1996), 110 Stat. 1936, Pub. L. 104-191.

Katz v. U.S., 389 U.S. 347 (1967).

McGinley, P. (1959). *The province of the heart, "A lost privilege."* New York: Viking Press.

Posner, R. A. (1986). *Economic analysis of law* (3rd ed.). New York: Little Brown & Co.

SEC Regulation S-P (2000), *Privacy of consumer financial information.* U.S. Securities and Exchange Commission, SEC Release No. 34-42974, 17 C.F.R. §248.

Report of the Secretary's Advisory Committee on Automated Personal Data Systems, Secretary of Health, Education, and Welfare (July, 1973). *Records, computers and the rights of citizens.*

Ruckelshaus v. Monsanto Co., 467 U.S. 986 (1984).

Sprenger, P. (1999). *Sun on privacy: "Get over it."* Wired News.

Statement of the European Data Protection Commissioners, Foundation for Information Policy Research, Sept.11, 2002. http://www.fipr.org/press/020911DataCommissioners.html

Strauss, J., & Rogerson, K. (2002). Policies for online privacy in the United States and the European Union. *Telematics and Informatics, 19*(2), 173-192.

Swire P. P., & Litan, R. E. (1998). *None of your business: World data flows, electronic commerce, and the European privacy directive.* Washington: Brookings Institution Press.

Swire, P. P. (2002). The surprising virtues of the new financial privacy law. *Minnesota Law Review, 86*(6), 1263-1324.

United States v. Carroll Towing Co., 159 F.2d 169, 173(2nd Cir.1947).

Westin, A. F. (2000). *Public records and the responsible use of information.* Interpretive Essay, Alpharetta, GA: Choicepoint.

About the Authors

John W. Bagby is professor of information sciences and technology at Pennsylvania State University. He researches the public policy of information sciences and technology, privacy, security, intellectual property, entrepreneurship and financial services regulation. His undergraduate and graduate instruction in these subjects has occurred at four doctoral/research-intensive universities. He has developed and delivered various executive and continuing legal education classes. His funded and interdisciplinary research is published in numerous journals in law, economics, business and engineering. He is co-author of several college texts and serves on various professional and institutional committees, including three terms on the Penn State Faculty Senate.

Sanda Berar R&D manager at Nokia Multimedia in Finland. Her key responsibilities include Mobile Enhancements Finland SW strategy, competence development and technology studies. She is also responsible for operational development in the Mobile Enhancements, Software area. Prior to that, she has been working in diverse project management and SW engineering positions in Nokia, Finland. She has over 10 years' experience in SW development, and also holds a PhD in business information systems.

Raluca Bunduchi is a lecturer in management at the University of Aberdeen Business School. Her current research focuses on technology management and the development and adoption of e-business in organisations. Prior to that, she has been a research fellow at the University of Edinburgh, looking at the development and adoption of e-business standards. She studied for her PhD in the Department of Management Science at Strathclyde Business School, examining the use of Internet technologies and their implications for the nature of business relationships within and across organizational boundaries.

Anindya Chaudhuri is lead researcher at the National Center for Education Accountability, Austin, Texas. He graduated with a PhD in public policy from the Lyndon B. Johnson School of Public Affairs at The University of Texas at Austin in 2005, after obtaining an MA in economics in 1999 from Jadavpur University, India, specializing in International Trade. In 1997, he was an Honors graduate in economics from the same institution, with a minor in mathematics. His research interests include telecommunications, education, international trade and research methodologies.

Ioannis P. Chochliouros is a telecommunications electrical engineer, graduated from the Polytechnic School of the Aristotle University of Thessaloniki, Greece, holding also an MSc and a PhD from the University Pierre et Marie Curie, Paris VI, France. He possesses broad research and practical experience in a great variety of matters relating to modern electronic communications. He currently works as the head of the research programs of the Hellenic Telecommunications Organization S.A. (OTE) in Greece, where he has been involved in different national, European and international R&D projects and market-oriented activities. He has published numerous scientific and business papers and reports in the international literature, especially for technical, business and regulatory options arising from innovative e-infrastructures and e-services, in a global converged environment. He also works as a lecturer, on the Faculty of Science and Technology, Departments of Telecommunication Science, Computer Science and Technology of the University of Peloponnese, Greece.

Stergios P. Chochliouros is an independent consultant, specialist for environmental-related studies, and holds a PhD from the Department of Biology of the University of Patras, Greece, and a university degree as an agriculturist. He has gained enormous experiences as an academic researcher and has been involved in various research activities, especially including options for extended use and/or applicability of modern technologies. In particular, he has participated, as an expert, in many European research projects relevant to a variety of environmental studies. Moreover, he has gained significant experience both as educator and advisor; he is author of several papers, studies and reports.

Tilemachos D. Doukoglou holds a diploma of electrical engineering from the Aristotle University of Thessaloniki-Greece (1986), an MEng degree from McGill University of Montreal – Canada (1989) and a PhD in electrical and biomedical engineering from the same University (1994). He was also a visiting research engineer and post-doc in the Massachusetts Institute of Technology-Cambridge, MA-USA (1994-1995). Dr. Doukoglou is currently the head of OTE's (Hellenic Telecommunications Organization) Labs and New Technologies Division. His interests are in the area of IP over DWDM technologies, Broadband Services over xDSL technologies (VoD, VideoStreaming, GoD, etc.) and development of platforms for services like TeleMedicine and TeleEducation. He has also been the ADSL Rollout project manager for 2004 and 2005. Since 1995, he has been involved in various EU RTD programs as technical responsible and project manager. Finally, he has more than 40 publications in international magazines, conferences and workshops.

Kenneth Flamm is director of the Technology and Public Policy Program and dean rusk chair in international affairs, The Lyndon B. Johnson School of Public Affairs, The University of Texas at Austin. He is an expert on telecommunications, international trade and the high technology industry. Dr. Flamm is a 1973 honors graduate of Stanford University and he received a PhD in economics from MIT in 1979. From 1993 to 1995, he served as principal deputy assistant secretary of Defense for Economic Security and special assistant to the deputy secretary of defense for Dual Use Technology Policy. Prior to his service at the Defense Department, he spent 11 years as a senior fellow in the Foreign Policy Studies Program at Brookings. Among his publications are *Mismanaged Trade? Strategic Policy and the Semiconductor Industry* (1996), *Changing the Rules: Technological Change, International Competition, and Regulation in Communications* (ed., with Robert Crandell, 1989), *Creating the Computer (1988) and Targeting the Computer (1987)*.

Shane Greenstein is the Elinor and Wendell Hobbs professor in the Management and Strategy Department of the Kellogg School of Management at Northwestern University. He teaches courses on strategy in technology-intensive industries and markets. He is also a research associate with the industrial organization and productivity groups at the National Bureau of Economic Research in Cambridge Massachusetts. His research interests cover a wide variety of topics in the economics of high technology. His most recent book is *Diamonds are Forever, Computers are Not; Essays in the Economics and Strategy of Computing Markets.* It is published by Imperial College Press. He received his BA from University of California at Berkeley in 1983, and his PhD from Stanford University in 1989.

Jarice Hanson is the Verizon chair in telecommunications at Temple University, Philadelphia. She is also professor of communication in the Department of Communication at the University of Massachusetts, Amherst. She has authored, co-authored or edited 15 books and numerous articles on media and society, and on telecommunications policy. A former department chair and associate dean, she also was the founding dean of the School of Communications at Quinnipiac University. Her next book will be published by Praeger Publishers in 2007, titled, *24/7: How the Internet and Cell Phones Change the Way We Live, Work, and Play.*

Jarmo Harno received his MSc in mathematical analysis from the University of Helsinki in 1983. After working in SW industry, he joined Nokia in 1987, and has worked as a systems analyst and manager in R&D, quality assurance and product management. He started as a senior research scientist on techno-economics with Nokia Research Center in 2001. In doing research on the future telecom technologies and service concepts, he has also taken part in the EU IST framework co-operation project TONIC (2001–2002). Starting from the year 2004, he has led a work package for "Mobile and wireless network economics beyond 3G" in the EUREKA's CELTIC co-operation project ECOSYS. Mr. Harno has authored several international journal articles and conference presentations, and holds some patents relating to telecom technology and services.

Meheroo Jussawalla is an emerita research fellow/economist at the East West Center, Honolulu, Hawaii. Her research interests in the economics of telecommunications has led her to research and publish 15 books and 200 refereed journal articles in the ICT sector. A festschrift was presented to her in 1998 titled *Communications and Trade: Essays in Honor of Meheroo Jussawalla,* edited by D.M. Lamberton (Hampton Press, NY). She has served on the board of directors of the Pacific Telecommunications Council and the International Institute of Communications. She is on the editorial board of *Telecommunications Policy.*

Dimitris Katsianis received the informatics degree, an MSc in signal processing and computational systems from the University of Athens, Department of Informatics and Telecommunications. He is a research fellow with the Optical Communications Group, participating in several European R&D projects. He has worked as an expert scientific advisor with several firms in the field of techno-economic and network design studies. His research interests include broadband communications and methodology of network design with techno-economic aspects. He has more than 40 publications in journals and conferences in the field of techno-economics and telecommunication network design and he serves as a reviewer in journals and conferences.

Ken Krechmer is lecturer in the Interdisciplinary Telecommunications Program of the University of Colorado, Boulder, USA. He was the founding technical editor of *Communications Standards Review* and *Communications Standards Summary* (1990-2002), technical journals reporting on standards work-in-progress in various national and international standards committees. Krechmer consulted on standardization strategies and actively participated in standards committee meetings 1980-2002 for various clients, including France Telecom, British Telecom, NEC and Intel. He received the first place awards in the World Standards Day paper contests in 1995 and 2000. Krechmer is a senior member of the IEEE and a member of the Society of Engineering Standards.

Youngsun Kwon is an associate professor of IT Business School at Information and Communications University in Korea. He is a senior researcher, leading research on the unlicensed use of spectrum at the Spectrum Engineering and Policy Research Center in Korea. In addition, he has been a member of the Gerson Lehrman Group Telecommunications Council Member since 2005. He is listed in the 23rd edition of Marquis *Who's Who in The World* (2006). His major research concerns are spectrum resource management, competition policy in telecommunication industry and the convergence between network industry and traditional industries including mass media industry.

Changi Nam is a professor at Information and Communications University in Korea. He received a BS in management from Seoul National University, Seoul, Korea in 1978, and a PhD in business administration (finance) from Georgia State University, Atlanta in 1988. During his stay in Korea Information Society and Development Institute (KISDI) from 1988 to 2000, he had been engaged in the research related to strategic management of post and telecommunications. Since 2001, he has been a faculty member at Information and Communications University, servicing as dean of the School of Business and director of the IT Business Research Institute. His current research interests include financial analysis and performance evaluation in the information and communications industry.

Hajime Oniki was born in 1933, Tokyo, Japan. He earned his BA and MA from the University of Tokyo, Japan, and PhD (economics, 1968) from Stanford University, USA. He is currently a professor at Osaka-Gakuin University, and a professor emeritus at Osaka University. His academic appointments in the past include professor at Chukyo University and Institute of Social and Economic Research, Osaka University; assistant and associate professor at Queen's University, Canada; assistant professor at Harvard University, USA; and assistant professor at Tohoku University, Japan. He served as editor of *International Economic Review* and as associate editor of *Information Economics and Policy*, *Economics of Innovation and New Technology*, *info* and *Telecommunications Policy*. Professor Oniki writes mainly in economics of information and communication.

Theodoros Rokkas received his BSc in physics in 2000 and an MSc in electronics and radio-communications in 2002, both from the National and Kapodistrian University of Athens, Greece. Currently he is a research associate and working toward a PhD at the Department of Informatics and Telecommunications at the same university. His research interests include mobile communication systems, broadband and wireless systems and technoeconomic evaluation of networks.

Thomas Sphicopoulos received his physics degree from Athens University in 1976, the DEA degree and Doctorate in Electronics, both from the University of Paris VI, in 1977 and 1980, respectively and the Doctorat Es Science from the Ecole Polytechnique Federale de Lausanne in 1986. From 1976 to 1980 he worked in Thomson CSF and in 1980 he joined the Electromagnetism Laboratory of the Ecole Polytechnique Federal de Lausanne. Since 1987 he has been with the University of Athens, where he is a professor in the Department of Informatics and Telecommunications. He has participated and managed about 30 National and European R&D projects and he has more than 100 publications in scientific journals and conference proceedings.

Anastasia S. Spiliopoulou is a lawyer, LLM, member of the Athens Bar Association. During recent years, she has directly participated in matters related to telecommunications and broadcasting policy in Greece and abroad, within the wider framework of the information society. She has been involved in current legal, research and business activities as a specialist for e-commerce and e-businesses, electronic signatures, e-contracts and e-procurement, e-security and other modern information society applications. She has published many scientific papers, with specific emphasis on regulatory, business, commercial and social aspects. She has mainly focused her activities on recent aspects of the European regulatory policies and on their implications in the competitive development of the converged telecommunications market. She currently works as an OTE (Hellenic Telecommunications Organization S.A.) lawyer for the Department of Regulatory Issues of the General Directorate for Regulatory Affairs.

YiJun Tian is a final year PhD candidate at the University of Technology Sydney Law School, and a postgraduate research associate at the Baker & McKenzie Cyberspace Law and Policy Centre, Australia. He was visiting scholar at the University of Washington Law School (Seattle), and summer associate at the Berkman Center for Internet & Society at the Harvard Law School in 2005. He has published a number of journal articles on international comparative law, intellectual property and Internet law in Australia, China, the United Kingdom and the United States.

Dimitris Varoutas holds a physics degree and MSc and PhD diplomas in communications and technoeconomics from the University of Athens. He is a lecturer in telecommunications technoeconomics in the Department of Informatics and Telecommunications at the University of Athens. He actively participates in several technoeconomic activities for telecommunications, networks and services within numerous European and national R&D projects His research interests include optical, microwave communications and technoeconomic evaluation of network architectures and services. He has published more than 40 publications in refereed journals and conferences in the areas of telecommunications, optoelectronics and technoeconomics.

Ilari Welling received his MSc degree in telecommunication engineering from the Helsinki University of Technology in 1996. He joined the Nokia Research Center in 1995, where he has been studying techno-economic aspects of telecommunication networks and is currently leading the research group focusing on this topic. Recently, he has been working on the EU project TONIC and is currently leading the CELTIC project ECOSYS, which concentrates on techno-economic modelling. Mr. Welling has authored/co-authored several international journal articles and has presented papers at conferences in the field of telecom techno-economics. He was also co-author of the book *Broadband Access Networks: Introduction Strategies and Techno-Economic Evaluation* (Chapman&Hall, 1998).

Qingchuan Zhong holds a master's degree in public affairs from the Lyndon B. Johnson School of Public Affairs, The University of Texas at Austin and an undergraduate law degree from Shanghai International Studies University, China. Zhong is recipient of various academic honors, including the Emmett S. Redford Award from the LBJ School and the Jones Day International Legal Fellowship. Zhong has worked for Public Strategies, Inc., Austin, Texas, and was a summer associate at the U.S. law firm Paul, Hastings, Janofski and Walker. He is currently earning his JD at the University of Michigan Law School, where his research interests include law and public policy in competition, development and technological advancement.

Index